Published under the aegis of

Center for Communication and Information Sciences

(Victoria University; University of Toronto at Mississauga;
University of Helsinki; Universidad Sao Paulo, Brasil; Indiana University;
University of Lugano; University of Ottawa)

Series: *Language, Media & Education Studies*

Edited by: Marcel Danesi & Leonard G. Sbrocchi

Cover: Cornelis Troost (1697-1750)
The Anatomy Lesson of Prof. Willem Röell (1728) - 200x310 cm

Anna Makolkin

Anatomy of Heroism

To students and
Colleagues at
Haifa University
from the author

Toronto, Canada
February 2003
a. Mak

LEGAS

New York   Ottawa   Toronto

Canadian Cataloguing in Publication Data

Main entry under title:

Anna Makolkin
  Anatomy of Heroism

(Language, media & education studies; 17)
Includes bibliographical references
ISBN 1-894508-12-2

1. Heroes. 2. Semiotics.   I. Title.

P99.4.S62M34 2001   302.2   C01-901638-4

For further information and for orders:

LEGAS

P. O. Box 040328   3 Wood Aster Bay   2908 Dufferin Street
Brooklyn, New York   Ottawa, Ontario   Toronto, Ontario
USA 11204   K2R 1B3   M6B 3S8

Printed and bound in Canada

Contents

Preface

As if by the twist of the post-modern irony, this book itself, originally entitled *Hero and the Concept of the Extraordinariness*, has a very extraordinary history. The idea of expanding the notion of the heroic and taking it to a higher level of abstraction, came to the author back in 1989-90, when she, one of the first four Frye Fellows at the newly formed Northrop Frye Centre at Victoria College, was laboring over her first book within the thin walls of Pratt Library, the old premises of the Centre. This honorary fellowship gave her the opportunity to work on my first book *Name, Hero, Icon: Semiotics of Nationalism* (to be published only in 1992 by Mouton de Gruyter, Berlin), as well as the honor and privilege to audit the last live lectures by Northrop Frye — on the affinities between the Old and New Testament narratives. Both were sufficient inspirations for the next book *Anatomy of Heroism* which would be completed only by 1993.

Due to the vicissitudes of the academic manuscript life, it would become possible to publish it only in the year 2000. It is up to the readers to decide if the manuscript has managed to withstand the challenges of the other works on the similar topic, published since 1993, but, given the nature of *universals*, the main philosophical category used in this book and applied to the *hero-sign*, the author hopes to have been able to accomplish her task.

The subject of the heroic is one of these paradoxical topics in discourse at large — familiar to everybody, and yet one of the most puzzling, intriguing and unresolved issues for nearly all oral and literate societies. Despite the omnipresence of heroes in life and in fairy tales, legends, sagas and myths, the first serious analysis of Hero as a *universal, transhistoric, transcultural* and omnipresent phenomenon was not undertaken until 1841, when Thomas Carlyle had published his famous and largely underestimated treatise, *On Heroes, Hero-Worship and the Heroic in History*. Amidst his own web of prejudice and bigotry, Carlyle still managed to describe one of the most powerful *cultural universals —Hero—* in the most profound and exhaustive manner, prophetically stating that "society is founded on Hero-worship. All dignities of rank, on which human association rests, are what we may call a *heroarchy* (Government of heroes), — or a Hierarchy, for it is sacred enough with all (1966[1841]:12).

Since the 19th century, the Carlylean *heroarchy* would be complimented by Vladimir Propp's classification of fairy tales (1921), Campbell's representations of heroes in myth (1949), Haddas' *Heroes and Gods* (1965), Hook's *Hero in History* (1967) and Butler's *Myth of the Hero* (1979). Considering the significance and the transhistoric and transnational nature of the heroic, the studies of the phenomenon have not received sufficient attention of the post-modern scholars, remaining one of the under-examined topics, left aside more as an anthropological curiosity.

This monograph not only renews the dialogue about the heroic, be-yond cataloging the faces of the heroes and stating the obvious, but takes the somewhat cynical modern readers back into the world of myth and fairy tale with a different purpose. With the *hero-sign,* we arrive onto the territory of the neglected *cultural universals* and their controversy, and approach a different level of abstraction. Hero is examined from the new, semiotic perspective and treated as a *universal sign.* Reaching the level of the hero-race, hero-nation, hero-culture, the hero-sign is examined in the process of evolution of the universal image, taken to a different concep-tual level or the comprehensive semiosis of the universal sign. The *arche-typal cultural sign,* the marker of extraordinariness, is followed from a sin-gle fictional character to a real group. It connects the traditional domain of folklore, literature, cultural anthropology with the history, philosophy, political science, and social psychology.

The purpose of such an investigation lies in establishing not only the most well-known pathway of human imagination, with the hero as its key structural element, but disclosing some misconceptions around the meaning of the sign- Hero. The hero-sign is dissected in diachrony — from Aristotle and Plato, and the Greek myths to Umberto Eco and the post-modern cultural mythology to illustrate the power of the heroic and its role in the construction of false beliefs, or *false signs,* such as ethnic and racial delusions, xenophobia, fixation on a particular culture and aesthet-ics. In the spirit of the modern debunking and search for the authentic motivations of the Self, the work illustrates the paramount role of the *heroic* in the European and World culture. The concept of the heroic is pre-sented as a vital part of Culture, a *cultural universal,* connecting the dis-connected, the fragmented Eurocentric world and the rest of the human cultural production.

The metatextual universe is formed by the works of Aristotle and Plato, Plotinus and Hegel, Vico and Carlyle, Dostoevsky and Tolstoy, Humboldt and brothers Grimm, Peirce and Leibniz, Freud and Barthes, Derrida and Jung, Haddas and Kerenyj, Eliade and Butler, among others, and various perceptions of the phenomenon of *extraordinariness.* This gives an opportunity to outline the developmental pathway around the topic of the universal hero-sign. The inclusion of Carlyle and others re-edits the historical and philosophical narrative, improving the collective philosophical memory, widening the cultural universe and connecting the postulates by the ancient, Victorian and contemporary thinkers.

The work questions the usefulness of some forms of heroism in the most acceptable cultural rituals, such as sports tournaments and beauty contests, undermines the solemnity of war history and military parades, monumental architecture and numismatic hero-worshiping, viewing them as manifestations of the *uncivilizing herophany*. It places the modern culture and modernism into the revisionist stage of *herophany*, examining the modern conflict between the democratic anti-heroic ethos of the time and the primordial heroic drive of humanity as the essence of the eternal search for the higher purpose.

Having demonstrated the role of universals and hero-sign, the work undertakes the task of classifying the most significant cultural signs, contributing thus to the neglected area of semiotics and complementing the familiar classifications of signs by Peirce, Eco, Sebeok and others.

The *hero-sign* helps to view revolutions and wars, beauty contests and sport tournaments, celebration rituals and sexual unions as manifestations of the similar semiotic phenomena. This post-modern revision of the heroic in culture ends with the analysis of the feminine Self through the *woman-sign* and its new meanings. The hero-sign, thus, assists in dealing with feminism, after patriotism, hero-worshiping, nationalism, cult of beauty, sport or political power.

In the time of the crisis of values and confused standards, one may also view this work as a post-modern, post-Derridean evaluation of the Self, both individual and collective. Who will be the future cultural heroes and what will be the future patterns for mimesis? Whose myth will be embraced next? Regardless of the suggested answers, the process of the sign-production will be still in place, and the ineluctable *hero-sign* would challenge us over and over again. The disclosed *anatomy of heroism* will hopefully uncover the semiotic possibilities of this *dominant universal sign*. In the post-modern universe, torn by difference, perhaps the shareable and the familiar might help us to deal with the existential dilemmas in a more productive manner.

The author extends her thanks to all the friends and colleagues, the members of the former Toronto Semiotic Circle, on whom the ideas had been first tested in the passionate Saturday morning discussions; special thanks to Dr. Roseanne Runte, President of the Victoria College who has made the publication of the book possible, and Mr. Jack Shen who transformed the manuscript into a computer disk.

Chapter One
Universals and Universal Hero-Sign

The Universal is common.
Aristotle

*Universals are the substance
of the world.*
Armstrong's *Universals*

1.1 *Boundaries of the Universals*

In his attempt to explain universals in the most accessible way, Thomas
Sebeok begins his famous essay "The Doctrine of Signs" with the recall of
ten particular situations, which involve a radiologist, a French language
teacher, a meteorologist, a historian, an anthropologist, a Kremlin guard,
a hunter, a peacock and a dog. All these different situations evolve
around the same process of decoding various signs which engage different sign-perceivers into the "same abstract operation which resolves each
episode to an instance of semiosis or sign-action" (Sebeok, 1986:35). A
less trained observer would simply state the differences between the peacock, the man and the dog. After all, the differences are far more obvious
than similarities, and most of our existential conscious and unconscious
experience revolves around establishing difference and differentiating
one thing, quality, action from another. But semioticians detect sameness
and similarity first. Paradoxically, both processes, the act of noticing the
common and the different are essentially *analogous* signs, as Aristotle
established in his *Metaphysics* and *Physiognomonics* (1984:2, 1552-7729)
Why does this occur?

First of all, despite the fact that the signs available for processing
could be different, our cognitive equipment for their decoding is always
the same. Human brain happens to be of a single general design and
helps us to respond, more or less uniformly, to temperature, colour, smell,
taste, spatial organization and shape. These features of common visual
perception, called "primitives" are the most basic *cognitive universals*
which assure our survival in the natural space, enabling us to produce
new *similar* or *dissimilar signs*. The cognitive 'primitives' also point out to
the similarities around us, by which we are all visibly united, such as by-
narism, symmetry, repetition, among numerous other *permanent signs*
(Makolkin, 1992).

Secondly, we all share the same complex and rich natural "empire of
signs" — planet Earth, which from time to time reminds us about its
potent significatory ability in the form of floods, earthquakes, storms,
avalanches, hail or drought etc. (Barthes, 1982; Yoshimiko,1990). Leaving
aside the varying responses and ways of decoding these *natural signs*, one

has to accept their determinism and primacy. An inhabitant of the New Guinea or an Australian bushman may react differently than the urban dweller of Melbourne or Rome to the flood or an earthquake, but all of them would never fail to acknowledge the signification of the *natural semiosphere.*

The *so-called "primitives"* have been instrumental in establishing this basic vital sign-decoding and sign —production system, which the Russian physiologist Pavlov labelled as the "secondary signalling system"— the *verbal signs.* The myriad of these new signs attest to the sophistication of our basic cognitive apparatus, which can not only process but produce new signs endlessly and incessantly. The fact that works of Confucius could be read in the language of Shakespeare and Pushkin is a sign of the *permanent universal sign* producer— Human Brain - and the best testimony to the *cultural and natural universals.* The possibility of translation and transmission of a single codal structure into a new one is the best illustration of the available universal semiotic decoding route, what Chomsky labelled as the "universal grammar." (Chomsky, 1968:27) Chomsky's theory of the universal grammar and the interrelationships between the single languages and all linguistic varieties is rooted in the Aristotelian dichotomy of the universal and particular. To Chomsky, "each language can be regarded as a particular relation between sound and meaning," while the universal phonetic universe and the universal grammar are the common territory of the linguistic empire of signs (Chomsky, 1968:17) The linguistic material is finite while its application is boundless. Chomsky suggests "that the study of the universal grammar, so understood, is a study of the nature of human intellectual capabilities" (1968:27) His deep and surface structure co-relationship has merely metaphorized the Aristo-telian binary opposition of the particular and universal, limiting it to linguistics or the territory of the *verbal signs.* His idea of the deep structure as "a bracketing of minimal meaning — bearing elements" is symmetrical to what many semioticians call the *seme* or the minimal unit of meaning. What Chomsky failed to mention in his hypothesis on the matter of the human mind was its universal ability to produce a metaphor, which could be revealed even at the pre-verbal stage of human development (Vico,1962; Vygotsky,1962; Danesi,1988; Paimegiani,1988).

The symmetry between the variety of the tactile, thermal, visual and other experiences and their analogous nature reveals the remarkable commonality of a deep and complex combination, such as meta-phor. To produce a metaphor means to be able to recall the past and transfer it on to the present, to observe something common between the two, obviously and seemingly uncommon signs, transferring one quality of a sign onto the other.

The *verbal sign* 'metaphor' owes its origins to the idea of transport, movement and transference. The ability to produce a metaphor reveals another, more advanced universal cultural activity, something beyond the cognitive primitives. To refer to a man as 'cold', either emotionally or verbally, or to associate rain with tears meant to move away from the natural semiosphere or *natural signs* to the man-made cultural semiosphere or *cultural signs*. Nature and its signs appear as a given, a matrix and the realm of the ordinary, while *homo-sapiens* manages to create the extraordinary through the metaphor and metaphoricity of the decoding process.

The current status of culture and the myriad of the *cultural signs*, above and beyond, or in combination with nature, make the boundaries of the universal rather obscure and invisible. It was much easier, in a sense, for Aristotle to observe and prove the existence of what is common than it is for Lévi Strauss or Chomsky. The deeply saturated modern cultural text presents itself as an empire of different signs, which seemingly do not share anything in common. But the irony of it all is that even this emphasis on difference is as profoundly universal as the process of seeing the other in the invisible "I".

We cannot escape the determinism of the *natural signs*, we still share the unpredictability of life, we still pass through its common stages of birth, growth and death. Our shareable *natural signs* stimulate the common rituals and symbolic practices around those *familiar signs*. Despite the superficial differences in those cultural practices and codes, the basic principle of *sign-production* and processing remains invariably universal. Paradoxically, the production of knowledge about differences is not different from the discovery of what is common. Oscillating between Nature and Culture and relying on metaphor, we communicate our existential experiences, invent ways of reshaping, re-describing both nature and culture, and the methods of this re-invention. It is a part of coping with the predictable, the ordinary and that which is boringly the same.

To produce new signs means to make the world strange and exciting, transforming the ordinary into the extra-ordinary, the non-heroic into heroic. It does not imply that *sign-producers* ever leave the boundaries of the universal. They simply extend them, repeating the same sign-producing rituals over and over again, until the new combination is no longer a *familiar sign*.

1.2 *Universals as Dangerous Signs*

The subject of *universals*, raised in our post-modern, post-computer, post-literate, post-space shuttle, confused, alienating and narcissistic universe, may seem somewhat odd. The oddity of it may be justified by the general climate of disintegration, separation and extreme obsession with the *particular* as opposed to the *universal*. The universal implies unity, while unity may be viewed by some as something strange, abnormal and even dangerous at a time when all the inhabitants of the global village are more preoccupied with separateness, separation, division, "differance" and difference. Some treat universals as an utopian concept which is often the culprit of many modern misfortunes and hostile outbursts in human communication. R.I. Aaron summarized this general climate around universals in his preface to *The Theory of Universals:*

> It is not denied that the contemporary attitude towards universals is frequently one of suspicion, nor that there are genuine grounds for suspicion (1952:VII).

The suspicion is rooted in the modern paranoia of communication, contact and fear of the "Other". The post-Freudian and post-industrial capitalist self is a deeply wounded "I", seeking refuge within the limited confines of the particular. The mythical freedom and existential bliss are promised precisely there, within the boundaries of the one's own, be it Body or Mind, i.e. the particular dichotomy. Thus, any other territory is perceived as a hostile, alien semiotic sphere that is bound to produce an *alien sign* and alien social force. Umberto Eco is well aware of the fact that

> The labour of sign production releases social forces and itself represents a social force. It can produce both ideologies and criticism of ideologies (1976:298).

The universals are feared as the signs, which may undermine the dominant ideology of the market place and consumption, disturbing the established exchange of signs in the macro semiosphere of neurotic production, speed and movement. Back in 1952, Aaron comforted those who were intimidated by the universals, having reminded that there was nothing to fear. To fear the universals means to fear one's own imagination, thought, to be afraid of thinking and how we usually think.

None of the ancient or the medieval thinkers were afraid to ponder about the universals and meditate about the Good and Evil, Truth and Falsehood, Beauty and Ugliness, Colour and Darkness. In fact, to be a philosopher has always meant to engage into an inescapable and endless debate about the universal and particular since the world is the uncomfortable unity of the two. Aaron (1952) and Armstrong (1991) agree that the emphasis on the particular was reinforced by Locke and Berkeley, eventually becoming pervasive in the Western European philosophy.

1.3 *Aristotelian Universals*

Aristotle had re-considered universals, having elevated them beyond the familiar objects, things, humans and animals to the relationships between them, as well as between the thoughts about those relationships. The pre-Aristotelian Western and Mediterranean thought sufficiently examined the objects, things and their qualities. It was only Aristotle and his followers who went beyond qualities and came to the conclusion that universals may be observed in the relations between things and people as well. In *Categories* Aristotle proclaimed that "the individual man belongs in a species, *man.* (1984: 4, vol. 1)" and so does a dog, a horse or any other particular object. Centuries later, Locke would deny it, stating that "all things that exist are only particulars." Aristotle had anticipated Lockean doxa in his *Metaphysics*:

> For it seems impossible that any universal term should be the name of a substance. For primary substance is that kind of substance which is peculiar to an individual, which does not belong to anything else; but the universal is common, since that is called universal, which naturally belongs to more than one thing (1984: 1639[1038] vol. I).

He distinguished the two basic levels of categorization, having labelled the particular as the primary substance and the universal as the secondary one. He simultaneously had mapped the route of thought, i.e. from the particular to the universal, from parts to the whole or from the singularity to multitude. Aristotle also made an effort to divide the semiotic universe into the two basic groups of signs, i.e. those that lead to Knowledge and those that lead to Belief which is not true knowledge. His essay "On Signs" could be treated as a possible anticipated response to his future opponents, who would deny and reject the universals, i.e. signs causing knowledge. The centuries of denying the universals had been foreseen by Aristotle, who would have treated such concepts as "signs causing belief" (1984: vol. 2, 2287).

Within the Aristotelian philosophical purview, Lock's and Berkeley's vehement rejection of the universals and fixation on the particular would have been regarded as a *possible sign*. Armstrong divided the two main schools of thought — the realist and non-realist, the realists being those who choose to recognize the reality of universals (1989:5). The non-realists included conceptualists and nominalists, the most representative of whom was Thomas Hobbes, who treated universal merely as a name "phantasm formed in the mind," having no equivalent in the world (Hobbes, 1839: 1, IV). It was Hobbesean idea that sign was merely another belief- causing agent, amidst the dominance of the particular. Aristotle might have anticipated it, along with the scepticism of the positivists, who would demand the empirical data on universals, when he stated in his *Metaphysics* "science and art come to man through experience (1984:vol 2, 1552).

In Berkeley's view, this experience is based on the memory of the particular, i.e. the image of a triangle is impossible without the experience of a real triangle, a particular thing. To this Aristotle had his answer, having established the division into the primary and secondary substances, as well as through the theory of resemblance.

1.4 *Resemblances and Recognition*

> *Man is a universal,*
> *Callias is a particular*
> Aristotle, *De Interpretatione,* 17.6.1.

This classical Aristotelian example might have inspired Charles Peirce to argue that resemblances could be established when the event of comparison takes place and "the resemblance of anything lies in the comparison of that thing with something else " (1931:vol, 1,155). Peter and Callias are indeed different individuals, particular men, but they resemble one another by being human beings, belonging to the same type. The famous Peircean type/ token ratio, perhaps, derives directly from the no less familiar Aristotelian man/Callias juxtaposition.

The contemporary theory of sign- production by Umberto Eco acknowledges *recognition* and *resemblance* as the primary preconditions of semiosis:

> The act of recognition may re-constitute the object or event as an imprint, a symptom or a clue, interrupt those objects or events means to correlate them to a possible physical causality (1979:221).

The entire process of communication is based on the assumption that the communicated message would be perceived and that the perception be possible due to the ability of the addressee to recognize the familiar, to see the *resemblance* between the new and old message. Despite the fact that Eco does not use the term "resemblance", it actually still is the essential part of his theory of sign-production. The *iconic signs* may be produced and perceived as iconic because there is a direct resemblance between the icon and the *proto-sign* — object. The variety of resemblances or the different degrees of similitude forces Eco to differentiate between an *iconic sign* or a *replica*, or an "absolutely *duplicative replica*" — all of which confirm Hume's theory of resemblance that is again a reworked derivative of the Aristotelian categories (1979:180).

Hume provides two accounts of resemblances in his *Treatise* — the so-called true resemblance when the two things actually share some properties, and when there is no actual resemblance at all. Hume's theory again returns us to the Aristotelian *Rhetoric to Alexander* where one is informed about the two main groups of signs, i.e. those "causing belief" and those "causing knowledge". Knowledge is created on the basis of establishing the true and testable resemblance, while belief is maintained by the seeming resemblance, which may or may not be present. Aaron, however, explains where the novelty of Hume's theory lies when he writes the following:

> He [Hume] wishes rather to explain the whole process of becoming accustomed to a recurrence of resembling entities in experience, and of associating a name with the recurrence, in such a way that hence forward the hearing of that name, or the seeing of it in writing, stimulates the mind to certain activities (1952: 79).

Hume, thus, arrives at the understanding of the process of perception via resemblance and recognition which enables us to form associations with the familiar and well-known past experience of the "I" and the "Other". According to Hume, language itself is already a storage of the *recognizable signs,* which are perceived because they resemble the concepts and images, carried by them through constant signalling, referring and pointing to the same thing, ideas, actions events and places.

Leibnitz, in contrast, rejects the search for resemblances in names / words alone and proposes to find them in the natural environment first, and then in the cultural semiosphere, constructed by human above it. Leibnitz proposed the notion of the universal characteristics that govern both Nature and Culture. He assumed it would eventually become possible to express the understanding of the world not through the inadequate signs- words, but through other objective alphabet of thought. Taking into account Leibnitz's fascination with numbers, one may assume that he intended them to become better substitutes for words, nonetheless the significant part of his teaching lies in the re-affirmation of resemblances as the innate quality of the mind, the thinking apparatus (Leibnitz, 1982 [1765]).

If Leibnitz, Lock, Hume and the predecessors choose to limit their focus, Kant manages to introduce a new aspect of resemblances, namely their selective choice *a priori,* or what modern philosophers label as Desire. To see the resemblance it would be necessary not only immerse oneself into the empirical, but to have *a priori* desire to do so. To observe the *universal sign* one has to investigate several sets of semiotic contexts and compare them, choosing to select the most important or necessary one, that which appears as such to the perceiver:

a̲bc bcda̲x fa̲x ya̲g lgla̲p

                        a̲ = universal or invariant

                        or

beda̲x   fa̲x

                        x̲

                        or

yag   eglap

                        g̲

The temporal span widens the sphere of semiosis and expands the field of observation. The greater the time span, the more visible the *universal sign* becomes and clearer is the pattern of its semiotic functioning, more evident in diachrony. At the same time, the excessive isolation of the segments of the semiosphere could totally obscure the presentment of the *universal sign*. The universal sign requires a wide semiotic space in order to be recognized as such due to the resemblance to the "Other".

Peirce would insist that a dyadic comparison is impossible at all

> For qualities cannot resemble one another nor contrast with one another unless in respect to a third quality; so that the resemblance of qualities is triadic (1931: vol 1250).

In other words, the comparison of *ba* and *cda* in relation to *eag* for instance, could result in establishing true resemblance or locating the *universal sign*, which is the goal of the present examination.

Nonetheless, the desire to reject the *universal sign* and deny its omnipresence is still quite strong which explains the ongoing controversy around the topic. There is no agreement whether the universals exist, even after the arguments had been repeatedly presented by numerous thinkers, such as Aristotle and Confucians, Leibnitz and Peirce, Aquinas and Vico, Van Dijk and Sebeok, Armstrong and Aaron, Freud and Jung. The debate about universals is still going on.

It is impossible to ignore the universals or *universal signs* which continue to re-emerge, re-signal and re-signify their presence in the most unrelated semiotic contexts. Despite the reluctant acceptance, they reappear in all cultural contexts, across all the temporal boundaries, amidst the no less forceful difference, variety and specificity of the particular. Despite it all, there still are and will always be signs, images, ideas, things, relations, perceptions, phenomena and structures, which could be invariably recognized for their resemblance to one another, be they called *universal signs* or "invariants", or "universal characteristics" (Leibnitz, 1702; Aaron, 1952; Makolkin, 1992; Maliuta, 1989).

Maliuta regards the necessity of the *invariants* or *universal signs* as the existential reality, "dictated by the principle of homo-centrism that accounts for the concrete human qualities in the process of human cognition" (1989: 6). Presumably unaware of Leibnitz's universal alphabet, he also feels that words failed *homo-sapiens* and a new system of symbols would be required to reflect the obvious universal inner and outer regularity of the existing systems of signs.

Continuing this search for the new signification of the canonical regularity, we would like to suggest that the repeated, recurrent particularity may be no longer treated as such, but be re-named as an invariable resemblance / universal or invariant — *universal sign* (Propp, 1928; Greimas, 1979: Danesi, 1993; Perron, 1993).

1.5 *Hero — Universal Sign*

Gilgamesh and Christ, Apollo and Homer, Buddha and Socrates, Confucius and Thomas Aquinas, Plato and Avicenna, Aristotle and Cromwell, Columbus and Peter the Great... what are the resemblances between all of the above names — icons, signs of particular semiotic significance? They all are signs of extra-ordinariness, pertaining to different epochs, different linguistic traditions, different cultural systems, heroes of various kinds. Being obviously quite different, they resemble one another in one quality — their heroic status in the collective memory of the global educated literate community.

Since the earliest days of existence and self-reflection, the introspective mind of the *homo-sapiens* had established common shareable standards, the evaluators of the human performance, and the *Hero-sign* had become one of such numerous measurement tools, measuring the existential performance. Heroes have always been, were and are being continuously chosen, sought, worshipped crucified, remembered, immortalized and defended in favour of the new extraordinary individuals (Propp, 1928; Bremond, 1970).

"Society is founded on Hero-worship" is the famous and the most precisely formulated universal by Thomas Carlyle, who had established Hero as a *permanent* and *universal sign* in the ongoing global semiosis. Paying tribute to his heroico-romantic nineteenth century, Carlyle, quite unexpectedly for himself, had re-introduced the Aristotelian universals and suggested to look at a cultural construction as a predetermined process where *hero-sign* plays a vital part.

Bill Butler re-described the *hero-sign* in his book, *The Myth of the Hero*, where he provided the following definition:

> The hero is an archetypal figure, a paradigm who bears the possibilities of life, courage, love — the commonplaces, the indefinable which themselves define our human lives (1979: 6).

To him, hero is everywhere where the existential situation tests human physical, mental and spiritual force. Hero is the *omnipresent sign* who can reveal his/her extra-ordinariness in every context where "frontier situation" occurs or any condition of stress may require such a presence (Carlyle, 1884; Butler, 1979; Campbell, 1949, Russell, 1963; Mark, 1982; Haddar, 1962; Hook, 1967; Makolkin, 1992). Law-making or law-breaking, war or exploration, hunting or fishing, martyrdom or tyranny, self-sacrifice or oppression of others — all may require the heroic performance.

Devil and angel, the Greek Prometheus or Polynesian Maui, Ivan Tsarevich or Cinderella, Gilgamesh or Chinese Kuan Yin, Egyptian Aster or Finnish Vainamoinen. "It is an ancient human tendency to deify heroes to make gods of man," — states Butler and makes no distinction while detecting the *hero-sign* between a Robin Hood and a Mafia Don, President Nixon and the Godfather. To him, they all bear the heroic markers which identify their positive or negative extraordinariness and are worshipped either through scandalous fame, envy or glorification. Their *"visible signs"*, as Butler labelled the societal reward for their heroic deeds, are "cadillacs, Long Island estates, Swiss bank accounts, and time on TV screen (1979: 32).

Butler, not referring to Carlyle, basically explains to the twentieth-century readers the famous Carlylean dictum and expands it beyond the limits of the cultural space designed by Carlyle. Odin and Dante, Shakespeare and Luther, Mohammed and the Russian tzar mark the boundaries of the Carlylean field of the heroic universe. Despite his perceptive conclusions, Carlyle does not attempt to convince his readers that hero is the archetype, the universal. His heroic pantheon is very small while Butler's heroic catalogue includes the global heroic legacy and provides a substantial evidence to the vitality of the *universal hero-sign*. Any particular meanings brought on by religious myth, political ideology, communal poesis, or a specific metalanguage could be all standing behind the Hero-sign. Similarly, a man could be Socrates or Mohammed but both would share their human characteristics. The semiosis or the production of a new message, the process of communication is an ongoing process, and any new meaning of a *hero-sign* may be added on, while the characteristic quality which identifies the sign's presentment and presence will be always the same, i. e. the extra-ordinariness.

The Hero-sign is omnipresent in all linguistic codes, linguistic monuments, such as dictionaries and encyclopaedias. Its numerous definitions may slightly vary but ultimately bear strong resemblances. The *Grand Dictionaire Universal du XIX Siècle* provides one of the most successful laconic disclosures of the meanings of the Hero-sign, as well as its transcultural, translinguistic occurrence. It states that the French word *heros* has its synonyms in

> Latin-*Vir*
> Sanskrit-*Vira*
> Greek- *Herôs*

which mainly signify "homme fort" (a strong man) or "grand homme" (a great man). *Homme fort* captures one of the most significant universal meanings, i.e. the physical strength of the individual which enables an archetypal hero to take part in a physical confrontation, such a battle tournament, mountain climbing or space exploration. *Grand homme* label encodes the notion of the extraordinariness:

> Homme qui possède certaines qualités certain mérites au plus haut degré (vol 9, p.24).

The highest degree of all other qualities beyond the individual's re-markable physique is one of the basic universal meanings of the *hero-sign*. This French interpretation of the sign bears the mark of the Cartesian Body/Soul dichotomy. The strong man is simultaneously the great man in all other respects. The strong/great ratio may be treated as a prelimi-nary semiotic base of the sign hero:

> Hero-sign =   *strong/great (fort/grand)*
> homme-hero

The forte/grand ratio is the ultimate message of the multitude of heroic legends, epic, myth and songs, dedicated to the heroic performance of the Hero. All which unites Achilles and Beowulf, Odin and Hildebrand, Attila and Gunnar, Siegfried and Cuchulainn, Finn (Fionn) and Kai, Roland and Marko Klalevych among many others adds to the mytholog-ical and real heroic legacy..

Somewhat similar semiotic strategy is employed by the *Living Webster Encyclopaedia Dictionary of the English Language* which defines "hero" as

> a man of distinguished valour, intrepidity, or fortitude; a central or prominent personage in any remarkable action or course of events; a man admired and venerated for his noble deeds or qualities, one invest-ed with heroic qualities in the opinions of others; the principal male character of a poem story play, or the like on whom the chief interest of the plot is centered (p451, 1971 ed).

The definition basically discloses the anatomy of the *hero-sign:*

> hero = grand/fore = principal protagonist;
> hero = grand/forte = the subject of a panegyric;
> hero = grand/forte = admired for actions;

hero = grand/fort = causing remarkable action;
hero = grand = capable of prominence;
hero = forte = man capable of remarkable physical action;

The structure would have been incomplete without the acknowledgment of the deity status of heroes in the mythological tradition, and to fill this gap, the dictionary mentions the classical mythological attitude towards heroes when they were presented as "intermediate in nature between gods and men" (p. 451). The image of this hero is given with the modern finishing touches, disclosing the American metaphor "hero", which in the U.S. colloquial language may mean "an oversize sandwich, made with a long roll or with bread cut lengthwise" (p. 451). The archetypal grand/forte characteristics is a complicated sign — edifice, represented by an *iconic sign* — sandwich which serves as another duplicate metaphor of a hero. The resemblance between the *grand homme* and oversize sandwich is precisely in the extreme size, the marker of extra-ordinariness or the precondition for the new metaphor (Nuessel, 1988 19-23).

The Webster's New World Thesaurus, edited by Charleton Laird the same year, provides the most complete list of meanings of the sign-Hero applicable in various societal codes:

military	sports	politics	history
brave man	athlete	idol	conqueror
victorious	general	champion	victor great man
combatant	popular figure	celebrity	a man among men
warrior	celebrity	popular figure	demi-god
fearless soldier	victor	man of courage	martyr
combatant hero	star	mettle	exemplar
		model	fearless soldier
		man of the hour	victor
			knight-errant
			master
			man of distinguished valour, saint

Simultaneously, the frequency of the used analogues captures the saturation of the heroic in the historic discourse where the account of the heroic deeds represents the discursive essence. Leonard Mades calls it "the heroic conception in history" and the description of the extraordinary as "heroization of men and women". He acknowledges it "an almost universal phenomenon:"

> The precise qualities of the hero in a given time and place vary, but, his basic exemplary function remains. The hero serves many social purposes. The society that heroizes him achieves, vicariously and collectively,

the realization of its values. In some societies, his mythicization serves to explain natural phenomena, to induce religious zeal, or to inspire men to great undertakings. By his superhuman achievements, the hero wins the fame — and with it the immortality that each man longs for (1988; vol 14, 144).

Most Western dictionaries of the Indo-European Languages invariably point out to the Greek origins of the word and to the Greek practices of the heroic cult, even when they acknowledge the universality of the *Hero- sign*. The Greek mythology which is permeated by the cult of the heroic is regarded as a convenient field for the observation of the heroic. Pagan system of worship was rooted in the recognition of the extra-ordinary of various kinds. Demi-god and demi-mortal were the parts of the *heroic sememe.* The Greek cultural code, being the deepest structure of the Western cultural text, has affected even such rigid codal matrices as dictionaries and encyclopaedias. The Greek expressive version of the hero-sign may be regarded as the heroic extreme with the utmost content and expression (Greimas, 1979; Eco, 1979; 84-120).

1.6 *Universal Heroic Pathway*

Despite this occasional tension all the slightly varying definitions of the sign-hero refer to the common semiotic reality, deeply ingrained in our cultural history and existential experience. One encounters *hero-sign* is all spheres of production of signs, be it science or religion, literature or oral tradition, politics or sports, dance or opera, sculpture or architecture, philately or numismatics. All extra-ordinary or heroic qualities which they embrace form a triad:

physical	=	strength
intellectual	=	genius
spiritual	=	courage

This triad of features may be treated as a precondition of becoming a hero and being a hero. These are the prerequisites but those which are by no means sufficient to achieve the *heroic status* within the group.

In order to gain the heroic status, or actually to become a hero, one needs to be recognized by the rest of the group. The process of recognition has two stages:

a) selection;
b) worshipping.

First, a group (a family, a tribe, a state, a nation, a party or a team) chooses the hero. Secondly, it establishes the way of worshipping and remembering the hero for his/her *heroic deeds*/actions. The group canonically singles out a potential hero, a heroic "Other" who may somehow stand out for his/her heroic qualities. A single hero/ine is usually selected out of the multitude of the potential ones, be it a saint, a ruler, a priest, a party leader, a poet, a film-maker or a TV personality. One may only recall our cultural rituals of honouring and selecting heroes, such as the Olympic games, beauty pageants, Nobel prizes, elections, awards and medals.

The strive for the heroic is ingrained in our collective psyche. After all, the notion of the best, the greatest is expressed either through the superlative degree of adjectives, or other linguistic devices, actualizing the canonization of the *Hero-sign*, and expressing the extreme quality for the extra- ordinary. The desire to measure and compare, perhaps, is the existential reason for the *Hero-sign*. After all, despite our eternal strive for the equal, equality and justice, we do see and acknowledge our difference, as well as the differences between the objects, things and living beings around us. It is with great reluctance that we admit our difference in physical strength, intellect, spiritual force and endurance, our hero-worshipping is the ultimate surrender, recognition of the superior qualities of the "Other". One outlives the other, one runs faster, one climbs better, one plays, sings, works better and faster, one sleeps longer, one eats more, and finally one earns more than the other... The endless list of inequalities, caused by natural or cultural conditions and predetermined by them, forms the primary layer of the extraordinary. If one had to establish the hypothetical genesis of the *hero-sign*, it would invariably lead to the natural re-accessment of this multitude through measuring, comparing and ultimately worshipping the Best.

The passage of a Hero is from the ordinary to the extraordinary, from the unknown to the famous, from misery to happiness and reward. The reward for the heroic deeds may not necessary come in the hero's life time, but posthumously, in the form of glory, remembrance and even size of the monument, be it an Egyptian pyramid or Lenin's mausoleum. The canonical hero has always been an individual, either above or within the group, selected, recognized, rewarded and revered by the very group. Thus, it is not incidental that, up until the institutionalization and protection of democracy, Hero has been an individual. With the establishment of democracy, *hero-sign* has acquired the expansion of the heroic meaning, transference from the individual to the group of individuals, who choose the heroic status among other groups, be it artists or scientists, politicians or fellow nationals. The shift in the semiosis of the archetypal *Hero-sign* has not undermined its basic semiotic structure, but has merely added another new dimension that could expand the canonical universal heroic paradigm (Zarnowski, 1914; Raglan, 1949; Carlyle, 1966 [1841]; Hook, 1967; Butler, 1979; Vico, [1730] 1968; Sartre, 1964).

Chapter Two

Universal Sign and Universal Narrative

Human psyche is the womb of all the
sciences and arts.
Carl Jung, *Psychology and Literature*

2.1 Hero-Sign and Fairy Tale

Carl Jung re-articulated the ancient collective thoughts about some obvious commonality of human attitude towards life experience through
his theory of archetypes and collective unconscious where he basically
summarized what the tellers of tales, myths and legends over the world
had been signalling all along. Jung pointed again to the universe of verbal signs which help

> to penetrate to that matrix of life in which all men are embedded, which
> imparts a common rhythm to all human experience, and allows the indi-
> vidual to communicate his feeling and his striving to mankind as a
> whole (1933: 172).

Fairy tales have drawn the attention of scholars as the most accessible
laboratory of human imagination, "the purest and simplest expression of
collective unconscious psychic processes" (von Frang 1970:1; Macleod,
1968; Christiansen, 1964; Propp, 1958; Groom, 1989; Eberhard, 1965).
They mirror the most endemic semiotic processes in their most elementary form, and the *hero-sign* happens to be the sign of the greatest *semiovalue* within this familiar *semiosphere.*

In the 18th century, heroes evoked scholarly interest which went
beyond mere collection of data, e.g. the works of Winckelmann, Haman,
Herder and Moritz who were drawn to the power of symbols and poetic
forms in a fairy tale. The 19th century, with its neo-pagan tendencies and
the expansion of the romantico-heroic paradigm, is crowned by the con-
tribution of brothers Grimm, in the area of comparative folklore and comparative cultural codes. However, it was not until the strides by Vladimir
Propp and A.N. Nikiforov when the idea of the *cultural universals* and the
universal hero-sign had been supported by the morphology of the fairy
tale. They came to a surprising conclusion that all fairy tales are uniform
in their structure, all of them invariably dependent upon the central performance of the main protagonist — the fairy tale hero. The Propp-
Nikiforov theory undermined the notion of appropriation of *cultural signs*
through the diffusion and migration, reinforcing the idea of a common
perception matrix, encoded in a seemingly primitive fairy tale plot
(Jakobson, 1945: 640).

The hero/villain dichotomy, an invariant in a fairy tale, has encapsulated the universal dichotomy of the world and its permanent expression in language, with its stable good/bad invariant in any code. The hero in a fairy tale stands for the positive existential forces which confront the negative ones in the desirable, just manner that fulfils the collective strive for justice, goodness and happiness. According to observations by Propp, "the hero and the villain join always in the direct combat (1928:47). The hero always performs some heroic deeds, suffering and enduring the oppression of the villain and his allies. The heroic abilities are tested in the process of overcoming the obstacles, be they physical or spiritual. The hero survives the period of martyrdom, non -recognition and is ultimately rewarded while the villain is punished. The victorious hero always stands for the occasionally unrealistic but most desired existential plot. His quest and victory signify the realization of the impossible dream when justice and goodness invariably prevail, despite the ordeal, persecution, danger and risk of death. The unrealistic happy end stands for the wishful thinking, the ideal fantastic world while the heroic pathway predetermines the universal map of extra-ordinariness that entails risk-taking and overcoming obstacles in the real life. The invariant fairy tale motifs record the canonical interpretations of the previous existential encounters. Propp's study of the Russian fairy tale would be reinforced by the work of A. Aarne and Thompson (1961), Claude Bremond (1970) and Greimas (1976) , all of which would point towards the uniform pattern of the heroic ascendance which invariably contains similar phases:

reward
glory
glorious return
departure/exile
battle with a villain
helper
heroic deeds
heroic test
series of villainous attacks
unusual intelligence and strength
suffering in childhood
birth unusual

The role of the helper on the way to recognition of the hero is that of the intermediary between the misfortune and bliss, a facilitator of the desired turn of destiny towards the happy events. The fairy tale narration captures the required shift in the actions of the chief actant-hero and his helper so that the ultimate heroic moment of reward could occur in a fairy tail. The events and actions are constantly changing their direction, leaning towards the ultimate happy end. Propp described them as the fairy tale invariant transformations, which could be treated as a precondition for the semiosis instigated by the *Hero-sign*.

The helper in a fairy tale could be described as a *sign-facilitator,* who assists the *Hero- Sign* in his/her predestined semiosis. Carl Jung treats the old man motif as a universal evidence of the sign-facilitator performance in "The Phenomenology of the Spirit in Fairy Tales".

> The old man always appears when the hero is in a hopeless and desperate situation, from which only profound reflections or a lucky idea —in other words a spiritual function or an endopsychic automatism of some kind— can extricate him. But since, for external or internal reasons, the hero cannot accomplish this himself, the knowledge needed to compensate the deficiency (1945 [1959]; 218).

The helper personified by the old man brings out the required "forces" of the hero who may again exercise his/her extra-ordinary powers on the road to success. Jung explains this eternal seduction by heroes in fairy tales as a manifestation of the unconscious, the universal collective archetype, as well as the projection of the collection ordinariness upon the individual extra-ordinariness, naming it as "animus-projection":

> The animus-projection gives rise to fantasised relations of love and hatred for "heroes" "demons". The favourite victims are tenors artists, movie-stars, athletic champions, etc. (1959:197).

Interested in the proof of the collective unconscious, with his "animus" and spirit, Jung stumbled upon a significant un/conscious universal — *hero-sign*. He included all the extraordinary public figures, selected and revered by the community, into the heroic personality catalogue, or what we renamed the *heroic pantheon*. The universal attraction to this *permanent hero-sign* he explained by the occasionally intense manifestation of the suppressed libido. He regarded the magnetism of the Hero-sign as powerful as human sexual drive, which is allegedly transformed into a collective intense admiration. Platonic love at a distance. Here, Jung argued with the ancient Greek interpreters of the heroic, used to who perceive hero as a son of God and a mortal woman, a product of Eros. To account for the existing myth and his own interpretation, in the light of anima/us archetype and its impact on the unconscious, Jung replays the famous exegesis in Plato's *Cratylus*. The erotic aspect of the hero-sign suggested by Plato helps Jung to emphasize its universality, naturalness and universal appeal.

Claude Bremond's *Morphology of the French Folktale* (1970) would also point out to the universal pattern of the heroic ascendance and the expression of the *hero-sign* through the heroic deeds, or a task accomplished in three stages. During the first stage, the so-called "deficiency", the hero is non-existent yet, appearing through the task which is set for him. The second stage, "the improvement procedure", is marked by the overcoming of obstacles and accomplishment of the task (heroic deed), while the third and the crucial stage, the improved state" brings recognition to the hero (Bremond, 1980; Propp : 1978 [1925]).

In the more complicated narratives, the improved state may not come immediately but be slightly delayed, and the "state of deficiency", or another trial may be set for the hero to be overcome. Bremond introduces then the extra phase, i.e. the procedure of restoration which is required to bring the hero to his/her final moment of recognition. Bremond divides the stages of the heroic semiosis in the fairy tale into the stages around the action, rather than around the actor/actant. The task or the heroic deed becomes the marker of the heroic progression along with the means or tools of activity. Thus, the morphological parts of the presumably French fairy tale encapsulate the canonical semiotic progression in any fairy plot, the prototype of any heroically-oriented narration.

The predictability of the fairy tale would later defy Lotman's theory of art and artistic text. According to Lotman, art is a system of signs, deliberately constructed in the most unpredictable manner so that "each artistic text is created as a unique sign with a particular content, constructed ad hoc" (1977; 22). Thus, a French fairy tale, in Lotman's view, would be a *unique sign,* having no resemblance with a German, Russian or Estonian fairy tale (Lotman, 1977). However, it is Lotman who correctly admits in the same work that "character is a paradigm" (257). The character of the fairy tale is a paradigm, with a far more significant role to play beyond fiction making. The *hero-sign* of the fairy tales is the first recorded acceptance of the universal existential principle, revolving around the dichotomy of the good and evil, life and death, failure and victory, negativity and positivity, love and hate. It is one of the primary organizing principles of existence. The order of things in the world is being permanently established   around   the *hero-sign,* the communal choice of the heroic taste and eternal improvement of the environment through those accomplishments and their remembrance (Bremond, 1980; Propp, 1978; Aarne, 1961; Brombert, 1968; Campbell, 1949; Godwin, 1984; Farnell, 1021; Fishwick, 1979; Haddas, 1965; Kerenyi, 1959; Makolkin, 1992).

2.2 Greek Hero-Type and Its Token

The striking Hellenic world, to which the entire Western culture is so greatly indebted, both in the area of the development of the natural linguistic codes, metalanguages and in the formation of the societal rituals, was deeply motivated by the *hero-sign* and the heroic. The idea of Beauty, Spirit, Intelligence and Relationship, the concept of Harmony, the image of the ideal Human Being who combines all the aspects of extra-ordinariness, the so-called Greek ideal, — bear all the qualities that are canonically associated with Hero-sign. The entire ancient Greek culture is inseparable, from the cult of the Hero (Farnell, 1970; Hook, 1967; Haddas, 1965; Haydon, 1941; Rose, 1953; Rose, 1960; Septman, 1960).

C. Kerenyi, in his book *The Heroes of the Greeks*, makes a claim that there is "an essential difference between the legends of heroes and mythology proper, between the myths of the gods and those of the heroes" (1959: I). He views heroes not as pure products of imagination, the *desired signs*, but as historical figures who were presumably responsible for the extra-ordinary re-description of reality, the actual historical transformations. In contrast, gods are perceived as purely mythological constructs, who may even surpass heroes in their heroic performance. "The gods demand heroes," — states Kerenyi and continues to press his argument further when he places heroes next to the ordinary humans. Thus, Kerenyi, suggests a heroic hierarchy which has presumably always controlled the societal rituals in the ancient world. The Greek gods, the mythical constructs, occupied the heroic pedestal. Their pantheon remained above the rest. Olympus, was a symbol of the ultimate extraordinary power, inaccessible to humans while the heroic pyramid metaphorized the traditional societal structure:

Deity
Olympus
Heroes
citizens
warriors
slaves
women or children

The cult of the heroes, the deity cult and the cult of the dead actually bore many resemblances, it had the same deference towards the tragic side of reality, and death unified them all. Kerenyi suggests that the birth of the so-called Greek tragedy has to be sought in the death rituals, mourning practices and customs of burials and that "tragedy is no less an act of cult than the sacred proceedings of the worship of heroes" (1959:14). The cult of Heroes and the divine cult also essentially manifest a dramatic plot. The Greek tragedy proper was a genre which, along with the panegyric to the dead, the mourning song, the heroic biography and *laudatio* used to describe the heroic deeds, tribulations of the hero, his martyrdom, conquests and his ultimate placement in the heroic pantheon. All of the above had been previously known and had their counterparts in numerous other traditions, in their legends, fairy tales, sagas and myths.

Eugene Waith treats hero as a semi-divine figure, an incomplete deity, who fulfils the aspiration of the rest of the mortals, releasing the heroic energies of society (1962;16). L.R. Farnell, inspired by the cult of the Greek hero, distinguishes seven *types* of heroes:

1. the *hieratic* type of hero-gods and heroine-goddesses, whose name or legend suggest a cult-origin;
2. *sacral heroes* or heroines, associated with a particular divinity;
3. heroes who are also gods, but with a secular legend, such as Heracles, Dioskouroi, Asclepios;
4. culture and functional heroes;
5. epic heroes of entirely human legend;
6. geographical, genealogical, and eponymous heroes and heroines, transparent fictions for the most part, such as Messene and Lakedarmon;
7. historic and real personages (1921).

Hadas and Smith speculate about the other possible interpretations of the *hero-sign*, drawing from the common aspects of the hero, the place of burial and sanctuary of the hero after his death. According to the author, the community actually demands the death of the hero and deity in order to worship freely and unobstructively:

> Hero denotes preternatural potency of some sort associated with a dead man... The hero in the technical sense must be dead (1965:10).

The *hero-sign* thus acquires more semiotic potency with time, after some distance from the actual heroic performance has been established. Haddas and Smith claim that death confirms the heroic status. Joseph Campbell adheres to the similar views. To him, death or departure represents the entire raison-d'être for the heroic life and is the symbol of recognition. He also subtly distinguishes between a hero-type and universes of functioning:

cosmos	societal universe
myth	legend, tale

Hero

Culture constructs its coding and signalling through one of the major sources — the heroic paradigm, with one major type-Hero and several tokens, such as hero-warrior, hero-lover, hero-redeemer and hero-saint (Eco, 1979; 179).

2.3 *Various Significations of a Greek Hero-Type*

What is remarkable about the ancient Greek culture, that, unlike other less complicated cultural texts, its heroic signification and system of universals simultaneously pointed out to various highly complex semiotic universes — fictionalized past and present, analytical examination of the natural environment, and control of nature and culture in the ancient world, actualized through the highly developed astronomy and mathematics, logic and civic legal code, economics and politics. The producers of *the cultural signs* in the ancient world valued equally the artistic and non-artistic discourses. In this respect, it is interesting to examine the most popular and well-known Greek myths. The Greek heroic dozen, the famous twelve Olympians signified not only mythical narratives, but also referred to some specific societal functions, be it politics or navigation, music or craft, medicine or military skills. Each mythical Greek hero carried many more meanings than the ordinary fairy tale character. Let us quickly list them again.

The mythical Hera, the Great Goddess, was a symbol of a promiscuous female, who had new babies every autumn and was glorified in the yearly spring resurrection. However, the same Hera symbolized the matrimonial kinship, and was the goddess of marriage and home. The *hero-sign* signified simultaneously the fictional world of disorder and the controlling force in the real society (Seltman, 1960).

Zeus symbolized patriarchy and the most powerful elemental force. In Homer, Zeus is the sky, a part of heaven, he is the omnipresent existential force:

> Full of Zeus are all the streets and all the market places of man; full is the sea and the heavens there of always we have need of Zeus; for we also are his offspring (Seltman, 1960:53).

Zeus was also a patron of commerce, as well as city architecture. Athene, Zeus' daughter, born miraculously through the head of her powerful father, became the symbol of the feminine wisdom and intuition. Athene, the Goddess of Wisdom, stood for this new possibility that females might think and act intelligently, also symbolizing the early feminist tendencies in the ancient Greek society. Hermes, the bachelor god, the patron of mythical thieves, a good singer and athlete, would be also known as the patron of poets and travellers in real life. Aphodite, the foam-born goddess, became the Goddess of procreation, fertility, religion and patron of love. Hephaistos, the lame servant of Zeus was the noble craftsman, patron of artisans. Ares, the most unloved deity and allegedly an alien, stood for the undesirable heroic foreigners who needed to be tolerated amidst the civilized ancient Greeks. His Roman prototype was Mars, the God of war Ares pointed out to the eternal source of conflict between the Greeks and barbarians (Hadas, 1965; Kerenyi, 1959; Seltman,1960). Apollo, who in the myth impresses with his extraordinary strength (at the age of seven months and four days attacking the serpent), would also become the sign of Youth and Beauty. He was one of the few gods who were entrusted with numerous other concrete societal functions, who had been also known as the God of music, philosophy and patron of the Olympic Games. The inscription on his temple represents the eternal challenge:

> Know thyself
> Nothing in excess
> The man is best.

This Apollonian dictum would become the *cultural sign* of the ancient Greek and entire Western civilized world. The cult of Apollo also embraced the civic criminal and constitutional code of this ancient tradition. The temple in Delphi, with the famous Apollo's pronouncements is, the *connecting sign* between the past and present cultural semiopheres, as well as the *permanent sign* of human wisdom (Graves, 1978; Makolkin, 1990; Makolkin, 1992). Apollo was the mythical guru and a model hero, capable of controlling Nature and Culture. Those, who followed the way of Apollo, presumably possessed lucidity, moderation, courage, tact and wisdom due to their self-knowledge and harmony with the world. Herbert Rose claims that Apollo is "the most characteristically Greek of all gods", the supreme Greek deity, the antithetical type to Christ (Rose, 1960;134).

Asclepios, not included into the Olympic dozen, was an " honorary Olympian" and the mythical student of Apollo and Athene who bestowed the art of surgery upon the Olympians (Seltman, 1960;180). He became the god of medicine. The connecting thread between the mythical and real significance of this god is immortalized in the famous Hippocratic oath which physicians of the world still take till this day:

> I swear by Apollo the physician, and Asclepios, and Hygieia, and Panaceia, and all the gods and goddesses calling them to witness that I fulfil, according to the best of my power and judgement, this oath and written bond, to honour as my parent, master who has taught me this art, and to share my substance with him, and to minister to all his necessities (Seltman, 1960:181).

Artemis, the mythical twin sister of Apollo, became the symbol of chastity and virginity. The temples built in her honour would become the models of architecture and the most trusted safety deposit banks in the whole Greek world.

Poseidon, the god of the sea, who in myth was symbolically responsible for earthquakes, but in reality would become more known in navigation. Again this *hero-type* also has a double function, the mythical and real. Demeter, the goddess of agriculture, encouraged enjoyment of labours on the land, a sacred barley water was made in her honour, she sponsored dance and singing. This hero-type had the most harmonious mythical and "real" functions, connected in the most grateful activity of cultivating the land.

Dionysus, the last, and the most feared deity, this Olympic dweller was allegedly of foreign ancestry. As it behoofs all foreigners, he was responsible was the disorder, disrespect and ruin of the civilized customs which he symbolized in myth. Scholars agree that the origin of the cult of Dionysus is Macedonia, the land slightly hostile to the Greeks. Otto Kerenyi labels Dionysus the "mad god", the god of frenzy and abandonment" (Kerenyi, 1959). He was a god of disruption and rebellion; his worshippers were persecuted, being regarded mad; most of his worshippers were allegedly women, who would abandon their families and children and indulge in sexual orgies and feasts in the mountains. In modern mythological layer of the entire Western cultural text, Dionysus is the mistaken god of wine, the meaning which he had acquired much later (Otto,1965; Makolkin, 1990).

To conclude this brief summary of the double-signification of the Greek *hero-signs* in myth one may justifiably claim a steady pattern. All the twelve Olympians are the signs which have series of fictional meanings and "real" roles to play in society. They point out to the imaginary and real activities of the people. The mythical deities perform the extraordinary mythical heroic deeds, as well as co-sponsor the ordinary activities of people in the extraordinary fashion. The ancient Greek mythology establishes the harmonious unity between the real and fictionalized semiospheres through the archetypal dozen of its hero-signs:

Olympus
12 Hero-signs

hero-making in fiction	hero-making in reality
signification of the unreal	signification of the real

The Greek heroic pantheon in myth, drama, philosophy and law is a catalogue of numerous hero- types and tokens, sustained by the real rituals, festivities and public re-enactment of the imaginary and heroic.

2.4 . Reduction of Hero-Types in Post-Pagan Signification

Paganism encouraged multideity and proliferation of various *hero-signs*, who could excel in the fictional and real world, either due to their physical strength or extraordinary intelligence. Heroes of the Western world, before the adoption of Christianity, would engage in violent battles to earn the heroic titles. Their physical vigour, attractiveness and survival, despite the obstacles on their heroic pathway, was their most important attribute.

The post-Christian heroes could be unattractive physically, weak and in frail health, but would still remain extraordinary, spiritually unshaken in their beliefs and martyrdom. The adoption of the monotheism was an occasion to reduce the number of pagan gods to one almighty God, and it signified a major shift in the heroic paradigm. The changes in the concept of the heroic or what constitutes the *hero-sign* would affect the number of signs and the criteria for their selection by society. The extra-ordinary act, the heroic raison-d'être had been changed. There was no need to kill a serpent, to destroy the villain physically. The heroic deeds and the meanings of the hero-sign had been re-interpreted. The battle, the physical (hero/villain) encounter were no longer regarded as the only extraordinary actions to be performed. A new heroic deed, the act of forgiving a villain, loving the enemy in return for viciousness, would become the new heroic model of extraordinariness, requiring new spiritual resources in order to adopt fully and completely the Christian doctrine and its heroic paradigm.

It was a turning point in the production of all *cultural signs*, when violence of the pagan heroes was condemned and deprived of its archetypal heroic value. The hero no longer needed be a destroyer, a killer of the villain, but the individual who could reform the source of evil, reshape the nature of the villain by loving him in return for his/her wrongdoing. It would be the strength of the spirit, rather than the physical strength that would be demanded from the post-pagan Christian hero.

This was also a turning point in the mythical process, aiming at the simplification of the sign production which would contribute to the additional layers in the collective imagination. The pagan heroic paradigm continued to function, the old heroes and multiple deities continued to rule human imagination, next to the transformed post-Christian heroic paradigm. Christianity as a semiotic process aimed at the transformation of the sign-producer, turning a violent energetic pagan *homo-sapiens* into a loving, thoughtful, self-denying ideal creature, a new extraordinary being, *a new sign*.

The post-Christian *hero-sign* would signify a new mimetic model, both for one's imagination and reality. The *new hero-sign* was the signifier of the eternal communal Love, the rejuvenated extraordinary force to be applied towards the new behavioural and imaginary patterns. The single hero —Christ— would restructure the ancient heroic pyramid, having changed the Olympic forum from the twelve domineering Greek gods to one single invisible and all mighty Lord. If the Greek Olympus had the divinity council, which presided over and controlled the heroic designation, one single central Christian myth would destroy it. It suppressed the pagan semiosis and the fictional processes dominated by the polytheistic consciousness:

12	1
Gods	Lord-Christ
Honorary	church servants
Olympians	disciples of God

The pagan Hellenic tradition was more liberal in the choice of heroes. It was sufficient to possess the physical strength and this quality alone would establish the heroic status. Since strong bodies come by quite often, hero-giants were quite in great supply in the pagan mythology and folklore of the Greeks and numerous other "barbarians", as ancient Greeks used to refer to the non-Greeks.

The ancient Germans had their Olympus named "Asgard(i)r," where they used to place their multiple deities. For instance, Baldr was the god of fertility, the prototype of the Greek Demeter. Thorr was the god of War, Surtr, was the patron of fire while Wode (Wodan) was the god responsible for human psyche (Tokarew, 1989:116-7). The Celts had their collection of deities which included Ogmios, god of furrow wisdom and eloquence, Esus, the god of Forests. The Slavs had their sun and wind, fire and husbandry deities — Svarog and Dazhbeg Volos and Perun, as well as the goddess Mokosh, the patron of the allegedly female house chores (Tokarew, 1989). The Zulus of South Africa had the celestial princesses who patronized the sacred agricultural activity.

Mircea Eliade summarized the pre-Christian sacred "herophany" around the *natural signs,* such as sun and moon, water and soil vegetation and animals, woman and man. The sky, in his view, had the utmost significance in mythology, as the source of most *sacred signs,* deities and *universal signs:* The sky, the locus of the universal extraordinary secret and mystery, "symbolizes transcendence power and changelessness simply being there," since "it is high above all humans on Earth" (Eliade, 1958:39). The natural macrosemiosphere has always been the major source of the production of the *sacred signs* — deities in the pagan cultural text. In this respect, a comparison between the Greek and Maori mythologies is very useful.

It is remarkable that the Maori deity collection approximated the Greek heroic dozen, but their semiotic significance somewhat differed. The Maori gods are divided into high and departmental gods. Tare, the god of plant life and fertility, Rongo, the god of rains, Tu, the god of wars, and Tangoroa, the personification of the sea and fish — all stand for the high gods, the *sacred signs* of the highest *semiovalence.* Ruarmoko, the "originator of earthquakes" was akin to the Greek Neptune/Poseidon (Irwin, 1984:36; Godwin, 1984).

The monotheistic signification has transformed the canonical archetypal source of divinity, the sky. Ultimately, there would be one *hero-sign* of the supreme *semiovalence, God* who would not share his heroic space with anybody else. Unlike the Greek Zeus or Maori Tu, the Japanese Amaterasu-Omikami (the Sun god) or the Egyptian Shamash, the Ewe god Manice or Masai, Ngai, who all had been homonoidlike and had similar existential habits, the god of the Christians would become a solitary inhabitant of the sky:

Heaven

God

Earth

God's servants and children

The mythical consciousness, which had to incorporate the real and the unreal, the fictionalized and the actual, the desired and the attainable, has divided the actual physical space into the heroic and non-heroic territory. The upper level of the semiosphere was reserved for the supreme *hero-sign,* the Lord, the appointed creator of the universe who possessed the complete control over the production of signs, both *natural* and *cultural.* This singular *sacred sign* would be entrusted with the regulation of the most mysterious and extraordinary world —the Universe.

Since then people, the products of the Lord's creation, would be entrusted with some extraordinary functions of a lesser degree which could never surpass the mission of the divine. The most extraordinary, the ultimate heroic deed would become the responsibility and privilege of the Lord, the *supreme sign.* The Christian teaching would establish the model of a heroic behaviour, the new pattern of an ideal man who could love, punish and forgive everybody, making it an impossible task to be performed only by the heroic few, represented symbolically by the canonized martyrs, the awarded, appointed heroes of the restructured post-pagan world. The rest of the God's children were never designated to become heroes. The heaven/hell dichotomy symbolically divided the sign-producers into the heroes and non-heroes. The sin concept conditioned the entrance into heaven, the idea of angels versus sinners would become the fearful model of the nearly impossible behaviour, the images of the heroic impossibility. Christianity as a semiotic universe has reshaped the heroic paradigm, making it an exclusive elitist heroic pantheon, in contrast with the more democratic pagan version.

The first Christians, who encountered hostility as any pioneers of Belief, would signify the universal rules of heroism, supporting selflessly a new myth, a new heroic legend. The entire history of Christ-ianity represents a series of heroic acts on the part of its believers, trying to disseminate, promote, enforce and defend their allegedly "right" belief, the correct formula of sign production. Its two-thousand history is a complex biography of Belief that had originated as a modest alternative to the pagan philosophy, ultimately having established itself as *tyrannical sign,* which would control states, empires and people for centuries. Paradoxically enough, the Christian teaching, which has emerged as a *seduction sign, with its philosophy* of Love and humility, would transform into the *tyrannical sign,* encouraging hatred and physical violence in the name of the *sacred sign* — Christ. Eventually, Christianity would be so powerful that it would control the cultural expression in the entire Europe. The Spanish Inquisition, the Vatican intrigues, the Russian Synod, the Church of England and the Catholic Church of the Latin America had been monitoring the production and exchange of *the cultural signs* and still attempt doing so. The church music, iconology and hagiography represented the powerful control over the expression and content of the Sign, and suppression of the pre-pagan signification. The positive meanings of the sacred signification wee the condemnation of violence, debunking of the archetypal sign-giant and elevation of the Spiritual

Pagan Hero	*Christian Hero*
Body	Mind
Beauty external	Beauty inner
Hate/Love	Love

The post-pagan heroism required inner strength, introspective vision and general inwardness. The Evil, the *heroic factor,* would function differently, no longer demanding the pagan valour, the visible physical outgoing expression of the Self.

This shift in the *heroic paradigm* was marked by the departure of from the external, the physical — the Body. If the pagan heroes celebrate their heroic deeds in the pleasures of the Body, the Christian martyrs deny them, obtaining their satisfaction from the awareness that their denial would ultimately be rewarded in the other world. The pagan heroes demanded recognition Here and Now as opposed to There and Later. To fulfil the demand for the extraordinary the Christian hero had been prepared to suppress the Body, to control its natural signification and neglect the canonical forms of heroic behaviour, such as war games, athletic competitions and musical contests. This new heroic code was being enforced through the liturgy, prayer, sermon literature and the intimidating discourse inside the ecclesiastical hierarchy:

> The monks were forbidden to have any private possessions; they were to love God and their neighbours conquer the flesh by fasting, give no man cause of offence and avert their eyes from-women (Makolkin, 1987:110).

Stifling the Body, suppressing its natural signification and promoting the Christian heroism was the essence of the new heroic code. The weakened body of a Christian hero, in contrast with the strong bodies of the archetypal folk, myth and legendary pagan heroes, would become a sign of the adopted Christianity (Momigliano, 1963).

2.5 *Pagan Antecedents of the Supreme Sacred Sign*

The Judeo-Christian cultural myth perpetuates the notion that monotheism owes its origins to Judaism and its Christian version in the New Testament, while the concept of the supreme power, supreme Being, i.e. the prototype of the monotheism, could be actually observed in many pagan mythological constructs. Irwin reports that Maoris and other New Zealand traditions had a concept of a supreme being who single-handedly ruled over the "departmental gods, district and tribal gods; inferior beings" (1984: 33). The cult of Io among Maoris, who were sometimes not even allowed to utter his name, is somewhat parallel to the Christian or Jewish cult of the supreme deity (Irwin, 1984).

The Maoris used to divide the *semiosphere* into the three realms, with Io, running the realm of the ultimate reality, placed in heaven, and ruling over various gods responsible for nature and human activity. The second realm was "the realm of the human" that included the remembered dead ancestors, chiefs, members of the religious affiliations, experts in art and talismanic objects. The third realm was the realm of the god of Evil and Hinenuiotepo, the guardian of the underworld (Irwin, 1984;17). All the three realms are interconnected and represent a harmonious holistic model of the world run by Io:

Io

humans

Ninenuiotepo

The world of Maori is a moving, revolving world, where gods conduct a dialogue or where signs affect one another. Io, the prototype of Christ and Yahweh, is the Maori version of the *sacred sign*. The Maori version of Olympus is very much like its ancient Greek prototype, with the postpagan attributes. The Maori world is an empire of signs that points out to a wholesome existential universe, but not without a pattern of the directed semiosis:

> Io (above)
> Rangi and Papa-tua-nukee = Adam/Eve (primeval parents)
> Wairua (spirits)
> Tipuna (ancestors)
> Mana (supernatural power)

The Maori vision combines the two familiar ones — the pagan Greek, and post-pagan Júdeo-Christian. Mircea Eliade reports that the Uralo-Altaic people also had their supreme Hero-God, Bai Ulgen. The people of Konde in Tanganyika had Kyala or Lesa as their supreme being. Similarly to the God of the Christians or Jews, Kyala/Lesa is a law-giving god. Their gods sometimes descend on earth in anger, assuming the body of a lion or a snake (Eliade, 1958:27). Baiame is sacred among the Australian tribes of Kamularoi, Wira Djuri, and Euahayi; he also lives in the sky. Mawu is the supreme version of the Ewe peoples in Africa, who, like Bantus and Pygmies, all acknowledge the power of the single force. Among the Tlingit Indians (North-West Pacific), the central divine figure is a crow, the primal hero and demiurge who made the world," writes Eliade (1958:53). The Samoeds worship Hum, while the Koryaks of the Central Asia call their divinity "the one who dwells in the sky", so do the Eskimos. The Akkadian Anu was the Father of all gods in the ancient Mesopotamia and, like all the gods- inhabitants of the sky, shared the same territory with all the rest of the mythological companions. The sky was the shared locus of the *natural semiosphere* where all the *sacred signs* had apparently originated. The high distance of heaven from the earth stimulated the imagination of the ancient people and the intense production of signs, inspired by the unknown and the unfamiliar. The high sky signalled remoteness and mystery while the empirical reality below was somewhat familiar. The inquiry into the origins of this reality was inaccessible to the ancient *homo-sapiens* who could only recreate the plausible genesis of the world through a metaphor, a sign of the familiar, standing for the unfamiliar. The high/low dichotomy was a convenient route, prompted by the natural signification; the sky/earth enabled the producers of *cultural signs* to signify their image of nature. The distance and remoteness of the sky, as well as its positioning above the inhabitants of the Earth, not only created the image of the vertically-oriented hierarchy, but encoded the societal transformations. The misbehaving gods could descend from above and be placed in the underworld, together with the demons, criminals or all other signs of Evil. In contrast, the extraordinariness of the ordinary mortals could have earned them their ascendance to the sky — the desired noble passage to the heroic realms that was upward-oriented, while the debunking of the extraordinary was downward.

The pagan and Christian mythological universes have practically worked out the future scientific essential symbols through the recognition of the *universal natural signs,* such as high and low, sky and earth, small and big, elephant and an insect, hot and cold, light and dark, white and black, etc..

The empire of the new signs had been constructed with the help of the existing and obvious *natural signs,* which heroes had either to tame, or learn to imitate. The *semiosphere* of Nature was the source of the new heroic deeds, which were to be performed either in real life, or in their imagination. Language, the secondary system of signification, was another semiotic layer above the natural semiosphere, which was to be interpreted by the rest of the passive and active interpreters. The *linguistic signs* communicated not only the observable natural signs, but the reaction of the observers to them (Danesi, 1988; 1993). The heroic stories recorded the awe and admiration of the early *homo-sapiens,* facing the semiotic multitude and reproducing them in the universal hero-signs, emerging and re-emerging throughout the vast territory of the multi-layered cultural space. In other words, the attitude towards the *hero-sign* guaranteed the vitality of the signifier and the intensity of the ongoing semiosis.

2.6 *The Heroic Biography — the Perceptual Model*

The myths, legends, fairy tales of the pagan and post-pagan era have registered the permanent human fascination with the extraordinary, having documented the stability of the narrative structure within which the deeds of various heroes are mediated. The universal narrative structure of all accounts of the heroic is the archetypal biography, the record of life from birth to death. The difference between a biography of the ordinary individual and the extraordinary is in the mode and degree of praise. Death, the culminating point in any biography, is particularly crucial in case of the hero since it is the moment of the recognition of the heroic worth and the beginning for hero-worshipping (Makolkin, 1987).

Biography, the complete life-story from birth to death, is the genre that captures the universal existential law and order. It is actually more than a genre, it is a universal cognitive model which attests to the human acceptance of the finality of dying and singularity of living. The formula of biography is birth and death with the production of signs in between.

Natural signs
B...............D
⇓
Signg production
(cultural)

The production of signs may be more or less influential for the community of the interpreters and more or less heroic. Nonetheless, the paramount influence of the heroic biography has been observed at various stages of civilization and in various cultural contexts. The criteria for measuring the heroic value of the *hero-sign* could change in the course of time, but, irrespective of the changing norms of the heroic behaviour, the heroic biography, the laudatory account of a life and deeds, would remain a constant, and invariable preferred model (Makolkin, 1987; 1988; 1992).

The framework of the heroic biography has proven to be the most comfortable semiotic ground for the expression of the hero-sign, sign-vehicle. According to Eco, certain signs may carry encyclopaedia-like series of meanings but they invariably point out to the characteristic *sememe* (Eco, 1979:105) The "circumstantial selections" or the changing meanings of the hero-sign, be it a giant, a deity, a political leader, a religious figure, a star, a philosopher or a scientist, merely contribute to the ongoing semiosis. The sign-vehicle, Hero, moves along the same pathway while the heroic biography is a universal perceptive model that captures its perpetual movement in the cultural space, regulating the entire collective process of *sign-production*.

The biographical poeticity is nourished by the *semiovalency or degree of meaning* of the *hero-sign,* while, in turn, biography, written and rewritten in a heroic way, prolongs the life of hero after death and satisfies the universal need of the heroic. The hero/villain dichotomy or hero/victim ratio seem to be the most preferred cognitive tools for approaching reality, production of signs and their interpretation (Aaron, 1978; Altick, 1965; Anderson, 1982; Anderson, 1984; Averintsev, 1973; Barakhov, 1985; Bower, 1985; Bertaux, 1981; Cockshut, 1974; Epstein, 1983).

Chapter Three

Romanticism and Reaffirmation
of the Universal Signs

3.1 *Abandoning the Sacred Sign*

For centuries, the heroic biographies of the Christian heroes-saints, martyrs and ecclesiastical leaders, and the sacred accounts of the Highest
Divinity used to dominate the Western cultural text. "The metaphysics of
One and Many", as Lehman puts it, would override the ancient pagan
multideity and the multiple heroes (1966: 93). The reductionist tendency
of the Christian *sign-production* was further promoted by Luther's radical
attitudes towards the Catholic practices and challenged by the development of science and technology. These new *cultural signs,* in turn, would
challenge the canonical *hero-signs.*

During the romantic revival of paganism, neo-paganism and the
industrial revolution, Carlyle's treatise *On Heroes* articulated not only the
transcending quality of the *hero-sign*, but the crisis of the *sacred sign* —
God, celebrating the heroic parade of the industrial revolution. The
achievements of science and technology in the nineteenth century,
changed the perception about the degree of the human extra-ordinariness. Train and telephone, photography and railroads, new chemical elements and new architectural structures, among many other extraordinary
deeds of humans shook the heroic pantheon, constructed by the Church
and Christianity (Carlyle [1841], 1966).

Carlyle articulated the Hero-worship as the universal religion,
embracing both pagan, Christian and post-Christian worship, that   is
simply "the transcendent admiration of a Great Man," the grand modifying element "of human thought" (1966: 11). He found the hero-worship,
the admiration of outstanding individuals, to be the shareable quality in
all types of religion and appreciation of great men in any society. To
Carlyle, Christianity was another form of hero-worship of a single of all
heroes — the unnamed and invisible one. He even defined history in the
light of the heroic paradigm:

> The History of the World is but the biography of great men (1996, [1841]: 29).

For centuries, this dominant great biography was the story of Christ, the
sacred hero-sign. In contrast, Carlyle proposed a totally new system of
signs, which could displace the supremacy of the Christian hero and
worship:

> By religion I do not mean here the church-creed which he professes, the
> articles of faith which will sign and in words or otherwise, assert; not
> this wholly, in many cases not this at all (21).

He viewed hero-worshipping as a characteristic and preferable signification that could be applied to any "great man", or any extra-ordinary
personality. The cult of a single hero had been destroyed by the comparative analysis of paganism, Christianity, and the general cult of the heroic in history and ordinary life. By establishing worship of the Hero as the
founding transcending form of knowledge, Carlyle has undermined the
sacredness of the *supreme sign- Christ:*

> Worship of a Hero is transcendent admiration of a Great Man (11).

He presented the common admiration of a Great Man-Hero as the
universal sign, the existential condition, regardless of the implied allegory.
The universality of this sign deprives the *sacred sign* — Christ of its singularity, uniqueness. In Carlyle's view, this sign is just one of numerous
others, in the past, present and in the future. The sacred quality of Christ
is challenged by the no lesser semiotic significance of Mohammed or
Yahweh. If the meanings of the *sacred sign* could be changed at least once,
they could be changed again, thus the semiotic forces prevail over the
persistent desire of the sign-producers to stop the process at a particular
signification point. Having proclaimed society to have been founded on
Hero-worship, Carlyle indirectly denounced the sacred sign-God and
reduced him to a symbol of temporary certainty. He dealt with prophets
in the similar fashion, treating them as transitional meanings of the *sacred
sign* and the preparatory stages for the new Hero — Man of Letters.

3.2 *Carlylean Hero*

Carlyle, the hero-worshipper, refuses to worship God and forgets to worship the king, "the ablest man". His society is symbolically represented
by a structure of bricks:

> Brick must lie on brick as it may and can.

His "able man" is placed in the upper layer of the societal brick-like
hierarchy, only ultimately to be displaced by the new divinity — the
Man of Letters. Although "the upper brick" — the "rulers" is a required
societal semiotic ground, it is not the most valuable to him:

> The Czar of all the Russias, he is strong with so many bayonets, Cos-
> sacks, and Cannons; and does a great feat in keeping such a tract of
> Earth politically together; but he cannot yet speak. Something great in

him, but is a dumb greatness. He has had no voice of genius, to be heard of all men and times" (114).

Formerly recognized as a given, the hero-ruler is dismissed, lacking the heroic power of a man of letters. This new hero is the true measure of success and heroism. In the Carlylean heroic pyramid, Dante is placed higher than the mighty Russian Tzar. The measure of the heroic ability is Logos, the power of verbal signification that transcends time and place:

Dante speaks to the nobles, the pure and great, in all times and places (100).

The efficacy of the *verbal sign* is his yardstick of all the other signs, the most heroic activity in the Carlylean semiosphere ruled by poets and writers, "the ablest man" of all. Having placed Poet on a higher pedestal, Carlyle attempts to demonstrate how *a verbal sign* may replace the visual image, or how the art of speaking may displace painting. He likens Dante's signs to the visual signs of painters:

I know nothing so intense as Dante, Consider, for example, to begin with the outermost development of his intensity, consider how he paints. (1966:92)

To reconstruct the Dantean visual world Carlyle appeals to the senses of the reader through the icons — *Red, Black, Pink*. The "red pinnacles", "red hot cone of iron glowing", "eternal black" appear next to the "fiery show". Dante's "seeing eye" captures the striking picture of Nature as perceived by Carlyle. His choice of the Dantean imagery is predetermined by his understanding that literature is an "apocalypse of nature", revealing its "open secret". Carlyle's choice of colours from the Dantean visual semiosphere recreates the familiar *natural signs,* such as Tree (green), (white) Snow, (red) Sun and (Brown) Earth. It is remarkable that blue, a *chromatic sign*, traditionally referring to the sky, is absent from the Carlylean chromatic universe. It is quite plausible that this avoidance of the blue sky image, had been influenced by his revised concept of the *sacred sign,* which no longer stood for the familiar Christian God. The new *sacred sign,* the Man of Letters, the painter is more comfortable with the archetypal "red sun" or "brown earth". These *chromatic signs,* selected for the support of the new hero-poet return the perceiver of the signs into the primitive pagan territory, the days of Fire and caves, hands of Odin and rebellious Luther, finally moving away from Raphael, the painter, to the verbal painter- Dante.

Carlylean chromatic upward-moving curve re-invents history, returning man back to the pagan heroic paradigm, only to connect him again with the new sacred sign — Poet. This new messiah is allegedly able to unite Paradise and the Inferno — he can punish and reward man with the simple wonders of nature. Carlylean sky is the sky of a black night where the "stelli literati" gloriously shine. While Dante sparkles as a "pure star", Carlyle addresses the imaginary perceivers, the heroic followers: "If thou follow thy star, Se tu segui tua stella" (1893;100). Star is the archetypal symbol of happiness, a *cultural universal*. The light of the star, as a metaphor, has traditionally stood for the light of knowledge. Carlyle invites the ordinary to follow the star — the poet who is the only hope for men facing the crisis of Christian beliefs and societal order. His new Hero-Poet not only has the skills of a painter, but he also possesses the "musical thought":

> A musical thought is one spoken by a mind that has penetrated into the inmost heart of the thing; detected the inmost mystery of it, namely the melody that ever hidden in it; the inward coherence which is its soul, whereby it exists, and has a right to be, here in this world. All inmost things, we may say, are melodious naturally utter themselves in song (1841: :92).

His newly invented *sacred sign* presents himself in the world of signs through the auditory stimulation, which, in his view, simultaneously conceals and reveals the essence of existence, the deepest form of signification. His hero, the Romantic poet, the resurrected pagan, connected with Nature and Culture through the early forms of representation, Orpheus and a new Homer, only he allegedly is the sign of the ultimate extraordinariness. This hero is endowed with the ability to reinvent the world of nature.

> The world of nature, for every man, is the Fantasy of Himself; this world is the multiplex "image of his own Dream." (1841: 29).

If the existing world is a dream, a fantasy of a hero, then every sign in this macro semiosphere is the mirror of the heroic self. The leap into the neo-paganism justifies the heroic deeds of the new hero, capable of reinventing the world in his imagination and "musical thought. Consequently, *the sacred sign* —God, loses his original meaning, beginning to signify the *verbal, visual* and *auditory* signs created by the hero-poet and his "divine caste", which are placed higher than the Christian and Pagan Gods, and a new secular God— *Roi, the King*. The longevity or immortality of the *verbal signs* seduces Carlyle, himself, a man of letters, who, like every mortal, is haunted by death. He wonders at the miracle of an utterance, the signification that never disappears. Writing enables Carlyle, the sign-producer, to leave a trace of his presence in the macro semiosphere, to perform his extraordinary act, which could save him from oblivion. Thus, Carlyle not only redesigns the heroic pantheon, but he also finds there a place for himself   as well. Frightened by the inex-orable flow of time and haunted by death, the "universal leveller of humanity", Carlyle justifies his own presence in the world through the symbolic image, the *sacred sign* — Hero (Frye, 1968; Andersen, 1982). He would not find any meaning other than in the life of a Hero. His scepti-cism of a post-rationalistic man precludes him from seeing his life through the Divine Hero and the Church, as well as through the Ruler and the State. The limitations of both are obvious while Hero-Poet seems to possess the unlimited power of signification, and thus the truly heroic essence (O'Neill, 1982).

The heroic "Other" imparts meaning to the ordinary "I". The dis-covered poetic double in the face of Dante or Homer places Carlyle, a Man of Letters, onto the new divine Parnassus, amidst the fortunate hero-ic "stelli literati" who may shine forever. The apocalypse of nature could be presumably averted by the heroic deeds of the *verbal sign*-producer, true " Divinity and Savour."

3.3. *Romantic Replicas*

Carlyle's formulation of the Heroic and his replication of the *hero-sign* are not accidental. It is part and parcel of the heroic age of the nineteenth-cen-tury Romanticism, the age marked by romanticizing the archetypal folk-loric hero. It was the age of the heroic Renaissance when the pendulum of the mythical awareness had turned away from the *sacred sign* — Christian God, i.e from the Christian monotheism, swaying back to the pagan multideity. During the romantic period, the inwardness of vision had been revealed in the extreme attention paid towards the primitive archetypal self, and along with it to the folkloric narratives of the past. In the light "of one and many", the heroic paradigm shift could be expressed as:

Polytheism	monotheism	polytheism
multiple heroes	Judeo-Christian	multiple heroes
	God	

The key signs of the Romantic discourse revived the primal arche-typal paired categories, such as Good and Evil, hero and villain, man and animal, barbaric and civilized, high and low. The frequently used verbal icons, re-registering the universal bipolarity of the world in literature and culture at large, juxtaposed the contrasting concepts:

day	night
freedom	war
good	evil

white	dark
small	big
young	old

Morice Pecham would define the romantic period as the "period of the establishment of the self" (Pecham, 1970). In fact, the romantic self redefined itself vis-à-vis the Christian self, through the heroic performance, amidst the struggle for democracy, be it The French or American revolutions, the parade of science (Darwin's *Origin of Species*), the revolution in the political economy and societal order (Adam Smith, Ricardo and Marx) or the Utopian myth of a new Communist proletarian paradise. "Disbelief replaced Belief", — diagnosed Carlyle the shift in the collective heroic performance. The plight for democracy, freedom, liberty and equality was based on the revolutionized model of thinking, the changes in belief, or the transformations in the collective mythical consciousness. The perception of the hero-sign had changed and affected the production of new signs, be they myths, or mythically instigated extraordinary actions and universes.

Christianity had been undermined and questioned, the ecclesiastical heroes, saints and martyrs were moved again to the periphery of Culture, giving place to the new heroes-revolutionaries and revolutionary thinkers, reformers of society and seekers of the new heroic deeds. "It was a revolution in the human mind", wrote Pecham. It was a new form of heroic signification that paradoxically revived the archaic pagan heroism, amidst the revolution in art, politics, economics science and technology of the pre-industrial society rejecting the agrarian mode for the new urban society (Pecham, 1970; Fry, 1968; Dakin, 1981; Karl, 1983; Alekseev, 1975; Bentley, 1963).

The neo-pagan renaissance concurred with the shift from the primitive agriculture-oriented world to the urban technology-oriented universe of railroads and machinery, steam and speed, which had opened new heroic vistas, presenting new heroic occasions and tests. Searching for the new romantic Self, the post-Christian Self simultaneously resurrected the *pagan signs*. The extraordinary deeds of the romantic heroes of the industrial revolution did not meet the mythical aspirations of the ordinary. Human anguish, quest for the unattainable paradise, despair and anger of the betrayed Self had revealed itself in the volumes of the passionate romantic poetry and novels, heroic music and a striking visual imagery. The romantic period would go down in history as the most intense, energetic and memorable time in the history of Culture. The sources for the production of new signs and the normative principles were widened and enriched by science, technology and art (Schenk, 1979).

Douglas Dakin describes romanticism as a reaction to the pressures from above, i.e. the dominating and sign-controlling societal institutions, such as Church, State and science:

> Romanticism had no exclusive ideology, no steadfast political affiliation and no firm artistic or literary precepts. Romantics went their various ways by intuition in defiance of ideologies, social conventions and religious traditions (1981: 5).

It was a mood of defiance and an alternate mode of thinking — a challenge to the existing models for the sign production. In opposition to certainty and firm beliefs, the romantics offered Doubt and scepticism, drawing attention to the pagan signs of the past, with their mystery, abyss of the unknown and the old *hero-signs*. The old heroes appeared to be the true heroes in contrast with the "forged notes", false Christian heroes of the post-pagan era.

If the eighteenth century was the age of the enlightenment, deep belief in Reason, power of the mind, the nineteenth century would embrace Feeling, or the attitude towards the Sign. In the light of the heroic, the romantic hero was not a thinker, but a doer, active rebel against all the forms of sign-production, be it church, industry, science or capital. The general feeling was that of debunking, rejection and disillusionment.

The Christian saint, a monk or a priest was as repugnant to the romantics as the industrial capitalist and inventor of speed, light, sound and engine. The new signs created by science or technology were intimidating, inspiring nostalgia for the old heroic folkloric universe. The paradigm of nature and the natural forces were perceived as an escape from the unknown and intimidating extra-ordinariness, produced by the artificial human hand — machine. Carlyle would summarize his fear of the new signs —technology and machinery— in his exalted narrative, dedicated to the pagan heroic past:

> The living Tree Igdrasil, with the melodious prophetic waving of its world-wide boughs, deep-rooted as Hela, has died-out into the clanking of a World-Machine. Tree and Machine; Contrast Two things, I, for my share, declare the world to be no machine'(1841; 196).

Anticipating the technocratic abyss of the next century, Carlyle condemns and rejects the eighteenth, the 'Sceptical century, the culprit of the misery for the ordinary.' Nature and its wonders are nostalgically represented by the *natural sign* — Tree, and the pagan mythological heroic universe by Hela. Carlyle would propose the basic formula for the century he lived in and its main essential ground:

Tree	Machine
Nature	Culture
Agriculture	Technology
Past	Present /Future

He also predicted that the conflict between the *natural* and *cultural signs* would eventually create the world dominated by machines, leading to the Apocalypse of the human world, the Orwellian hell in Art and Culture. The Carlylean tree/machine ratio anticipates the technocratic madness of the twentieth century and the future crisis in the successful production of new cultural signs — music, painting, literature, which he labels as "spiritual paralysis amidst the "mechanical life" (1966: 171).

Frightened by the possibility of such dangerous semiosphere that could enslave *homo-sapiens*. Carlyle proposes a new religion, a new semiotic cure through the *hero-sign* — Man of Letters. The mythological cartography of his own making where the social hierarchy is signified by the "bricks" —signs of various classes— is eventually adjusted to the needs of the new sign-poet:

	p	o	e	t	
p	a	i	n	t	er
s	i	n	g	e	r
m	o	n	a	r	ch

The new hero-sign is empowered with such a *semiovalence* that he may challenge even "the checks and balances", the sacred signs of the newly developing industrialism and capitalism. Carlyle rejects the entire new system of signs, inspired by capital at the expense of what he labels as "spiritual paralysis". "Machine" represents the archetypal evil, which includes the economist, industrialist and technocrat, not possessing the "vital forces" of the Man of Letters, nor his imagination.

Northrop Frye's attention to the imaginary and Deity in the next century would result in the circular semiotic model where the unknown and the engine-so-to speak would be placed in the middle, while the Carlylean model is a rigid square:

	N.Frye		Carlyle
	myth time		poet
			myth-maker
	nature		rulers
	culture		technocrat
myth time	mysteries	myth time	capitalist
	Hero		banker
	nature		clergyman
			saint
	myth time		pagan deity

Heroism is the belief in the extraordinary, in the world of possibility while the sceptical pre-technocratic ethos is disbelief, the denial of the heroic. Carlyle's heroes are the characters of the Nordic sagas and ancient Greek myths, the "sincere" men, the ideal human individuals. The sceptics of the eighteenth century were his hostile enemies of the heroes, who have allegedly destroyed the pure and sincere beginnings, the foundation of the true *hero-sign*. Having deprived man of the heroic status, they instead transferred the extraordinary possibility onto the man-made objects — machines, the helpers. This transfer of meaning from the *hero-sign* to the helper was very repugnant to the romantics of the nineteenth century, who were willing to "enhance the individual grandeur" of man via human imagination, the *cultural signs,* such as art, history, national culture, politics or economics (Cantor, 1988: 3).

The Romantics expressed the semiophobia or fear of the new *cultural signs* which would stifle the producer of signs, his/or her semiotic power. To prevent this creative apocalypse romantics elaborated the philosophy of the heroic deeds, such as struggle for freedom, equality, social welfare and return to the pagan folkloric roots. The replication of the *hero-sign* occurred in a new semiotic environment. The image of "folk", so much cherished by the romantics, was associated with purity, sincerity, the Tree of unlimited knowledge and the truly heroic boundless universe. The romantic movement was the age of debunking the Judeo Christian philosophy and its heroic models. In contrast, it offered the escape into the Hellenic pagan heroism and search for its heroic tokens, analogues in each particular tradition. The revived and transformed heroic paradigm of the romantics included the individual and group heroism.

The individual heroism, inspired by the Faustian or Byronic versions, or Hellenic tokens co-existed with the intense group heroic drive, seeking the heroic title for its particular community. The Hellenic heroic cult stimulated the production of new *hero-signs,* amidst entire   groups, searching for their own collective heroic stock of the past, the parallel paganism, integrated into the national mythology. The quest for the heroic ultimately and logically formed the foundation for the heroic context between groups. Carlyle's theory of the nation-hero is not clearly formulated in his treatise *On the Heroic,* but already serves as a precursor for the mythical heroic delusions of the twentieth century (Bentley, 1963).

Greece was the European cultural matrix for the individual and collective heroism, the desired collective hero, despite the fact that the Greek polis was a rather timid prototype of the future national state. The Olympic deities were equally worshipped in all cities-states but some islands could claim to be the birthplaces of particular heroes. For instance, Delphi could take pride in being the heroic territory of Apollo, the prototype of the national pride for the future Western national states and so much admired by Nietzsche and the ideologues of the German national socialism. Hero and national hero vis-à-vis heroic clusters, nation-heroes — these were the key points within the shifting romantic heroic paradigm. The Romantic hero was anti-Christian in its basic essence, i.e. particularity versus universality was its prevailing meaning of the reconstructed heroic semiosphere. The Romantic ethos provided the semiotic basis for the ideology of the so-called national-liberation movements, which represented a violent competition for the collective heroic title — Nation-Hero. The nation-hero as a sign signified a collective heroic identity of a single group, which presupposed the saturation of the extraordinary and superior.

The Christian heroic paradigm had failed on a collective basis, which was first revealed in the revision through Reformation, second, through Calvinism, later puritanism and ultimately as a post-enlightenment syndrome. The Marxist theory of the heroic impoverished masses was an attempt to save the Christian heroic mode and to impose the heroic behaviour pattern upon the poorest of the global village. The Christian God-father to humanity was replaced by deity — Marx, demanding the extraordinary universal *homo-sapiens*. There was inner saturation of the heroic in the Marxist mythical territory, all members of the proletariat were encouraged to become revolutionary heroes, battling the *corrupt sign* — capital. They were also defined as members of the single brotherhood, the dwellers of the new Marxist Olympus. The Romantic myth undermined and destroyed the Marxist myth which had rejected the primacy of the particular.

The key icon of the romantic discourse was Folk-volk, the particular collectivity, symbolizing the heroic self of a particular group. The precursors of the romantic future delusions may be observed already in Luther, who juxtaposed in his *The Christian Nobility of the German Nation* the key icons-Folk and Nation, creating the first significant anti-Christian meanings within the Christian discourse. Since the Christian man is a loving brother to all human beings, the specific heroic Christian status of the German Christians strikes as a new and hostile meaning of the accepted signifier, a preference of a particular selected heroism, i.e. German Christianity.

Luther's subtle infatuation with the particular collective heroism could be linked with Herder's 1773 essay on Ossian and the later research by brothers Grimm. Jakob and Wilhelm Grimm, guided by their philological and paleontological interests, had collected the early German sagas and fairy tales. By Christmas of 1812, their collection of German folklore became the most widely reading material after the Bible (Snyder,

1952: 51). The obsession with folklore did not limit itself to Germany, all European nations at that time had been in a state of frenzied search for their roots, folk heritage and extraordinary collective psyche, something that would be later labelled as the national character, or national fate. The serenity of the Victorian European culture had been destroyed by this collective neurosis, that would eventually lead to the energetic heroic contest among groups for the title of the most extraordinary Hero-nation. The supreme hero —God of the Christians— had disappeared to be displaced by the new post-Christian heroic multitude-national poet, national hero, national leader, nation-martyr and so on.

The Carlylean hero-poet would be later replaced by the national hero-poet, the cult of the Man of Letters be challenged by the variety of cults, such as particular language, particular art, particular way of cultural construction, particular heritage. The Romantic mode encouraged the intensification of the semiotic heroic process along the lines of the particular. The motif of struggle, a part of the heroic plot was the predominant feature of the Romantic *semiosis* and the Romantic *heroic replica* evolved as a result of this cult of struggle and tensions within the heroic paradigm:

> Hero-nation
> hero-poet
> hero-national poet
> hero-leader
> neo-pagan hero
> hero- romantic revolutionary

The Romantic Self was in the state of turmoil, confusion and intense mass rebellion, ultimately imitating the archetypal folk Self and focussing on the elimination of the societal constraints, such as monarchy, capital, church and partly the scientific activity. The rebellion against the *sacred sign* resulted in sharp criticism of Christianity, and a satirical portrayal of the clergy. The romantic imagination gave rise to the neo-pagan myth, the new Christian religion of Marxism, disguised as atheism, all of which could flourish within the canonical heroic paradigm. The geographical territory of the heroic deeds of the romantic heroes was vast — from Europe to Asia, Africa and Australia and New Zealand (Bentley, 1963). If the folk hero could be satisfied with the results of his heroic deeds within a small territory of a village hut, city, or kingdom, the Romantic hero demanded more physical space and consequently a larger territory of worship. For instance, it was not enough for Napoleon to be a French national hero. His heroic drive led him to Russia and Egypt. The shadow of the ancient hero-Alexander of Macedonia — provoked a new heroic mimesis. The declaration of independence of the United States enshrined another system of signs, driven by the grand heroic plans to create a nation-hero.

The Marxist heroic schema envisioned in the distant future the collective heroic tribe of the happy labourers, living in the paradise of equality, dosaged labour and benefit. The Russian revolution was not only the re-enactment of the Marxist heroic drama, but the display of the eternal enchantment with the heroic. (O'Neill, 1989). Romanticism was not only the fertile semiotic ground for the *hero-signs*, with their enormous destructive and constructive energy, but it also produced the *disenchanted hero*, exemplified by the post-Byronic depression of the Russian hero — poet, Lermontov:

> Sadly I look at my generation.
> Its future is empty and dark.
> Oppressed by cognition and doubt,
> It will age in inaction.
>
> We love and hate by chance,
> Without sacrifice to either,
> A secret cold reigns in our hearts,
> While fire boils in the veins.
>
> A gloomy and soon forgotten crowd,
> We shall pass without a noise or trace,
> Without a single thought, or labour proud.
> [1838: "Duma" (Thought)]

Lermontov's hero is the Carlylean "unable" individual, disenchanted Byronic hero, the marginalised social "actant", suffering   from his own ordinariness, his lack of the heroic endowments, who experiences the agony of death anxiety, the fear of dying "without a trace," his mark in the cultural *semiosphere*. Lermontov's *disenchanted hero,*   immortalized in Pechorin, is   the main protagonist of his novel, a *Hero of Our Times*, who has embodied the anxiety of the "able man" and his failure to reach the boundaries of the extraordinary. Lermontov's hero   is the romantic anti-hero, who has failed the heroic expectations of his age, community and the   higher   standards,   imposed   by   the   romantic   heroic   paradigm. Pechorin is the *anti-sign*, contrasting other European cultural heroes, such as Goethe's Faust, Schiller's Willhelm Tell, Casanova, or Napoleon, among others, Lermontov's heroic replica imitates the Byronic *anti-sign*, Child Harold or Corsair, whose extra-ordinariness basically revealed itself in the rejection of the ordinary multitude, rather than response to its heroic demand (Makolkin, 1992).

3.4. *Sources of the Carlylean Heroic Semiotics*

Carlyle's definition of the universal semiotic pattern through the prevailing heroism could be traced to Shelley and Fichte, Hume and
Rousseau, Seigei Ouvaroff, Thomas Taylor and Hobbes, Milton, Coleridge and Schelling (Babbitt, 1919; Froude, 1884; Lehman, 1966). The
Fichtean "divine Idea of the world" gets replaced by the heroic human
concept of the man-made "empire of signs", while his reality is only a
stage towards the highest supreme moment. In contrast, the Carlylean
semiosphere, driven by the heroic, is the contemporary," here and now",
which is possible precisely due to the heroic deeds of humans and their
supreme heroes -men of letters, producers of the *verbal signs*. His familiarity with the Fichtean semiosphere, ultimately ruled by the *sacred sign*
— God, by no means could imply a direct "borrowing" from Fichte, as
Lehman suggested (1966:121-2). The Fichtean *heroes* are the servants of
God, while Carlyle's heroes are the leaders of the ordinary, serving
humanity through their extraordinary power.

Carlyle's Divinity-Poet is the Confucian Master, who may not "know
it all", but who is guided by his concept of the Whole, the connecting
thread, "fantasia" or imagination (Confucius, 1956). His poet is the
Vicean creator of metaphor, the source of knowledge, the engine of cognition and ultimately the civilized being ,who reasons and talks, rather
than uses the spear (G.Vico, 1744). The Vicean heroes were barbarians
who fought and used to be proud of their physical force. The heroic age,
in the Vicean sense, was a stage of shame and violence, which humans
should rather forget. Carlyle did not share the scepticism of Vico, nor did
he idealize the after-heroic age, the supreme stage in the developmental
stage of humanity. Vico had a negative connotation behind the *hero-sign*,
which, to him, stood for a violent dialogue of the giants and ultimately
death of the weakest (Vico, [1744], 1962). Carlyle re-described the meaning of the *hero-sign*, that   no longer represented the force of the Body, but
the force of the mind, the imagination, which is able to produce a new
metaphor, conduct a civil exchange of verbal signs. His semiotic law was
formulated in the shadow of Keats and Coleridge, Byron and Shelley,
Scott and Words-worth and their creative attempt to liberate the Self.

Rousseau's natural man, with his limited goals and desires, was a
small hero, who needed a small heroic territory. Carlyle's *hero-sign* was
nourished by the cult of Genius, titanic figures that inspired and disturbed the romantic poets, the Hegelian worship of the Greek physique
and Schiller's myth of resurrection of the Greek totality. He remained
indifferent to Johann Caspar Lavater's heroic *face-sign*, his preoccupations with phrenology and the worship of the extraordinary exterior
(Lavater, [1775], 1891). The Carlylean dictum, regarding the foundation of

society on hero-worship pays equal tribute to "necessarians" (Hume, Hobbes, Collins, Leibnitz, Priestley, etc.) and advocates of liberty and free will — Clarks, Beattie, Butler, Price etc. (Reed, 1989: 35). The *hero-sign* appears since his emergence is a necessity, an expressed need for the heroic, and he is able to act heroically since he possesses the freedom to signify. However, this aspect is less emphasized by Carlyle, whose hero needs his own will to create *the verbal signs*. The Carlylean Hero unifies the Hebrew messiah, the Babylonian Gilgamesh, the Confucian master, Machiavelli's Prince, Plato's philosopher and the Plutarchian politician, along with the numerous other heroic antecedents. His hero-sign asserts himself not through logic, but via poetic intuition, the metaphor and *verbal signs*. According to him, "to get into the truth of anything is ever a mystic act — of which the best Logic can but babble on the surface" (1898; 65-66). Carlyle's infatuation with the intuitive, mystically penetrating reasoning contradicts the theory of Peirce, who worship's the logical understanding and elevates cognition through the omnipresence of the Sign.

3.5   The   Peircean Hero-Sign

According to Peirce, "all human affairs rest upon probabilities" and the extraordinary actions may be performed, based on the extra-logical ability of the mind to access them. Thus, the extra-logical in Peirce is the essentially the   heroic:

> The very idea of probability and of reasoning rests on the assumption that this number is indefinitely great (1932, vol. II;397-8).

Peirce's hero is the logical individual, who "would sacrifice his own soul to save the whole world". At the same time, Peirce does not demand this capacity from all, since not all are capable of being so "logical":

> It is not necessary for logicality that a man should himself be capable of the heroism of self-sacrifice. It is sufficient that he should recognize the possibility of it, should perceive that only that man's inferences who has it are really logical, and should consequently regard his own as being only so far valid as they would he accepted by the hero (1932, vol II: 398 ([2:654]).

Peirce does not impose the judgement of the other sign-producers upon the design and pattern of the *hero-sign*, but rather allows it to develop freely one's semiotic capacity, revealing one's heroic, i.e. the logical power to the community.

Peircean heroism rests on the doctrine of chances, the logical understanding of its essence and the limited heroic horizons, since his heroic *semiosis* is not unlimited. No matter how successful the hero is, the end of one's heroic performance is eminent and unavoidable. His heroism, rooted in the appraisal of the sign-production and sign-arrangement, has three key attitudes, which Peirce calls "sentiments" around the perpetual functioning of the heroic paradigm:

> namely, interest in an indefinite community, recognition of the possibility of this interest, being made supreme and hope in the unlimited continuance of intellectual activity, as indispensable requirements of logic (2,655, 1932, vol II; 399).

The Peircean *hero-sign* has a highly moral, ethical meaning. Unlike the Carlylean supreme Hero-Poet, who stands above the ordinary, the Peircean hero is a logical appraiser of the heroic possibilities and serves the community of the ordinary. His image is more humble and more connected with the Christian moral philosophy.

3.6 *Peircean Secondness as a Romantic Invention*

According to Charles Peirce, sign is a triadic form which is parallel to the existential triad, possessing the Aristotelean beginning, middle and end:

> The beginning is first, the end is second, the middle in third.   (1,337)

At the same time, the first is the "presentment of the sign", which evokes feeling and attitude of the perceivers towards it. The Firstness of the sign is its presentment, while Secondness is feeling and struggle, as Peirce argues, contradicting himself and dwelling on Secondness. Secondness is the character, the essence of the presented sign, which secures further production of the new meanings in the future (1,344). A little later in the same volume, Peirce imparts the third with the same qualities he had earlier defined as the expression of Secondness:

> The third is that which bridges over the chasm between the absolute first and last, and brings them into a relationship. (1,359)

The Feeling and Struggle would   become his   key reactions to the Romantic signification, which was greatly dependent upon the forces, aroused by the intense functioning of the heroic paradigm. The heroic semiosis demanded the natural choice between the more ordinary and most extraordinary heroic phenomena to direct the course of the familiar process into the most orderly fashion, towards the supremely heroic. It is remarkable that Peircean triadic formula of the principles of signification includes such Romantic icons, as Feelings and Struggle. Peirce demonstrates that the semiotic field at any given moment remains very much affected by the emotions of the perceivers around. In the case of the *Hero-sign,* the reaction to it was always highly emotionally charged. Hero was inseparable from the romantic sign- Feeling. The foregrounding of the heroic in the romantic signification also meant emphasis on the extreme and radical feelings. The romantico-heroic paradigm could be defined as the cult of Secondness, the prolonged phase of semiosis, while Eco's "continuum", as he would name,   the advanced stages of semiosis, is allegedly prepared for further manipulation by the *dominant signs.* In case of the dominant *hero-sign* it was a "vicious circle" where the hero was invented to evoke emotions or the intense emotions eventually led to invention of the hero (Peirce, 1932; Eco, 1979; Makolkin, 1992a).

Chapter Four

Hero-Sign in the Delayed Secondness

4.1 *Hero, Logos, the Secondary Heroic Meta-Tale*

Wilhelm von Humboldt's treatise *On Language* is very much a part of the romantico-heroic signification of the nineteenth century which would lay the foundation for the future heroic delusions of the 20th century. His meta-discourse on language assisted in the construction of the myth of the superior languages, superior family of languages and superior nation-hero. It continues the heroic saga of the superiority of the Greek nation, Greek language and culture. For Humboldt, Logos is the heroic sign, the expression and embodiment of a special heroic particularity:

> Language, is, as it were, the outer appearance of the spirit of the people, the language is their spirit and the spirit is their language (1988, 46).

Language is the signifier of a particular heroic force of the collective pro-ducer-nation. The Greek language, in Humboldt's view, is the superior verbal embodiment of the heroic people and their special heroic spirit. It possesses a special "grace fullness", like a skilful dancer. He grants the Greek language its heroic title and status among other Indo-European languages (Humboldt, 1988). Latin and its close family of the Romance languages possess a slightly lower status in his heroic hierarchy. The German language is described as the re-designer of the ancient heroic verbal signs, after Sanskrit, Greek and Latin. Humboldt's heroic linguis-tic saga has many elements of the fairy-tale, with the only exception that the hero is not a single individual, but a group, a collective producer of the system of *verbal signs*. His comparative linguistic account is a sophis-ticated heroic representation of the lives of the strong, vibrant and cre-ative species- languages, such as Sanskrit, Greek, Latin and German, ver-sus the "weaker", allegedly less civilized ones, such as the monosyllab-ic Chinese, or agglutinative Finno-Ugric family!?

At the root of his comparison, there is a simple heroic matrix, lan-guage-hero, produced by the heroic group. The metaphors used are — tree, family, inheritance, male and female line. German appears as the strongest offshoot of the linguistic tree family, with the best inherited linguistic genes/properties of the *proto-sign* system— the unmentionable Indo-European, the venerated Sanskrit and Greek languages. His organ-ic model of analysis used in his comparative study is focussed on inflec-tion, as the manifestation of the viability of the particular language-specie and simultaneously as a marker of higher civilization. The high/low and barbaric/ civilized ratios are his basic tool in the creation of the heroic hierarchy of languages and nations (Tong, 1993: 29-47). According to this model, the non-Indo-European languages, lacking inflection, are deprived of the vital force and possess no heroic future. The Chinese language, in Humboldt's classification, is a non-heroic specie and, thus, neither are its carriers, the speakers of Chinese, the able intellectual species!?

The Indo-European family, particularly, Sanskrit, Greek and German as their fundamental parts, are elevated to the status of the heroic signs, and in the future, the dangerous borderline between the ordinary and the extraordinary *verbal signs* would be drawn, as a semiotic base for the heroic delusions and the dangerous continuum of racism. From a general sign-logos, Humboldt proceeds to the design of the particular Hero-Logos, whom he leaves undone, understated, only to be vigorously improved by others. If a language could be the measuring yardstick for the assessment of the mental development, then the languages, with the allegedly weaker powers, could be shared by the supposedly mentally weaker species. The seeds of social Darwinism had been pre-planted in the Humboldtian organic model, only to be replanted on the different soil, i.e. the socio-political context of the future Europe, obsessed with the heroic origins of some of its inhabitants. Ultimately, the table of the Indo-European Languages would become the heroic pantheon of the verbal semiotic systems, where only the strongest and the most "civilized" species could be included. The majority of the languages of Asia, Africa and Australia and New Zealand had been excluded as the inferior Other, the ordinary unsophisticated symbols of the inferior mental development.

The colonizers of the New World would rely heavily on Humboldt's linguistic Darwinism and equate the differences in the presentment of the *verbal signs,* with the deficiencies of thought. The monosyllabic Chinese would stand for the primitive organization of thought. Wharf's study of the Hopi language and the observation of the poor expression of colour in their linguistic semioshpere would lead him to the erroneous perception about the alleged limited chromatic capacity of the Hopi. Similarly, Umberto Eco would repeat the same false strategy in his study of the words standing for colour and people using them (Eco, 1991). On the basis of the assumed role of number of icons, standing for colour, Eco would construct the entirely new theory of cultural types. Unlike Wharf or Humboldt, Eco would not associate "many" and "poli" with civilization. In contrast, the multitude of verbal signs standing for colour would signify to him the primitive barbaric nature of a particular culture. Eco would imply in the twentieth century that the cultural text of Eskimos, with the numerous ways of describing snow, is allegedly inferior to the cultural organization of the Greeks, Romans and modern Italians, who are presumably colour-blind and whose languages reflect the poor chromatic semiosis (Makolkin, 1993). In his own way, Eco subverts the old Humboldtian one/many ratio and manipulates the continuum in such a manner that the monosyllabic *verbal signs,* or poli-inflected signs no longer stand for the high/low ratio. On the contrary, they become totally irrelevant, Eco departs from the qualitative approach in the analysis of signs and instead suggests the quantitative one, i.e. the quality of thought, rather than quantity of linguistic elements. However, Eco does not reject the high/low ratio in the comparative analysis of the sign production. Some, such as the Greek, Roman, Italian, German and English, are presented as the superior sign-systems and superior sign-producers, while others, like Eskimos, Russians and some Indian tribes, are treated as inferior. To Eco, the absence of the *verbal signs* signifies the presence of the higher unspoken, invisible semiotic of the superior, heroic cultural text (Eco, 1991; Makolkin, 1993).

4.2. *Grimm's Morphology as a Metabase*

Humboldt's theory of the linguistic "heroism" originates in and greatly owes to the philological comparativism of brothers Grimm, whose emphasis on the phonemes, particularly vowels, had led to the basic unification of such distant linguistic species, as German and Sanskrit. Having established the semiotic affinity between the various codes, brothers Grimm had invented the heroic tale of the proto-language, its alleged developmental history, ultimately determining a rather unique place of the German code within the Indo-European family. Brothers Grimm had perceived the German language, as the strong vital young growing part of the Indo-European body of languages and the carrier of a particular heroic spirit. The myth of the strong North, Nordic, Teutonic spirit permeates their classification of languages, exploiting the upper/lower semiotic ratio in the design of the famous table. It is not accidental that the more "heroic" codes, such as Icelandic, English, Saxon, Prussian and Germanic are placed at the top of the table, while the root codes, that had stimulated borrowing of the vital abstract vocabulary, such as Greek, Sanskrit or Hittite are situated at the bottom.

The Body metaphor, another competing *romantic sign,* plays a significant role in Grimm's appraisal of the linguistic signification and construction of the *verbal signs.* They distinguished the three stages in the development of language, which fulfil the metaphoric prescription of the beginning, middle and end. The beginning is the metaphor, standing for the pre-verbal, "childhood" stage of gestures and sounds and naming of concrete objects, the so-called "noun-stage". The second, is the vital youth period when most of the creative activity would have occurred, the so-called" verb-period". The third, although a metaphor of age and wisdom, was still regarded as a phase of decay (Kamenetsky, 1992: 108).

The second stage in the development of the *verbal signs* was the time for the production of more complex systems, such as epic, poetry and tale, representing more complex semiotic structures and being still very transparent semiotic layers. They still reflect the true self of the young, vigorous human body which is capable of the heroic action. The folklore and fairy tales, studied by brothers Grimm and others, had been treated as semiotic constructs, marking of the heroic phase in the developmental history of the language and were the key operative categories. They signified youth and vitality of the Body in its heroic phase.

Their *naturpoesis* assisted brothers Grimm in reconstructing the archaeology of cognition as they perceived it, i.e. through the Romantic quest for liberation of the mind and healing the Body. Their semiotic universe had two basic levels — the level of the popular culture via fairy tale promotion, and the meta-discourse level via the theory of language development. However, both of them manipulated the youth/old age ratio at their deep semantic level, trying to rejuvenate the heroic paradigm. Their theories about fairy tales and concepts of languages had boosted the heroic paradigm and substantiated the return of the pagan hero-signs. Brothers Grimm inspired the global infatuation with the heroic past. The natural sign- replicas, such as fairy-tales, sagas, and epic tales had been at the root of the semiotic process, the natural organic *proto-morpheme* of the collective heroic *mythopoesis*.

The myth of Rousseau's natural man, Herder's folkloric beginning, Luther's supreme Christian and Friedrich Schlegel's search for the "holistic spirit of the past" — all stimulated Grimm's heroic archaeology of the semiotic universe. The Hegelian heroic hierarchy would arise from the similar epistemological sources and would complement the traditional heroic paradigm.

4.3. *Hegelian Perfect Signs*

The Hegelian philosophy and aesthetics are also largely rooted in the concepts of the heroic, having been constructed around his heroic hierarchy, where God /Spirit is the *supreme sign*, the source of the *perfect signs*, the manifestations of the spirit. Hegelian *perfect signs* are the heroic individuals, heroic groups and heroic collective activities, such as art, poetry, drama, painting, music, architecture or philosophy (Makolkin, 1992, b:57). After his *supreme sign*, spirit, Hegel places the hero, the performer of the most extraordinary actions, actualizing the universal spirit, since he treats action as a universal sign, hero is a *universal sign* as well. To Hegel, heroes are individuals, who act independently, driven by their desire to lead and perform a deed that is right and moral (1975, vol I: 185). Heroes are endowed with the utmost intelligence , enabling them to determine the moral, legal and ethical parameters of their preplanned collective activity for the group.

The Hegelian heroic theory appears "as a time, in which virtue, in the Greek sense of *agape*, is the basis of actions (1985, vol I: 85). And its ideal heroic age is the Greek cultural past constructed by the will and virtue of the individual heroes, unlike the Roman age built on the communal law and order. To Hegel, Homeric heroes and mythical Greek gods were the manifestation of the heroic particularity, unlimited freedom of the "willing and achieving". Should the actions of the heroes be immoral, the responsibility and guilt be shared by the rest of the group in the heroic age that knows no separation between the individual and collective:

> Of such separation the Heroic Age knew nothing. There the guilt of the ancestor descends to his posterity, and a whole generation suffers on account of the original criminal; the fate of guilt and transgression is continually inherited (1985, vol I; 188).

Hegel's ideal Heroic age is the time of Homer and Agamemnon, Hesiod and Pindar, ie.e the Greek past constructed by the ideal heroes and recorded in its legendary epic. Epic, the account of the utmost bravery and morality, is the perfect form of heroic signification. Hegel judges cultures according to the presence or absence of this genre in their artistic history. Hegel claims that the Chinese cultural text is void of epic, which is indicative of their non-poetic particularity. The poetry/prose ratio assists Hegel in dividing all cultures into the poetic (civilized) and prosaic (less civilized). The same he applies to the folk song which serves as a criterion of barbarism:

> Peoples who have only got so far as poems of this kind and have not reached a higher stage of lyric or produced epic or dramatic works are therefore for the most part semi-barbaric with an undeveloped organization and with transitory feuds and catastrophes (1985, vol. II;1125).

Since Chinese, according to Hegel, do not have epic, they have not developed beyond the semi-barbaric stage. In contrast, the Greeks, the producers of epic and drama, the heroic tragedy and visual arts, are the *perfect sign-producers* in the universe of the *cultural signs*, who occupy the highest place in the Hegelian cultural hierarchy controlled by the heroic. Hegel consistently and persistently attempts to establish the heroic status, either of a particular genre or language. Being aware of Sanskrit and Hebrew, Persian and Latin, Slavic and Germanic languages and literatures, Hegel still struggles with the multitude of the sign-producers and semiotic texts. The vast heroic paradigm forces him and enables him to place a sign, or a series of signs either higher, or lower in his ideal *semiosphere*. The epic/folk song ratio. enabled him to place the entire Chinese cultural text below the Hebrew and Arabic, Persian and Sanskrit, while the lyrical narrative assisted him in juxtaposing the German and Slavic literatures and poetries. The heroic principle or "the principle of personality", as Hegel calls it, helps him to classify the German and Slavic cultural texts, having placed the latter clearly below the German:

> This principle is effective in the most perfect and unclouded way in the case of the Germanic races, while the Slavonic ones, on the other hand,l have first to struggle out of an oriental immersion in the universal substance of theirs (vol II, 1985:1153).

The Greeks, the producers of the ideal, heroic lyric, drama, epic and other forms of glorification of the particularity are the *perfect signs*, the manifestation of the supreme spirit, the holders of the ultimate heroic ideal. They are also the alleged signifiers of the most *semiovalent sign* — the heroic civilization. The Greek language is his favoured system of the most *seductive signs* — Greek words, in which the heroic, poetry drama and epic had been written. Hegel's fascination with the Greek verbal signs echoes the Humboldtian attitude and the general cult of the Greek ethnocentrism in the Western culture. Hegel juxtaposes the North/South and East/West ratios, using them as the classificatory principles in the description of the cultural text, obsessively searching for the *perfect signs,* the ideal producers of the heroic.

According to Hegel, the Chinese, who did not have the epic poetry dedicated to the particular individual heroism, were somewhat deficient in their production of *cultural signs*. Similarly, the Slavs, clinging more towards the oriental universalism, are to a certain degree inferior to the Germans, who clearly distinguish between the qualities of the individual and the collective specific ities. Hegel is not consistent in his critique of the group identities, in the light of their attitude towards the hero-signs. Ultimately, he is guided by the desire to establish the heroic hierarchy, where the Germans, the sign-producers of the *superior signs,* would be justifiably placed above the rest of the Europeans and the Orientals. Being aware of the rich cultural texts in the East, or Mediterranean regions, he gradually constructs his heroic pyramid. Initially, Hegel has to dispense with the mysterious Orient. The monosyllabic Chinese, lacking the epic and poetry, makes Hegel lean towards the archetypal barbaric/civilized dichotomy of racism, where the allegedly less sophisticated Chinese language itself locks the Chinese sign-producers into the inferior semiosphere!?

Guided by the kinship between the languages of the Indo-European family, Hegel, similarly to many other European thinkers, mistakenly assumes that all the Other, unfamiliar codes that do not share this linguistic codal relationship, are presumably limited in their capacity to signify and create new meanings. The Indo-European kinship, manifested through the common linguistic root, would become also a sign of the linguistically superior code, which through inflection has the infinite possibility to develop new form and meanings. It would produce the myth of the cultural hierarchy, built in into various codes which would eventually nurture such *dangerous signs,* as Eurocentricity, around the French, Italian, English, German or other superiority (Tong, 1993).

Hegelian tendency towards the *perfect signs,* the Greek ideal cultural icons, expressed itself not only in his classification of languages, verbal art and his general attitudes towards the hero-signs, but to the visual arts as well. In Hegel's view, the Greek sculpture and architecture were the other set of perfect signs ,produced by the superior sign producers —the Greeks, the supreme hero-signs in the heroically elevated European cultural *semiosphere.* If analysing languages and verbal arts Hegel resorts to the familiar primitive/civilized paradigm, while approaching the visual arts, he uses the aesthetic function of the sign, the beautiful/ugly ratio. The Greek sculpture presumably expresses not only its own beauty but the beauty of its producers, ancient artists. Hegel echoes Leonardo's dictum of the European renaissance which insisted on the beauty of the artist as a necessary precondition for the production of the beautiful images or *beauty-signs* (Leonardo, 1802:131). The followers of Leonardo shared his belief into the organic aesthetic unity between the sign and its producer, the mechanistic transmission of the aesthetic function, imparting some physical, nearly biological quality, to the external presentment of the Sign.

Hegel reiterates Leonardian rule of painting when he marvels at the beauty of the Greek *face-sign:*

> In the ideal formation of the human head we are confronted above all with the so-called Greek profile. This profile depends on a specific connection between forehead and nose; in other words, on the almost straight or only gently curved line on which the forehead is continued to the nose without interruption (1975; 727, vol II).

In his view, the Greek profile would have the permanent function, signifying the superior aesthetic form and thus be regarded as the superior *face-sign.* It would, in turn, be treated as the heroic matrix, the yardstick, against which all other faces of other races and nations be measured.

Moreover, Hegel attributes special meanings to the different parts of the Face-Sign. The "mouth paradigm" would allegedly signify the animalistic qualities, while *human signatum* be represented by the nasal cranial bridge. Reinterpreting various parts of the Face-Sign, Hegel recreates the history of the human species, allegedly encoded in the movement from the mouth to the nose and ultimately to the eye:

high	forehead	= sign of intellect/highest order
	eye	= sign of spirit
	nose	= sign of beauty
low	mouth	= sign of the lowest order/indicator of animalistic nature

The mouth, a tool for food consumption, the signifier of the shared primitive biological existence, i.e. kinship with animals. Somehow, he forgets that mouth is also the active organ in the production of the *verbal signs.*

Guided by the high/low ratio, Hegel postulates that the upper part of the face, namely the forehead, is the sign, standing for the higher stage in the development of the humans. The higher the forehead the more intelligent, civilized the *homo-sapiens* appears. According to Hegel, the Hellenic face, represented by the ancient Greek sculpture, is the most parallel representation of the *proto-sign,* the actual Greek head, which signifies to him the ideal heroic face, the ideal form of human development. The Hegelian Hellenic profile signifies the desired, ideal, heroic biological species, as well as the ultimate *cultural sign.*

Since most Hellenic sculptures do represent the paragon of the aesthetic, religious, referential and poetic functions. and do portray the perfectly balanced, well-proportioned heads and bodies, Hegel further supports the European cultural myth about the Greek superiority in the sign-production. In the Hegelian rendition, not only the representation of the Body is beautiful but the *proto-sign,* the actual body is indeed exceedingly beautiful, the superior or *ideal sign.* It is also the symbol of the heroic cultural text-the Greek civilization. The Greek face, established as the ideal pro-sign to be emulated in sculpture and painting, was also designated the supreme civilizing function, it became the marker of a higher civilization:

Good	Bad
human	animal
intelligent	dull
civilized	wild/barbaric
beautiful	ugly
Greek	non-Greek

Hegel does not stop at the elevation of the physical features of the Greeks, he continues to promote even the Greek way of adornment as another marker of a more civilized societal behaviour. Even the Greek hairstyle is depicted as *seme* of a high aesthetic function (Mukarovsky, 1978; Hegel, 1975):

> The barbarians let their hair hang flat or they wear it cut all round, not waved or curled, whereas the Greeks in their ideal sculptures devoted great care to the elaboration of locks, a matter in which modern artists have been less industrious and less skilled (737).

Even the Greek hairstyle is presented as a sign of a superior cultural tradition and labelled as the ideal sign of civility and highest expression of "the aesthetic function", which corresponds again to the archetypal binary heroic model:

Heroic	non-heroic
Greek	non-Greek
face	face
hairstyle	hairstyle
en chignion	love
beautiful	ugly
civilized	uncivilized

Even nakedness, the traditional marker of the barbaric culture, is excused in the Greek art as the representation of special Freedom, void of the evil barbaric sensuality. The Greeks, in Hegel's view, were not aware of their own nakedness and supposedly displayed complete indifference to their own bodies. Their Eros is utterly naive, and the naked bodies in their cultural text were mere *aesthetic signs*, representing ideal forms, the heroic bodies, which were utterly immune to any barbaric perversion. However, since nakedness would be still a marker of the primitive sculpture, Hegel suggests to concentrate on the busts, the most demonstrative *perfect signs* in the ideal semiotic space. In order not to deal with the lower part of the body and the "erotic function", Hegel ignores Eros and censors the undesirable signs which could affect his concept of the heroic. The Hegelian attempts to suppress Eros and replace it by the aesthetic function of the *face-sign* reflect his organizing efforts, within the yet unformed heroic structure, the common recurrent attacks on nakedness and flesh, usually undertaken by the extreme moralizing right of any society. The Hegelian definition of the hero bears a moral dimension, the acts of the hero are always moral and right, so the naked body could somewhat destroy the ideal heroic definition. The insistence on the absent lower parts of the Body and present Face indicates the fear of the non-heroic, equated with the erotic... The Hegelian Hellenic bust is the perfect cultural sign, signifying the no less perfect proto-sign — the Face-sign of a civilized, superior and cultured Greek, the member of the venerated heroic race, the symbol of the temporary victory of the radical moral right (Hegel, 1975; Mukarovsky, 1978; Ponzio, 1990).

4.4 . Collective Hero-Sign -Race

The production of any sign is largely a collective enterprise, actualized by the group after a certain period of deliberation. The producers of signs have to agree on the adoption of a particular form of signification, ,regarded as more urgent, suited for a particular moment in the existential history of the group. What is traditionally described as a popular belief is actually a form of signification, which would have already passed the collective censorship, prior to becoming the *dominant sign.* They eventually serve as the unwritten laws which sustain order within the cultural semioshpere and may act quite oppressively upon the societal expression. They may either suppress the further semiotic efforts of the sign-producers or transform at any given point in the life of the group, or be dominated by the new dominant signs. For instance, the pagan values of the Western society had eventually been displaced by Christianity, a system of new dominant signs, that would later lose their original semiotic value in the face of the dominance of science and technology, a new layer of dominant signs, subsequently having overpowered this religion (Makolkin, 1987).

However, amidst this continuous process of sign selection and affirmation of power, there are signs, exercising their permanent and persistent dominance. Among them, there are the sentiments of kinship, ethnicity, shareable cultural rituals. They resurface and exercise their semiotic power largely due to the myths about the heroic superiority of a particular collectivity. It is never enough for a group simply to share certain physical space. The collective Self is invariably involved into the competition for the heroic status among the other Selves (Holland, 1977; Gergen, 1991; Lyons, 1978; Gizgus, 1981).

The ancient Athenians, for example, used to regard themselves intellectually, physically and spiritually superior to the non-citizens of Athens. Aristotle, not a native of Athens himself, appealed to the collective ego of the Athenians, praising their intelligence and physical beauty over the other inhabitants of the various parts in the ancient Hellenic world. In his famous essay, *Physiognomonics,* Aristotle designs a protomap for the future dangerous ethnosemiosis when he suggests to use the size of the facial features as the markers of different intelligence:

> The small-minded have small limbs and small delicate lean bodies, small eyes and small faces, just like a Corinthean or Leucadian (1984, vol I: 1242).

Leucadians and Corintheans stood for the allegedly inferior race, juxta-posed against the Athenians.Aristotelian bias against non-Athenians is an endemic Atheno-centric attitude, which was persistently cultivated to elevate the heroic social status of Athens vis-à-vis the rest of one hundred fifty eight city states (Kerenyi, 1959; Rose, 1960; Brumbaugh, 1981). The myth of the centre, the superiority of the selected centre is a *universal cul-tural sign* in itself, intricately based on the myth of the hero, be it individ-ual or collective (Raglan, 1936; Butler, 1979; Brombert, 1969; Bentley, 1963; Campbell, 1949).

The nineteenth-century scientific discoveries would revive the *arche-typal signs,* the nostalgia about the heroic race. It is remarkable that the Darwinian theory of evolution and selection would emerge parallel with the strong revival of the heroic mythology, the nostalgic look into the heroic past of civilization and an attempt to find the hero-race. There is a marked symmetry between the myth of the hero in biology, sociology , economics and politics. The re- carving of the geographical maps of Europe used to occur simultaneously with the vigorous collection of the heroic sagas, fairy tales, propaganda of national liberation, and the cult of the heroic particularity, the semi-scientific classifications of languages and races (Barzun, 1941; Bentley, 1963).

Grimm's law in comparative linguistics, Humboldt's search in social linguistics, Darwinian theory in biology, Marxist revision of political economy and Gobineau's treatise on the inequality of races share their common preoccupation with the heroic collective particularity. If, for Marx, this particularity is of a common social nature —the hero-prole-tariat of every race, nation or creed— for Grimm, it is the German par-ticularity (Barzun, 1941). For Gobineau, it is the Aryan hero-race. He divided all the human varieties into the "three basic races, white, yellow and black", within which he attributed all the heroic features to the white Europeans. While he admitted that blacks possess excellent physical strength, the same heroic quality paradoxically disqualified them from the heroic status among the other races. The physical strength, the heroic attribute of the fairy tale giants, is the sign of the lower level of civiliza-tion in his social mythical hierarchy of civilizations. What is heroic in the imaginary world is non-heroic in the real existential world, where physi-cal force is a sign of barbarism, the primitive cultural development. The civilized man has allegedly lost the primordial physical power at the expense of the development of the brain. Trying to prove the higher developmental level of the so-called "yellow race", Gobineau states:

> The yellow man has little physical energy, and is inclined to apathy, he commits none of the strange excesses so common among Negroes (1970, 136).

If Gobineau's black race, capable of violence and enjoying killing "for the sake of killing", "the yellow race is the exact opposite of this type", as he says, and is therefore superior. Gobineau's theory of inequality strives towards the Hegelian *perfect sign*, but his postulates on the yellow race represent this middle voice, the Derridean "differance" between the extreme lowest and extreme sentiment of racism, based on the highest heroic performance (Derrida, 1972). His mythical yellow race stands above the Negroid, whose "mental faculties are supposedly dull, or even-non-existent." The high/low ratio is used to establish the position of the two compared cultural and biological entities:

intellect	low	yellow	low	strength
	high	black	high	

The alleged higher physical strength lowers the status of the mental development among the black race, while the physical apathy of the yellow race allegedly elevates them.

Despite the fact that the yellow race he rates higher intellectually, Gobineau still assesses its collective creativity not very favour-ably:

> He [the yellow man] does not dream or theorize; he invents little, butcan appreciate and take over what is useful to him. His whole desire is to live in the easiest and most comfortable way possible. The yellow races are thus clearly superior to the black.
> But no civilized society could be created by them; they could not supply its nerve force, or set in motion the springs of beauty and action (1970,136).

In contrast, Gobineau's white race does possess all the necessary prerequisites for the construction of the so-called civilized society. Gobineau acknowledges that the white race is also capable of cruelty, violence and a certain degree of barbarism. However, this race collectively possesses the "extraordinary attachment to life, guided not by the mere violent impulse, but by "the principal motif of honour". Honour, as a symbolic value, becomes his yardstick in the assessment of the extraordinariness of the heroic race, along with its superior intelligence. Gobineau imparts the white race with a higher, more sophisticated creativity. The ability to produce signs of a higher order, i.e. signs above the existential responses to the *natural signs*, the signs regulating the relationships within the group, is are the truly heroic prerequisites of Gobineau's hero-race, the white race.

Gobineau is aware of the lack of physiological homogeneity and the complex mixture of racial types, but views it as a heroic deterrent, something which precludes the utmost heroic performance of the hero-sign.

According to him, the influx of the "foreign elements" distorts the heroic image of the hero-race. Moreover, it eventually leads to the death of the superior civilization:

> If, like the Greeks and the Romans of the Later Empire, the people has been absolutely drained of its original blood, and the qualities conferred by the blood, then the day of its defeat will be the day of its death (1970, p. 69).

Gobineau subtly implies that the fall of the ancient heroic civilizations was due to the lack of the genetic purity. The cause of the heroic downfall is in mixture with the Other, presumably inferior races. The mixture of the races is a *dangerous sign,* in Gobineau's purview, not only due to the biological interference and genetic interplay, but also to the destruction of the social heroic pyramid. Allegedly, the mixture of races leads to harmful equality, undesirable distribution of the social wealth and destruction of the heroic impulses within the group. Thus, Gobineau's heroic paradigm is constructed on the two basic foundations — the biological and socio-political. To him, the mixed races do suppress the biological heroic impulse of the extraordinary specie and simultaneously undermine the social pyramid, which legalizes inequality and rule of the strongest and fittest, be it an individual or a group.

Sensing the trend of the historical process towards democracy, the fearful anti-heroic social construction, and playing on the nostalgia for the monarchy and tyranny, Gobineau uses this fear of democracy to promote his version of the heroic race. The white race, imparted with the qualities of the extraordinary, provided its purity is secured, has a given right to rule and control the inferior others. Gobineau provides the twofold justification for the white supremacy:

	Superior	
	ruler	
	white race	
	Europe	
	pure	
servants		servants
yellow		black
Asia		Africa
mixed		mixed

Gobineau successfully manipulated the collective death anxiety, the desire to rule and colonize, dictating that racial purity is the only guarantee against revolt, disorder and ultimate death of the superior civilized species. Endangered by mixture and contact with the alleged inferior races, the white race has to remember that:

> The purer a race keeps its blood, the less will its social foundations be
> liable to attack of the general way of thought will remain the same (1970;
> 90).

Having placed the while race at the top of the ladder, Gobineau proceeds
further, pushing the limits of the heroic paradigm and attempting to
establish the inner heroic ladder within the heroic race itself.

His inner heroic universe is limited by the English, German, French
and Spanish, whom Gobineau aligns with the Sanskrit/Hindu cultural
texts. The impact of the Indo-European classificatory linguistic myth is
evident in Gobineau's final semiotic strategy. The "Aryan variety", the
umbrella term used by Gobineau, embraces the collective supremacy of
the not so white race while the "Practitii", the female, and "Purusha", the
male, are the principles, guiding him towards further division into heroic and not so heroic collective entities. "The English are superior," claims
Gobineau "in strength of the fist, i.e. they embody the male principle and
possess the most heroic vitality. However, at the end of his observation of
differences and inequalities, Gobineau finally chooses his most favoured
hero-race — the Germanic race:

> The Germanic race was endowed with all the vitality of the Aryan vari-
> ety and needed it in order to fulfil the role to which it was destined
> (1970: 190).

Thus, the final version of Gobineau's heroic ladder places the Germans
above their European relatives. It is remarkable that the collective term
"race" acquires a different meaning, applied next to the sign "German".
It begins to mean the "purest race" subgroup. within the group "race" or
the "white race":

Hero-Race —	monarchial
German	threshold
English	
French	democratic
Spanish	threshold
Sanskrit	
	Slave Borderline
yellow	
Negroid	

Gobineau's theory of difference, racial purity and hegemony of the
Germans, as the most civilized sign-producers, would be later used in
the Nietschean heroic prophecies and in Arthur Rosenberg's vicious
heroic narrative of the 20th century, which would be used as the ideological master tool in the Nazi purification technique. Honour — the
marker, prominent in both Gobineau's and Rosenberg's heroic univers-

es, is Peirce's *qualisign,* the unifying mythical construct for both semiotic strategies in both theories of racism (Peirce, 1931).

4.5. *Rosenberg's Sacred Sign*

Gobineau's heroic ladder absolutely ignores the power of the *sacred sign* — religion that preaches universal love, tolerance, acceptance and reconciliation with the Other. It dogmatically imposes the notion of purity, not realizing its practical obstacles. Rosenberg, whose doctrine of the heroic owes greatly to Gobineau and Nietzsche, represents an evolution of the concept of purity and offers a semiotic strategy for the practical realization of the mythical heroic paradigm. He assures the twentieth-century sign-receivers and producers that the forces of the heroic would be driven by the myth of pure blood, blood, becoming the *dominant sign* in this new, 20th century heroic context:

> Today a new belief is arising the mythus of blood; the belief that the Godly essence of man itself is to be defended through the blood (1970:82).

Following Gobineau, Rosenberg teaches that the survival of the heroic race and its superior cultural text is dependent, first and foremost, upon the biological purity. Rosenberg is aware of its impossibility and that the visible heroic performance of the Germans would be impaired, if the mythus of blood is not sold to the general public. It is not accidental that Gobineau labels this belief "mythus", implying that this is just another construct, utopian in its essence but presenting itself as a *true sign.* The key to the ruling of the masses has traditionally been the ability of the rulers to present the *false sign* as a *true sign* (Aristotle, 1985).

Rosenberg acknowledges several key signs, such as Love, Pity, Honour and Duty, labelling them as the "spiritual essences "; to him, they are the *universal dominant signs,* controlling the general production of *cultural signs.* The sacred Western sign —Christianity, with its Judaic roots, and the central sign— Love, were the main ideological obstacles in the creation of the myth about the pure Germanic race. Love of the Other presupposes the widest possible contact, including the physical intercourse, intermarriage and the feared mixture of the races.

In order to sell the idea of the German purity and heroism, Rosenberg first eliminated the *sacred sign* — Christianity, having condemned its key concepts. He explained how a Christian could condemn the Christian dominant sign — Love, and justify hate and destruction of the Other. Rosenberg was aware of the fact that it would have been impossible to stimulate hate within the Judeo-Christian paradigm. After all, Christ was presumably a Jew and preached brotherly love for "all children of God." A new semiotic universe had to be designed to justify genocide and ethnic cleansing (Mosse, 1970; Gordon, 1984).

The first step was to destroy the old universe of the *sacred sign* — the Judeo-Christian universe. Appealing to the historical facts, Rosenberg convincingly argues that this old semiotic system is nothing but a cluster of *false signs*, that

> the thought of love was never able to penetrate the leadership of the church establishment. The expansion of the Roman system, from the first day on has been characterized by dogmatically principled and consciously intolerant organisation, one which has taken a negative, if not hostile, attitude towards all other systems (1970, 105-6).

Rosenberg appeals to the *true signs*, i.e. historical incidents of the Judeo-Christian intolerance, manipulation and dealings with the State, directly contradicting the essential semiotic structure of Christianity as a system of the *sacred signs*. The history of the Christian cruelty towards non-Christians, the Judaic intolerance towards the non-Jews and the overall hypocrisy of the believers had been a valid semiotic base for the destruction of the Judeo-Christian universe. Having dispensed with the old system of the *sacred signs*, he could introduce the new ones, the desirable *dominant signs*, such as honour and duty, which would replace love and pity. According to Rosenberg, love of Christians was not only a false, but a *dangerous sign*, harmful to the Europeans in general, and to Nordic Europeans in particular. Instead of the universal brotherly love, Rosenberg suggests a new particular love, love for the mythical hero — Nordic man, and a new religious system, revolving around Honour.

In contrast with the old system of *sacred signs*, confined within the boundaries of the Judeo —Christian semiosphere and dominated by the allegedly *false sign* —Love, Rosenberg proposed an utterly new semiotic system, governed by the true dominant sign— Honour. This new mythico-religious system would be the Nordic religion of the pure or purified blood. It would not revolve around love and compassion towards all human beings, but around a particular love for the ideal Nordic homo-purities:

Nordic	Judeo-Christian
pure	impure
honour	love
life	death
health	illness
victory	failure
strength	weakness

The Nordic mythical system of the sacred signs promised a higher level of development in all existential spheres, and cure from the imminent danger of mixing which the Judeo-Christian concept of brotherly love invariably entailed and advocated. It was presented not only as the alternative system of signification for the sake of signification but as an ultimate preventative measure against the presumably inferior Asiatico-African-Phoenician "pestilence", as Rosenberg labelled the Other, foreign, and dangerous influence (1970).

The Nordic mythopoesis also exploited the nostalgia for the heroic and archetypal doctrine of the superior *homo-sapiens*, the ultimate archetypal hero, for which any group secretly and passionately longs. If the Judeo-Christian system of signs nurtures the myth of the collective hero, "the chosen people", Rosenberg's Nordic mythical structure does not dispense with it either, merely replacing the key heroic signification. Instead of the Hebrew heroes, Rosenberg introduces the Germano-Nordic heroes, even suggesting that Christ could have possibly been the Nordic archetypal hero, a German and not a Jew.

Rosenberg designs the strategy of the cultural purification first, and his justification of the actual physical purification comes second, involving the replacement of Love by Honour, universalism versus particularism, appropriation of the heroic myth and its transfer onto his own territory of the new sacred signs. His suggested system of signification aimed at the separation from the cultural "Other". Manipulating the icons "health" and "death", and the natural death anxiety of the species on the collective level, Rosenberg would suggest that the heroic species, i.e. the Nordic man, could be revived through the physical separation from the foreigners.

The pathway to the ideal heroic status of the Nordic race lies through the Nordic religion and concrete steps of purification. The replacement of the meaning of the *familiar signs,* such as Soul, Love and Life, has helped Rosenberg to construct his model of exclusion. The universal human soul, replaced by the particular *German Volk soul,* universal brotherly love by the self love — all in the name of healthy existence, constituted the skeleton of the new heroic paradigm:

Hero
German
Volk
Love
Love
Health
Life
Nordic Religion

Rosenberg's hierarchy of the dominant sacred signs represented an alternative to the Marxist heroism, which was perceived as a cluster of *dangerous signs,* amidst which the victorious Nordic man could become an endangered specie. Instead of loving all the poor brothers, he suggested to love the next of kin, the German brother — the carrier of the Nordic genes, the follower of its religion and worshipper of its iconology. The rejection of brotherly love, the old universal sign of harmony justified the possibility of cruelty towards the Other. Rosenberg's replacement of the sacred signs shifted not only the heroic paradigm, but the attitude of the perceivers towards it. If the contemporary philosophers could not imagine how Christians could agree with the mass destruction of the people, a simple analysis of the redistribution of signs in Rosenberg's doctrine offers the explanation of its paradoxical logic. Indeed, within the Christian sacred semiosphere neither Christ, nor his relatives, the ancient Hebrews, stand for the non-tolerated "Other".

However, the Nordic sacred semiosphere allowed for the displacement of the traditional signs and meanings, whereby the shift in the collective perception of the heroic could redefine the new behavioural norms. The Roman Catholicism was dismissed as a corrupt system of the pseudo-sacred signs, while the beliefs of the ancient Indians and Greeks be embraced as the foundation of the new Aryan Nordic Religion. The Nordic man would be the goal of the mythical excavation beyond the layers of the Graeco-Roman world, the so-called genetic cultural and biological matrix of the most heroic specie — the German volk soul carriers.

4.6. *Russia as a New Sacred Sign: Danilevsky versus Dostoevsky*

The ethnocentricity has been acknowledged as one of the cultural universals, or what Dissanayake labels as the "common human predispositions" (1992: 49). Another example of its manifestation is the famous Slavophile versus Westerners debate, going back to the 19th century and revived in the 20th century, after the dismantling the Soviet Union. The Russian versions of Gobineau and Rosenberg, Spengler and Vollgraff, Lasaulx and Carlyle would be embodied in the philosophical systems of Danilevsky and Dostoevsky ,who promoted the myth about the sacredness of the Slavs and their messianic role in history. Their new *sacred sign* —Russian nation or race— was produced, based on the studies by Lamarque and Darwin. The notion of a strong surviving specie in nature led historians, philosophers and writers to the production of the new sacred sign —Unique Culture. Danilevsky, trained as a botanist, perceived culture and its producers as a universe which was parallel to the natural semiosphere. According to him, nations, states and cultural texts represented signs, akin to the varieties of plants. He developed five basic principles which presumably govern the development of all cultures and states. His first law defended the idea of "philological uniqueness", something that constitutes the "cultural-historical type" potential. The second law advocated the need for political independence. The third law professed the closed boundaries of the cultural text:

> The civilizing essences of a single cultural and historical type are not transmitted to the people of a different type. Each nation develops it for itself, under the influence of the alien civilization, past and present (1869[1966];95).

The fourth law required segregation of the ethnographic elements within each national political federation. The fifth and the last law likens people "to perennials, producing a single fruit, whose growth could be indefinitely long but whose blossoming period is relatively short" (96).

His cultural-historical types include twelve cultural traditions:

1. Egyptian;
2. Chinese;
3. Asian-Babylonian-Phoenician-Chaldean or ancient Semitic;
4. Indian;
5. Iranian;
6. Jewish;
7. Greek;
8. Roman;
9. New-Semitic;
10. Germano-Roman-European;
11. Mexican:
12. Peruvian.

According to him, only these cultural historical types were the "positive actants in the history of mankind" (1966:91). Such a small group as Finns was regarded as having very little historico-cultural significance and therefore "negative" (1966:98). The rest of the various civilizations, in Danilevsky's view, were still on the level of "the ethnographic material" ,or historically and culturally insignificant. In his view, the Graeco-Roman influence upon Europe could be likened to "a good fertilizer for a plant or a nutrient for an animal" (1869[1966]:105). The highest cultural type-European- has been presumably formed out of the Graeco-Roman "cultural fertilizer", in the primitive botanical sense. Moreover, the heroic title of excellence, in his view, belonged to the Germans and English, who supposedly "share the glory of advancement of sciences to the level of perfection" (163) Ultimately, Danilevsky proposed the idea of the more advanced level of the cultural and historical development, embodied in the Slavic or Slavo-phile type :

> After God and his sacred Church, the idea of Slavdom should become
> the highest idea, above freedom, above science, above education, above
> any foundation for the existence for any Slav-Russian, Czech, Serb,
> Croat, Sloven, Slovak, Bulgarian (and desirably Pole as well) (1869
> [1966]: 193).

In his division of the cultural types, Danilevsky clearly advocated the hierarchical, heroically-oriented approach. The progressive trend in this
heroic hierarchy was towards the ultimate elevation of Russia, as *the*
leader of all the Slavic nations. The heroic predestination of the Slavic
cultural type had been attributed to its alleged uniqueness of the spiritual psychological make-up, revealing itself in the lack of the desire to
conquer, generosity and their preferred worship in the Orthodox manner,
elevated to the degree of the exemplary group behaviour. The difference
between Orthodoxy and Catholicism is explained in the simplistic
truth/falsehood dichotomy, which would be later appropriated by Yury
Lotman, the Russian — Soviet semiotician (Lotman, 1968).

According to Danilevsky, each nation, deserving to be classified as
the cultural-historical type, preferably Slavic, has to uphold the idea of
statehood, and all the sacrifices in the name of the state are proclaimed
"sacred". Of all the sacred deeds, Russia is indeed endowed with the
most sacred mission — leading the Slavs towards their cultural and historical glory. The idea of contamination by another alien and inferior culture is the central idea of his book *Russia and Europe*, where Europe was
perceived as a source of some Slavic malaise and dangerous contamination in all spheres of life. He advocated the idea of cultural independence and cultural-political hygiene, rooted in the Byzantine "spiritual
heroism." For Danilevsky, Russia consequently stands for the Byzantine
Olympus, facing the alleged European ordinariness (1869[1966]: 345). In
contrast, Europe stands for danger of assimilation and cultural extinction
and imminent cause for military struggle.

Danilevsky was regarded as the Russian antecedent of Spengler, his
views were shared by Toynbee, earlier by Dostoevsky and Carlyle.
Danilevsky's idea of spiritual heroism is very much reminiscent of the
Carlylean heroic vitalism. His familiarity with Carlyle in his epigraph to
the Chapter ten taken from *Sartor Resartus*. Carlylean metaphor-nation as
a battery charged with vitality and energy was very much appealing to
Danilevsky who interpreted it in his own way:

Russia	Europe
battery	battery
hunger	money
spirituality	lack of spirituality
vital force	love

healthy body	sick body
positive	negative
present/future	past

The similar good / evil dichotomy characterizes Dostoevsky's vision of Russia and Slavdom. Similarly to Danilevsky, Dostoevsky advocated the sacredness of the Russian literature, culture, psychological make-up and spirituality. Dostoevsky's Russia and Russian orthodoxy are the sacred signs, sharing similar meaning with Rosenberg's "new Nordic religion. Dostoevsky's Russia is also somewhat akin to Rosenberg's Germany, where the Slavic Orthodoxy is granted the analogous *semiovalence*. In Dostoevsky's view, the Russian writers, such as Pushkin, Gogol, Nekrasov and others, embody the genuinely Russian uniqueness, which has neither parallel world, nor bears any similarity to any other European cultural icon.

However, Dostoevsky does not call for cultural segregation, the general universal human interests are and were always a part of the Russian cultural particularity, the essential human quality of all Russians. On the contrary, the ability to reconcile with and absorb the Other is the inherent Russian character, the characteristic collective "I", which exhibits the quality of peacefulness, forgiveness and capacity to empathize with the entire humanity:

> He [the Russian man] lives in peace with everybody and accepts everything. He empathizes with all people, regardless of nationality, blood, or roots. He finds and immediately accepts the national behind anything, which has some general human value *(Dnevnik Pisatelia* (Writers' Diary) 1873, 24-5).

The uniqueness of the Russian national character lies in the capacity to synthesize the universal and particular. The particular heroism is achieved through the recognition of the universal and particular worlds. Dostoevsky, the writer, the amateur psychologist, who himself had greatly benefited from the non-Russian cultural signs, comes to Danilevsky's extreme "spiritual heroism" through the tolerance of the heroic Other. Eventually, he would also worship the "third global idea" — the Slavic idea, as the culminating point in the universal human development. Dostoevsky's Slavic idea is the Russian Orthodoxy as a superior sacred sign after the Catholicism and Protestantism. As carriers of the particular and superior religiosity, Dostoevsky's Russian people have to believe in their unique spiritual essence, as well as in their supposedly unique global mission:

> Any great nation believes and wants to believe, if it wishes to live long, that the saving of the world rests on its people, and solely on them, and their entire existential purpose is to lead all the [rest people of the world] and to entice them into the communion with these great people (Dostoevsky, 1877: 13).

The heroic status of a particular national group could thus be secured only by the belief of one's uniqueness and unique mission. Moreover, only those "nations have a right to a higher existence, who are empowered by this belief," claims Dostoevsky. (1877:15)

On the other hand, the essence of the Russian spiritual superiority lies in the capacity for the truly Christian love:

> I do not care that you are more talented than I, cleverer than I and more beautiful than I. Why should I? Just the opposite, I admire your superiority because I love you (1877: 53).

This Christian love would and could essentially save the Russian people and elevate them above the rest of the world. Dostoevsky recognizes the cultural achievements of the Europeans, from the cultural contacts with whom, he and the entire Russian civilization, had greatly benefited. He painfully accepts the obvious superior wealth of the Europeans vis-à-vis the then capitalist Russia and proclaims this economic prosperity harmful and unnecessary for Russia. He perceptively saw the impossibility of the Russian capitalist Empire to reach the economic prosperity level of the Western Europe, proposing instead the revisionist approach of reconsidering the need of wealth. Consequently, his dichotomy of signs bears many similarities with Danilevsky's bipolar world

Russian	Europe
free	in slavery of money
loving	hating
truly Christian	unchristian
Constantinople	Jerusalem/Rome

Dostoevsky's slogan "Constantinople will be ours" would be eventually re-invented in Lotman's numerical topology of cultures and the mythical narrative about the Soviet popular culture, all of which would essentially emphasize and glorify the superiority of the Russian Orthodox faith and Church , versus the Catholicism and other beliefs. The Russian nationalistic myth, resurrected by Dostoevsky and the 19th and 20th century Slavophiles, would be very useful for the Communist propaganda of the poverty virtue and heroism of deprivation. The myth of the unique Russian soul, its generosity and love would help to denounce the corrupt modern West in the Communist-socialist era.

Lotman's essay *Semantika Chisla i tip kul'tury* (Numerological Semiotics and Cultural Types) is remarkably symmetrical, on its deep semiotic structural level, to Danilevsky-Dostoevsky mythical delusions when it concerns the grandeur of Russia and Russian Orthodoxy. In this brief and sketchy work, Lotman has outlined the three basic cultural types, according to their attitude to numbers — Catholic, Russian Orthodox and Hebrew/Judaic. Dante, Virgil, Lomonosov and Masons respectively represent and symbolically embody Judaism, Catholicism and Russian Orthodoxy. Lotman sees a concordance between "the moral anomalies" or ethics and attitude to numbers (Lotman, 1968:229). In his view, Dante and Virgil stand for a culture of "a paradigmatic type", where "the symbolic significance of numbers is not only emphasized, but whose morality is predetermined by this negative numerological obsession. *Sin* and *Number* signify the morally corrupt religious systems and a paradigmatic cultural type. In contrast, the Russian culture and religion, non-numerological ly obsessed, is thus moral, correct and syntagmatic:

Lotman	Dostoevsky
sin good	sin good
Rome/Jerusalem Moscow	Rome/Jerusalem Constantinople
corrupt saintly	corrupt saintly
inferior superior	inferior superior

Lotman's paradigmatico-syntagmatic dichotomy has a solid semiotic appearance and conceals the less visibly semiotic delusions about the alleged glory and extraordinariness of the Russian culture and religion. His attitude towards numbers stands for what Dostoevsky simply called the "slavery of money", or what Bacon had earlier defined as the "idol of the market place." Lotman's essay and other works on the typology of culture provides a new metabasis for the myth of the Russian sacredness and its alleged new messianic role in the 20th century. His work, largely written in the presence of the vigilant Soviet censors, carefully formulates and semiotically justifies the future post-*perestroika* nationalistic discourse. What he had failed to utter in 1968, he would openly profess in 1990, in his book, *Universe of the Mind* where Russian culture parades as a superior *sacred sign*, analogous to Rosenberg's Nordic religion. Lotman, would talk there about the "cultural infection" in the process of contact with the foreigners!? Lotman's *Universe of the Mind* clearly echoes the protectionist slogans of the cultural guardians of the 19th and 20th century, who, in their turn, had also been re-inventing the *dangerous signs*, created by Gibberti and Gobineau. Lotman's fear of the cultural "infection" and imminent death of the Orthodox Empire originates in Gobineau's purity principle:

> But if a people, like the Greeks and Romans of the Latin empire, has been absolutely drained of its original blood, then the day of its defeat will be the day of its death (Gobineau' [1853] 1970:70).

Lotman's concerns and preoccupations with the "Other", being infected by the Other, anticipate the resurgence of the nationalistic sentiments and Zhirinovsky's ethnocentric slogans in the nineties. The sacred image of Russia, the sign of love, poverty and self-denial would reappear again, next to the delusion of grandeur and new recycled old myth (Barthes, 1957; Greimas, 1992; Greimas, 1993; Murray, 1960; Ohmann, 1962; Lotman, 1990). However, Lotman's semiotic system provided a firm pseudo-scientific foundation for this new modern ethnomyth:

> On the frontiers of China, of the Roman Empire, Byzantium, we see the same thing: the technical achievements of the settled civilization pass into the hands of nomads who turn them against their inventors (142) (Lotman, 1990:142).

Heroic Occasions

5.1. *The Social Pyramid*

The *hero-sign* repeatedly signifies its presence and justifies its social significance in the fictional and real narrative. Myth, drama, song, fairy tale, novel and play — all have canonically paid tribute to the extraordinariness of the hero. Any elitist, class-divided, caste-separated, dictator-ruled or even democratic society philosophically relies on the concept of the hero and the heroic myth mechanism (Carlyle, 1966 [1841] Buttler, 1979; Hook, 1967; Campbell, 1949; Makolkin,1992). *Politics* by Aristotle, already in antiquity, had demystified the heroic and dissected the hero-sign. Denouncing tyranny, the rule of a single individual, Aristotle deprived the hero-ruler of his heroic significance, having suggested instead to apply the collective wisdom and collective heroism in the process of governing. Despite the ancient skepticism and rejection of the individual capacity to rule, the overwhelming number of societies are in variably attached to the social pyramid, generally based on the heroic mode of thinking and the dominance of the hero-sign.

All known societies pay significant tribute to the heroic contest, and the ongoing process of the heroic competition, so vital in any social signification. However, the stable social pyramid, with its upper, inaccessible heroic layer, is the most preferred semiotic model. Even in the modern democracies, all the social rituals pay tribute to this nearly organic and vital symbol — Hero, undermining the very core of a society based on equality. Hero is unequal to the rest, he defies the group. The British spectators, crying at the wedding parade of lady Diana and Prince Charles or public hysteria at the funeral of the Syrian President Al Assad — are the best illustrations of the vitality of the *hero-sign*. This modern re-enactment of the fairy tale is the acknowledgment of the semiotic power of the *hero-sign*, even when the actual power in society is purely ritualistic, royalty still signifies the utmost extraordinariness, be it deference for pedigree, or purely exaggerated veneration and hero-worship. The emperor, ruler, king, tzar or president are the *archetypal hero-signs* of very high *semiovalence*. They are disliked and worshipped signs, which are needed for the support of the heroically constructed social pyramid. Arnold Toynbee summarized this transcultural, transtemporal and transnational fascination with the upper layer of the social pyramid in the following statement:

> The source of action is never the society itself but always the individual (1947, vol I: 533).

...bee's heroic ... ... ro. vital societal source of progress, growth and ... ... the m... ...is, imitation of the heroic qualities of the genius, saviour or super human genius.

According to Toynbee, *hero-signs* are the *permanent signs* whose presence actualized the fermentation of the decaying and developing civilizations:

> In a growing civilization the creator is called upon to play the part of conqueror who replies to a challenge with a victorious response, in a disintegrating civilization he is called upon to play the part of a saviour (1977, vol I: 533).

At any stage of the societal development the *hero-sign* (conqueror or saviour) exercises not only his (predominantly his and not hers) power, not only demonstrates his heroic faculties and sets the precedent for the extraordinariness, but also stimulates the process of the recognition of the sign.

Toynbee gives a list of thirty heroes, which covers twenty one civilizations from Minoan and Hittite to the Eskimo and Mayan, invariably demonstrating the power of the Carlylean "able men". All the cultural texts organize themselves through the societal drill, called "mimesis" and the recognition of the matrix for imitation. The majority in any society are unable to create their own heroic narrative and merely imitate the Other. The Heroic Other represents a permanent challenge to the sign-perceiving community, who are either unable or not permitted to signify independently. "Brick upon brick as it may and can." — proclaimed Carlyle, having resurrected the archetypal model, based on the heroic hierarchy. Carlyle's metaphorical model of society is even more categorical than the ancient Greek pyramid; Carlyle's brick upon brick"— model suppresses any heroic impulses of the majority, any extraordinary mobility, aiming at any social change. It reflects the particularly strong social pyramid, ingrained in the social text on the British Isles, reinforced by centuries of deference towards class, wealth, origin and order. The British cultural text has historically exhibited strong affliction with the heroic *status-quo*, where the distribution of the heroic parts was stable, predictable and recognizable. Carlyle's theory of the heroic produced on the British Isles appeared almost simultaneously with Marx's *Communist Manifesto*, which stood for the complete heroic *reversal*, professing from the centre of Europe an entirely new heroic doctrine for the global community. In Carlyle, let us remember, the hero-king is the "able man", the skilful navigator of the ship called society, which needed to be saved from the destruction of the social pyramid. He is confident that:

> We will hail the French Revolution, as shipwrecked marines might be the sternest rock in a world otherwise all of baseless sea and waves (1901; 231).

Thus, the safety of the sign —arrangement and the societal "naviga-tion" represents a form of signification, totally dependent upon the law of the *heroic paradigm,* the *semiovalence* of the hero-sign and passive recog-nition of the heroic code. Carlyle's *Roi,* — king is the supreme *hero-sign,* the *true sign,* that perceivers are to recognize and accept unconditionally in the name of Order, permanent and stable social signification. There is also another feature of this heroic signification — absence of noise, or what Carlyle calls "silence" of the *Roi.* He draws the opposition between the speakers and non-speakers, the silent and noisy:

> The noble silent men, scattered here and there, each in his department; silently thinking, silently working (1901:257).

In his theory, the society is divided into the gesturers and producers of the true, meaningful signs and speakers, whose signs do not count. Their signs are allegedly void of meaning and constitute mere noise. The social pyramid and the societal matrix of the heroic are best revealed in a defined social code, where the power of the supreme hero is unani-mously recognized either as monarchy, military dictatorship, or any other individual power placed at the top. There, the upper position of the supreme hero vis-à-vis the rest of society, acknowledges the *hero-sign* in its full semiotic capacity. There are no limitations placed on the *hero-sign,* selected to reveal its utmost *semiovalence.* The pyramid seems to be the most suitable arrangement of signs for the selection of the *supreme sign,* the very sign, intended to fulfil all the promises of extraordinariness. The collective expectations of the sign-producers and perceivers, below the pyramid top, are fulfilled to the utmost degree in the light of their myth-ical heroic delusions. All the unfulfilled ambitions and desires of the indi-viduals at the bottom of the pyramid could be transferred onto a single hero at the top, along with the anxieties, anger and traumas which the existential signification entails. The vertically-oriented pyramid, despite all the oppressiveness is a mutually agreeable system of the *social signs,* enabling the *Hero-sign* to function freely.

5.2. Revolution and Reversal

If the vertical pyramid embodies the most convenient semiotic envi-ronment for the *hero-sign,* any attempts to destroy the established struc-ture disrupt the canonical process of the heroic signification. Any social revolution, aiming at the different rearrangement of the *social signs,* is paradoxically creative and productive at the same time. Revolution is another heroic occasion to expose the old, allegedly false, heroes and to install the new, presumably, true heroes (Le Bon, 1913; O'Neill, 1989).

Carlyle, uneasy with his new heroes, Men of Letters, finds escape in the socially convenient royal pyramid that divides the social "actants" into the Able and Unable men. His unable men are the potential revolutionaries, the dangerous sign-producers and false heroes whom he vehemently denounces:

> This is the history of all rebellions, French revolutions, social explosions in ancient and modern times. You have put the too Unable Man at the lead of affairs! The too ignoble unvaliant, fatuous man (1901: 227).

The traditional pyramid, in Carlyle's view, is an existential necessity, "the law of gravitation", according to which, the hero possesses the power to attract the sign-producers and perceivers below. He is the vital source of gravitation without which any society might collapse. Carlyle's concerns and suppositions resurface in the contemporary anxieties of the political analysts and futurists, who try to predict the Eastern European social post-Communist order, unable to imagine it without the familiar pyramid and the supreme hero. If not Yeltsin or Havel, Valesa or Tuchmann, who else? Who is able to govern the ungovernable? Hero has become an atavistic attachment amidst the farce of democracy.

Revolution is defined by Carlyle as the insanity of the disenchanted sign-producers, taking over the social pyramid and destroying the healer, the chief psychiatrist — the ruler. Society is the meta-phorical house for the insane, the bedlam, ruled by the *Roi*/King. Liberty and equality, the chief slogans, the key signs of the pyramid destroyers in the French, American or Russian revolutions are falsehoods, the collective delusions of the bottom, the dangerous symptom of the societal heroic malaise. However, any revolution is the satisfied desire for the shift in the heroic hierarchy. Those, who could not be heroes under the pressure of any societal pyramid, obtain the opportunity to express their extraordinariness in the changed semiotic setting, where the supreme sign had lost its centricity. Eventually, the gravitation towards verticality persists even within the changed social structure. The sign-producers desperately compete for their locus in the upper layers of the newly rearranged pyramid, for the leading role in the social signification.

The Christian doctrine and its dissemination, for example, was a revolution, aiming at the reduced member of the *sacred signs* and eventually reaffirming the signification of the single sacred sign-Christ. The sign obtains its supremacy not in isolation, but in a semiotic environment, amidst the other signs, which may also compete for dominant signification.

Any revolution is a *displacement* and dislocation of the signs, first and foremost, and a re-arranged semiotic ornament, whose design is decided by the apathy and involvement of the sign-producers and sign-perceivers, as well as by the *semiovalence* of the resurfacing hero-signs. The direction of this displacement is invariably upper, vertical, despite the efforts of some perceivers to keep the signs below the visible signification locus (Le Bon, 1913). Any successful sign-displacement success is secured by the preliminary mythical signification of the ideal, ultimate and desired paradisiacal state. The Christian paradise was needed to emphasize the desired state of the existential bliss, not Here and Now, but "Later and Then" , in order to justify simultaneously the injustice, poverty and misery of "this world". The symmetry between the *sacred signs,* God and Ruler, secured the temporary arrangement of signs, which would reinforce the stable authoritarian order.

The American and French revolutions not only undermined this order but violated the canonical symmetry, defeating the ground for the extraordinary. The icons of equality and liberty presuppose the diminished chances for the individual heroic expression, reducing the heroic possibilities. Simultaneously, the industrial revolution would reshape the myth of paradise. The reward had no longer be removed, the consumer bliss and acquisition of the tangible capital, the signs of exchange accumulated "here and now" had actually rewritten the mythical script. However, the anxiety of obtaining those signs by the largest possible community contributed to the Marxist myth of paradise, where the signs of exchange are controlled rigorously and precisely. The shifting mythical narrative predetermined the semiotic environment for the future displacements;

Christian	Industrial	Marxist
Paradise	Paradise	Paradise
Later	Now	Now
hard labour	hard labour	easy labour
intense production	intense production	slowed production
intense exchange	intense exchange	slow exchange
slow motion	speedy motion	slow motion
equality	inequality	equality

As it is evident from the comparative schema of the key signs the Marxist myth has obviously borrowed some basic signs from the Christian structure and exploited the universal human need for instant gratification. The success of the Russian revolution, unpredicted by Marx, lies precisely in the semiotic affinity between the Christian and Communist key signs. The Russian Orthodox Church had a more powerful hold over the sign-perceivers than the industrial Russian capitalist elite. The signs of exchange were circulating admits the producers and perceivers at a lesser speed than in other Western societies. They were less visible and consequently the circumstances for the displacement/revolution were more intense than anywhere else. S. Hook claims that the Russian revolution was not a heroic deed of a single individual hero, Lenin, but the inevitability of the circumstances (Hook, 1967: 209-10).

The success of Marxism in Russia was guaranteed not so much by the intensity of the local heroic paradigm itself, or the external correct Marxist assessment of the processes of the societal signification, but rather due to the general regularities of the mythical processes. The myth of paradise offered by the industrial capitalist revolution did not function in Russia, since the tangible signs of exchange and reward were not accessible to most of the members of the group. The unhappiness with the myth, the sense of betrayal, created the semiotic environment which could have been required in order to destroy the old myth and old heroic significance (Barthes, 1957; Liszka, 1989; Makolkin, 1992a).

The Marxist myth of paradise seduced with the promise of ease, slow effort and less intense movement. The external man-made signs, which had enslaved and entrapped humans during the industrial revolution, threatening the vital signs, the sacred natural sign — the Body, became so oppressive that they needed to be dispensed with. The legislated slow motion of the Body rewarded with the sufficient signs of exchange — the material goods for everybody according to their need - was a very seductive mode of the co-ordinated natural and societal signification. Carlyle predicted that speed would become the dominant force of the societal semiosphere and the undermining *destructive sign*, hostile to the Body. With Man, the sign-producer, becoming an addendum to the sign of exchange-Machine, Carlyle suggested to turn the" seeing eye " of an artist, the able sign-producer, into a new sacred sign, slowing down the process of cultural signification, swaying away from science and technology , the metaphors of the industrial evil. He offered a revolutionary perception of the Body — "seeing eye" of an artist which could bring the most desired paradise-immortality. Instead of the artificial consumer paradise of things — signs of exchange and means of fast movement, Carlyle suggested to turn the "seeing eye" of the artist either inside one's soul, or outside, towards the natural semiosphere, the Empire of the truly sacred signs.

The technological revolution of the 20th century revived again the myth of paradise, using the familiar structural elements, such as happiness, abundance and speed. Fast moving automobiles, fast-connecting telephones and mail, fast-changing images and fast-selected pieces of TV information — all are the *familiar signs* of this technocratic century. They all carry the myth of ease, effortlessness, usefulness, betterment and improvement of one's daily life. The computer revolution would change little in the general societal signification. It seduced the perceivers with the myth of paradise, where leisure, effortlessness and happiness reign. The obsession with the computer as a new sign, signifying the paradisiacal values only reinforces the *permanent desirable signs* which never leave the universal cultural codification. Having replaced the human hand and paper with a silver screen and buttons, society orchestrates a drastic *displacement* of the familiar, which is both imposed, feared and desired. The computer would ultimately offer this heroic opportunity of moving faster in the physical and cultural space. The faster mode of exchange satisfies the eternal heroic impulse to excel, but it nonetheless does not answer the question "why"? Why is there a need to exchange signs faster and to a larger group of perceivers, ,who may not be even particularly interested in that? Who benefits from it? Like any other revolution, the computer revolution has displaced the old signs for the sake of displacement, and not necessarily for the sake of improving the general quality of life. The meaning of the sign was ignored for the sake of the striking extraordinariness of the signifier, meant to surprise, baffle and, perhaps, confuse and control the perceiver with the false promise of liberation and construction of a new paradise.

Despite the denial of the primary signification sphere —Nature— there is an invisible connecting thread between the numerous sign-displacements which occur during any revolution. The signification of the tired, ailing, restless, aging and decaying Body is the ultimate stimulating mechanism behind any desire to design a new system of *the cultural signs.* The Christian system manipulated the fear of the dying Body and seduced the perceivers with the promise of immortality through after-life. The notion of glorious poverty would indirectly remove the need to toil hard and abuse the Body for the sake of new signs of exchange, expressing the excessive wealth. The Body was promised a better care within the supremacy of the Christian signification.

The industrial revolution used the same strategy, appealing to the eternal concern about the Body. The human hand was extended through a machine, which could expand, increase and improve the production of new signs. The machinery created a secondary system of signs, whose deep meaning was very seductive, i.e. to help the Body, to free the Body. Labour has been traditionally perceived as the undesirable necessity ; humans kept persistently designing ways of avoiding it. The social pyramid devised slavery as the labour-avoiding channel, with the unwanted activities displaced onto the group of the social outcasts. This unappealing form of *displacement* would be eventually replaced by the more agreeable one — the Machine. Instead of another human, performing the unwanted task, there has been designed an addendum, a man-made slave — a Robot. People have always fantasised about the paradisiacal world without labour; the fairy tales are full of stories about effortless meals, ready clothes, built houses and instant gratification of any imaginable desire. The underlying dream and desire of labour-free existence and the Body-preservation-motif are the key-signs, continuously manipulated in any displacement. The twentieth-century technology has partly materialized those eternal paradisiacal desires (Afanaciev, 1945; Aarne, 1961; Propp, 1958 [1928]).

The Freudian psychology would ultimately attempt to improve the production of signs in order to satisfy the Body as well. In Freud's view, the discontent of the civilized humanity was in the suppression of the libido by the cultural taboos. It used the same archetypal promise to free the Body and seduced the sign-perceivers with the same *dominant sign-Sexuality* (Freud, [1936] 1977; Freud, [1905] 1983).

The fashion revolution in the female attire of modernity was remarkably symmetrical to the Freudian fear of civilization and Nietschean Dionysian prophecy. The exposed parts of the female body would signify liberation from the taboos, imposed by the oppressive cultural code, again deploying the archetypal tactics. The Body, clothed in liberating attire, signified the desire to liberate Nature from the oppressive Culture. The naked/clothed ratio had been redesigned, using the nakedness which no longer stood for the negativity and barbarism, but for a new approach to a happy existence. The eternal sign-myth of paradise would resurface again in the fashion system (Barthes, 1967; Barthes, 1976).

The space exploration efforts would represent another form of the utmost extraordinariness. The inability to offer paradise on Earth, through the societal displacements (wars, peace treaties, revolutions, laws and cure) stimulated a new paradisiacal structure — Life on other planets, where presumably the Body is better preserved and Mind is in peace (Bettelheim, 1976).

Any displacement is offered to the community of actants, who are to embark on its actualization through the *recognizable signs* —a promise of improvement of the sacred sign-Body. The revolution in the food production— restaurant chains, factories, street vendors etc, — is the dominant visual signification. The success of the North American industrial societies partly lies in the successful manipulation of the anxiety over the Body. One don't have to strain oneself with the chores of cooking, buying, cleaning — one is liberated from the drudgery of taking care of one's body when, by a touch-tone telephone call, the North American consumers may obtain all the signs of exchange to please the Body, i.e. food, clothing, titillating entertainment etc. TV has replaced a more strenuous reading and activated the perception of the visual signs, dulling the capacity to invent the new sign, beyond the visual domain. The visual imagery on the silver screen has revealed the growing emphasis on the Body and its versatile manipulation, used to control the mind of the global multitude.

The goal of the genetic research at its deepest semiotic level aims at the perfect Body and Mind void of all the defective genes, exploiting the same archetypal mythology and the same paradisiacal desires. The ultimate dream is to create a truly extraordinary body and duplicate it endlessly in a controlled semiotic environment.

The sexual revolution of the sixties was not only another signification of the new *social sign* —new ideology and new distribution of the gender roles— it was a challenge to Nature. By controlling their reproduction, humans managed to compete with the primary and dominant signification of the macro semiosphere and challenge it dominance through Culture. The signs of the Body could no longer prevail over the intended signification process, designed by the owner of the Body. The sacredness of the *natural signs* was challenged by the extraordinariness of the interference in the most mysterious semiosis — the interplay within the natural and the organic systems. The female body was no longer a passive recipient of the natural signification. The birth control pill was another promise of happiness, another form of ascendance and heroic conquest. Again, as in many other previous heroic attempts, the myth of paradise was offered. Presumably, the Body, liberated from the burden of the unwanted procreation, could influence the production of the other, more pleasurable signs. The interrupted semiosis of the Body promised satisfaction, if the sign producers be engaged in mutual voyeurism, eroticism, intense production and consumption. The heroic reproduction of numerous offspring still worshipped in some societies was condemned as barbaric. The taboos of the traditional sexual signification were challenged. The sexual revolution in the Western society displaced the canonical order, having discarded the traditional values and embraced the Freudian prescription — to follow the signals of one's libido, the most sacred modern and ancient sign.

The birth-control devices reshaped the notions of the extraordinariness. A spinster or a bachelor, an *exotic sign* of the past, would benefit from the sexual liberation, since they would be liberated from the social awkwardness, the stigma of their exotic social status be removed with the dismantling of the traditional family. The unattached male or female, engaged in the production of the other signs and consumption of culture, would be a temporary ideal in the post-Freudian modernist society. Virginity, a heroic norm in the pre-sexual revolution time, would become obsolete. The reversal of the extraordinariness would occur — what used to be regarded as ideal, be now seen redundant or archaic,e.g. societal rituals, such as courting and marriage ceremonies, no longer signifying realities, but being re-enactments of the past cultural obligations, without the old inferences. For instance, a white dress, a sign of purity and virginity, would be transformed into a *false sign*, a replica of the old true sign. Similarly, a single woman, a social outcast in the past, would transform into a post-modern heroine, the symbol of a new progressive value system.

The designers of the artificial intelligence project would exploit the eternal desire for extraordinariness and heroic performance. Their final product has been intended to supersede the intelligence of the producer, to create the heroic intelligence, capable of surpassing the collective intelligence of all the previous generations of the sign-producers. The same promise of leisure is rooted in the advertising of its usefulness. The most labourious, intense and extraordinary activity, the ability to create sign and signify meaning, — would be redundant, transferred onto the sign — AID— artificial intelligence device, enabling the human brain to attain the impossible state of the long-desired leisure. Why? Isn't it in order to redefine the boundaries between the extraordinary elite and the ordinary multitude? Or isn't it an example of a pure and simple *ostension,* the "most elementary act of active signification" (Eco, 1976: 255).

5.3. *War or Violent Display of Heroism*

> *Here, with one stroke, I have killed forty mighty*
> *knights and a countless host of lesser warriors*
> *Ivan the Simpleton* (a Russian fairy tale)

The social continuum may be manipulated in various ways, through the very intense and rather violent signification. The stability of the heroic hierarchy within a given text or between the texts is periodically disturbed by the heroic impulses of the individuals and groups. The motivation behind the impulses to change the iconic edifice of a given kind could vary. It could be done in the name of the historical memory, restoration of the heroic glory of a single or collective hero, simple biological survival, whim of a single hero, the heroic collective delusions of the presumably superior cultural organization, or the mythical offence to the collective pride of a group (Makolkin, 1992a).

War is this extreme collective measure to which a group may resort in order to change the present undesirable arrangement of icons for the sake of the alleged progress. It is the most violent outcome of the lengthy mythical tribulations in the collective consciousness of the leaders and groups when they exploit the heroic paradigm to its fullest. War is the most extreme heroic occasion, where groups and individuals satisfy their craving for violence, as much as for the display of the heroic. War is the collective heroic enterprise where the forces of mimesis energetically push the duplication of the heroic matrix in individuals and groups. The unseemly , to say the least, sight of the military actions, the so-called "theatre of war" and the emotionally disturbing vision of the mutilated or dead bodies, the trauma and tragedy — these rather *confusing signs* are easily interpreted as a societal necessity, as the obligatory form of the heroic signification. Their need is justified by the noble causality of this signification, by the Other, the signs beyond the physical destruction and death. For instance, Agamemnon's heroic commitment and deeds were performed in the name of revenge for the rape and robbery by the son of King Priam. To avenge for the rape of Helen and stolen treasures Agamemnon assembled a thousand vessels to the delight of the proud and wounded Trojans (Aeschylus, 1925).

Some revisionist historians try to justify Hitler's heinous modern conquest by the spiritual wounds of the Germans, whose kindness, generosity of spirit were allegedly abused by the evil "strangers", who had the misfortune to settle among them. Paradoxically, the dignity of the displaced and tortured Jews would be later used as a mythical reason for carving the borders in the Middle East and create the zone of perpetual violence in the region, a post-modern tragic heroic contest. The heroic impulses of this group had been suppressed for centuries of migrations, persecution and exclusion, finally giving an outlet by the creation of the artificial mythical state, which cannot escape the perpetual theatre of war. The battle in the Middle East is justified by the heroic Biblical narrative, nurtured by the mythical, assumingly uninterrupted historical past, which defies the true existential conditions of the present and even some past. The state of Israel is the best illustration of the submission to war as a way of life, way of revising history with the help of the dangerous heroic myth. It is a voluntary act of creating a territory for the permanent tragedy, where the dead are constantly counted and new strategies of revenge are being perennially revised. The myth of the collective nation-martyr, being transformed into a collective hero, modern Israeli nation, with the Biblical heroic legacy, are the key signifiers, controlling their cultural text (Wolf, 1970; Rose, 1916; Snyder, 1952; Wistuch, 1985).

The Yugoslavian war of the nineties bears all the heroic prerequisites of any military battle, perfectly fitting the canonical heroic pattern. In the name of the mythical glorious past, the people are asked to perform actions of pointless heroism and participate in the childish conquest. Who has a more civilized mythical past? Whose cultural fabric is more refined and closer to the heroic Greek? Why can't we have our independent state? Like the Jews, like the Germans, like etc... (Watson, 1905; Kohn, 1933; 1967; Mitchison, 1980).

The icon "independent" has become the nemesis of this century, the heroic dictum of modernity. "Independent" also carries the taboo meaning of "racially pure", which had been collectively condemned by the collective global and individual history. "Independent" has begun to mean "heroic", stoically defying the biological, social, cultural and rational needs. It also carries the traditional semiotic validity of killing, for the sake of the future improved order, so that the mythical descendants would enjoy the mythical bliss in the mythical "independent" society. Independence from the Other, physically and spiritually, despite its impossibility has become the justification for modern war, its just cause.

War is always the re-enactment of the heroic encounter of the two sides, the replay of the eternal duplicity of the Good and Evil, the most vivid display of physical, i.e. the most admired and vivid extra-ordinariness. The replay of this adult heroic game is daily observed in children's games, with the assumed roles of slaves and masters, winners and losers. The global folklore, the most cherished cultural heritage, is largely the heroic pantheon of humanity where heroism of the Body is most graphically displayed (be it conquests of Hercules, deeds of Apollo, travels of Gilgamesh, martyrdom of Christ or cosmic fight of Ch'in Yu). The physical strength and military victory are the archetypal heroic features of any hero of the fairy tale (Eberhard, 1965; Eliade, 1958; Eliade, 1963; Farnell, 1970; Groom, 1989).

Combat and death of the enemy are very powerful semiotic events, exercising the sacred symmetry with the ultimate semiosis of the Divine mystery. The grand designer of the ultimate heroism may be imitated in the state of war. That, which could be stopped by the unknown sacred signifier, may be easily duplicated in a state of war. This grand displacement of the sacred meanings may shed the light onto the eternal seductiveness of war. The military commander and soldier share the heroic grandeur of controlling life and death of the Other, interfering with the signification of the semiophere — Nature.

Leo Tolstoy would denounce and demystify war in his world famous novel *War and Peace:*

> They would get together as yesterday to kill each other, kill and mutilate tens of thousands of people, and then would serve liturgies and worship the numbers killed, (frequently exaggerated numbers) and announce victories. The greater the number of the people killed, the greater is the achievement (1949, vol II: 208).

Tolstoy rejected war as a result of the individual will, having debunked the entire heroic interpretation of history. To him, war was the social heroic contract between the individual heroes and masses, who are willing to go beyond the existential ordinariness. Masses willingly commit acts of heroism, not only blindly following the individual hero, but pushing their spiritual boundaries to the limit. Apparently, the heroic impulses reinforce the nearly innate behavioural pattern of each individual, and the heroic circumstances merely evoke them. Some heroes-leaders are more successful at the heroic arousal than others, but some circumstances are more heroically predisposed. For instance, many Russian soldiers during the Second World War would throw themselves into the most ferocious battles and be ready to die uttering Stalin's name. Frequently, it was not a blind infatuation with the Hero-ruler, but a self-motivating device, used in the psychological preparation for the tragic war play. The name of the Hero would recall the entire set of the hero-signs at the disposal of the group and would distort the meaning of death. The opportunity to die heroically in a battle would seem superior to a mundane death from old age or ailment. The occasion to die for a patriotic cause decorates the moment, distorts the usual expected meaning of the morbid *natural sign* -Death. The role of the individual, orchestrating the war lies in misinterpreting the natural signification for the sake of the presumably future collective good. It imparts the extraordinary meaning to the ordinary act of dying. During the war, the re-description of Death occurs at various levels. There is a shared willingness to down-play its meaning and significance on the individual and collective levels. It is never imposed only from above, there is an inner dynamics between the rulers, their wills and those of the ruled. Tolstoy calls it a "special power transfer" when the entire groups agree to act heroically and take part in the dangerous war drama :

> Power is a co-ordination of the will of the masses, transferred by the oppressed or a silent agreement by the rulers who had been selected by the masses (1949, vol II: 698).

Tolstoy has captured the mutual interdependence of the wills and desires, whose displacement constitute the integral part of the social semiosis during the military actions. Wars, winning and losing never occur at random, by a chancy display of the meanings of the single *hero-sign*. All major societal shifts and displacements never happen as a result of the individual mood swings. In Tolstoy's view, the social actants are locked into the eternal heroic paradigm, having to react both individually and collectively to its inner dynamics. The sum of the cumulative meanings of the *hero-sign* allegedly orchestrates the heroic spectacles, which require more than individual extraordinariness.

The preparatory stages for the extreme display of the heroic during the war involve the manipulation of the mythical consciousness of the sign-producers, testing their collective cultural memory and their heroic appetites. Usually , decades or centuries prior to the actual war, its script-writers energetically manipulate the heroic memory. The past of the groups is revived as the heroic glorious past and the group is seduced by the myth of the collective extraordinariness. The archetypal evil, the other group or groups, is presented as the real obstacle to the revival of the for-gotten heroic status, and the necessity of war as the only means is con-vincingly argued.

Any preparatory stage heavily relies on the power of myth and the war participants. Any war carries the message of noble reasoning and promises to be the last display of the physical force in the name of the future eternal peace and prosperity. The sentiments of revenge and the desire to re-describe the past and present sign-arrangement are the uni-versal for any military preparation. Traditionally, it is the other war or wars which inspire the present, allegedly the noble war. The barbaric nature of the enemy and the alleged cruelty of the past invaders serve as the noble necessity for the present cruelty. Any war is rooted in the hero-ic collective mythology. The necessity of war is excused by the desire to restore the unrecognized heroic status of a particular group. The myth of the martyr and the past collective pain nourish the pre-military mythopoesis of any war.

A significant portion of the pre-Second World War mythology was dedicated to the myth about the abused kindness of the Nordic man, a victim of his own generosity and love. The original intention of the Fas-cists was not to destroy the enemy, but to expel the outsiders beyond the boundaries of the heroic Nordic purified state. The martyrs of the Second World War, the enemies of the Nordic race, those who have survived, have used their collective grievances for founding a new homogeneous state of the war victims. Paradoxically, but quite logically, the martyrs have established their heroic state in the Middle East only to be persis-tently engaged in the military drama with their new/old neighbours. The mythical Biblical reality, the mythologised past has been successfully transplanted onto the present to create a new heroic occasion — the Middle East drama. The dream of the Fascists about the inferior Asiatic people, destroying each other, has been fulfilled through the historical consequences of their lost War. Their war and their lost battles are being presently fought elsewhere by the non-heroic mythical Other. The impos-sible dream of purity and homogeneity is behind every mythical inde-pendence notion and among the causes of the present nonsensical war in the former Yugoslavia. All the sides are equally guilty in their search for the culprit, the inferior Other, who presumably suppresses their innate heroic nature, exclusive Culture and deprives them from the profitable sign exchange.

All the previous wars were wars for the expansion of the heroic boundaries, be it Alexander of Macedon, Napoleon or Hitler. The twentieth century post-colonial time is witnessing wars for the enclosure of the small boundaries, presented as the just wars for the independence and preservation of particularity in the linguistic code, cuisine, dress and even music. It is the modern obsession, the modern heroic goal, be it Estonia or Armenia, Tatarstan or Moldavia. The modern myth of uniqueness, extraordinariness of the endangered particularity inspires the modern displacement drive of the global tribe, whose global heroic feverish state calls for the urgent cure from the heroic mania. The nuclear war could be the last plausible human heroic encounter, with no sinners or martyrs, and the awareness of its possible danger is being used as the most effective cure from the heroic delusions and the forceful displacement (Derrida, 1992; Kristeva, 1991).

5.4. *Games and Sport Events — Signs of Physical Extraordinariness*

Sport tournaments are similar to wars, in terms of the solemnity of heroic occasion for the display of one's physical extraordinariness, but unlike wars, they do not have the equal immediacy and existential urgency. Their impact on the participants and sign-producers is rather limited. All good soldiers ought to be physically fit to engage in the display of the vital heroism, so sport competitions have traditionally been and are the grand rehearsals for the theatre of war. Healthy bodies signify physical well-being, mental stability and readiness for real battles, genuine display of their fitness. The fit Body has been the universal sign of one's physical and mental health *(mens sana in corpore sano)* and the contest of the fit bodies has been one of the most popular cultural rituals, immortalized in myth, song, saga or fairy tale. The collective mythopoesis has invariably and eternally been fixated on the limitations of the Body and expanded the natural signification by imparting the imaginary physical qualities. Thanks to the myth, the Body is able to decay and be rejuvenated again, to excel in all the extra-ordinary physical tasks. Its pure survival in the bio-semiosphere required the state of fitness and health to withstand the hardship of the physical competition with the other stronger and better adaptable bodies. This existential demand was satisfied by the natural selection in making attempts to improve the *natural signs* or assist their signification.

The ritual of sport games had been invented not only as a display of the "heroic " — physically fit Body, but as an opportunity to improve the natural signification. The physical fitness and beauty of a Body have become one of the most ancient archetypal signs of heroism. To be a hero one needed to be strong, particularly in the primitive societies. The Western cult of the Body is largely inscribed into the ancient Graeco-Roman matrix of the Body, ought to be proportionally built, extensively trained in games, exercises and military battles.

Strength and Beauty have always been and still are frequently synonymous, the size of the bodily parts carries the same mythical meanings as the other powerful natural signs. The larger size is always associated with the larger and greater capacity. The treatises of the ancient authors on the Body reveal the archetypal human obsession with height, length and weight. Small eyes were frequently associated with lack of vision and even sincerity (Aristotle, *Physiognomonics*, 1985, pp 1237-50). Accordingly, small foreheads stood for the lesser intelligence and generally small humans were not regarded as beautiful. The pagan mythical *homo sapiens* had to be of a big height, big-eyed and large-headed, with strong long arms, legs, muscles and impressive weight, exaggerating the ordinary human body. The Christian signification re-defined the physical realm of a hero, who no longer needed to be strong, large, heavy and generally physically fit. However, despite the strong impact of Christianity, the physical heroic standard in myth and in the minds of many groups has not significantly changed. The call "to love thy neighbour" and forgive one's enemies has not changed the nature of human encounters. It has not eliminated the heroic sense of occasion in a war, nor did it make a strong warrior image obsolete.

The ongoing Western, and now global, staging of the Olympic games exemplifies a symbolic tribute to the ancient Greek heroic pantheon, as well as to the universal archetypal fascination with the Body. The Olympic Games, this cultural atavism, has now been globally embraced. The politicians wish to create an illusion of peaceful entertaining spirit of the Olympic events, frequently staged to continue the political debates, using it as a political control tool (South Africa, China/Taiwan). The effectiveness of the sport teams in displaying the political statements had always been a part of these events. For instance, the gold medals won by the athletes from the former Soviet Union meant to represent not only the state of their sport training, but the heroic superiority of the social system which staged it. The failure of the non-Socialist teams was interpreted as a failure of their societies to prepare their fit heroes. Paradoxically, the same heroic yardstick was and is still being used to judge the quality of life and socio-political relationships in a given society.

Olympic teams and champions are the heroic matrices, shaping and controlling the desires and goals of many individuals, who imitate them or aspire to achieve the same. The Olympic champions are the hero-signs, modifying and manipulating our interests in the Body. They are the *rec-*

ognizable signs, displaying the physical heroism, traditionally valued the most. In fact, the analysis of the North American popular culture reveals this obsession with the physical side of the heroic, far more prevalent there than in Europe. The Canadian hockey or American baseball represent these large areas, where the heroic Body is displayed, worshipped and enviously examined. Sports and games in the North America also signify the fulfilment of the heroic political myth. Presumably, the heroic blissful society has been created where the Body is superbly fed, clothed, trained, and protected from the premature aging and decay. This neurotic display of the heroic body in games, tournament and fitness classes satisfies the paradisiacal myth of eternal youth and happiness, enshrined even into the American constitution. The cult of the Body and the myth of fulfilled paradise are intertwined and subordinated to the myth of the hero-nation-America. The individual physical extraordinariness fits the myth about the collective one.

The case of the mistaken replacement of heroic signification — a silver medal instead of the golden one for the Canadian swimmer, Sylvie Ferchette, is another example of myth fusion. The Olympic swimmer, who had spent sixteen years training for the prestigious contest, did not initially receive her gold medal due to a simple mistake of a Brazilian judge. The sponsors and supporters of the heroine, as she was referred to at the end, would eventually stage the gold medal award ceremony postfactum, imitating the Barcelona Olympic podium in Montreal. It was not only the celebration of the corrected error, but a hero-worshipping carnival in the honour of a French Canadian swimmer. Her Quebecois origins played a significant role in the celebration. Her extraordinary skills, personality and behaviour — all combined and emotionally emphasized during the ceremony, which was transformed into the celebration of the "Quebecois heroism". Silvie Frechette underwent the iconic transformation, from the Olympic Champion, the sports hero to the champion of Quebec, with the political meaning, embedded into the myth about the French Canadian heroic uniqueness. The word "extraordinary" came up several times in the speeches of the presenters of the champion and the lyrics of the Quebec famous tune were changed to include the extraordinary Sylvie Frechette — the sign of Quebecois grace, patience and stoicism. The two myths were fused in one:

$$
\begin{array}{ccc}
 & \text{extraordinary} & \\
\text{French} & & \text{Canadian} \\
 & \text{heroine} & \\
\text{extraordinary} & & \text{extraordinary} \\
\text{swimmer} & & \text{person}
\end{array}
$$

The post post-modern mythical forces, re-enacting the archetypal heroic fairy tale plot, do adjust the *universal signs* of the deep strata to the surface signification of the day. The archetypal giant, reincarnated in the modern Olympic swimmer, appeals to the recognition skills of the sign-perceivers.

The individual physical fitness threshold reached by the swimmer stimulates the forces of the heroic and the collective imagination produces a new *hero-sign,* a Quebecois national heroine. Being a woman, she also stands for the allegedly feminine type of the Quebecois ethnicity which cannot yet be recognized as an independent state. Thus, the contemporary heroic fairy-tales usually carry several mythological messages, the *hero-sign* is pushed to the limit to activate the societal semiosis on a variety of levels (Makolkin, 1992a).

Similar myth strategy could be observed in the story of the two skaters — Nancy Kerrigan and Tonia Harding who not only stand for the intensity of the Olympic competition, professional rivalry and American desire to win, but they also individually carry the signification of the inner social stratification. Tonia Harding visually fits the stereotypical image of the low income white American, stereotyped as the "white trash". The American reporters did not miss her pony-tail, excessive make-up and the general "waitress-like" looks. In contrast, Nancy Kerrigan, tall, noble, swan-like beauty stood for the upper class America. The previous attack on Nancy Kerrigan added extra layers of meaning to her as an Olympic contestant and a potential American hero. Nancy acquired a heroic status even before the games. The fact that she would recover before the Olympic performances, having endured the physical injury, would merely elevate her in the eyes of the American and global viewing public. It would fit the grammar of the heroic myth perfectly well. The drama of the contest and the ascendance towards recognition was precisely in accordance with the fairy-tale tradition and the archetypal heroic model. Nancy, the martyr and symbol of goodness and beauty, met the heroic expectations of the sign-perceivers. The mythopoesis associates beauty with goodness and suffering with sainthood. Her victorious performance reinstated her heroic status. Despite the fact, that she earned a silver medal in figure skating, in the hearts and minds of her compatriots, she was the Olympic and American heroine. Beauty, wealth, goodness and martyrdom prevailed over the mythical ugliness, evil, poverty and maliciousness. Despite the fact that Tonia's implication in the physical attack on Nancy prior to the games was a judicial dilemma, this unfortunate athlete would serve as a temporary *evil-sign*. The collective American myth-making distributed the mythical parts in the desirable way:

Nancy	Tonia
America of Success	America of Crime
beauty	non-beauty
wealth	poverty
upper	lower
good	evil
high	low
pride	shame
queen	servant
owner	slave

This polarity revealed not only the general tendency towards the extreme categorization, so much endemic in the process of choosing a hero, but certain collective American mythological specificities, rooted in the particular societal signification and the specific symbolic meaning attached to it. Nancy became the sign of Americanness, the ideal American female, who had reinforced the American existential philosophy of victory, success and happiness.

The 1994 Olympic drama did not end with the Nancy-Tonia plot. The climax came when Nancy had to take a second place after the young Ukrainian skater, Oxana Baiul. Oxana's gold medal lowered Nancy's heroic image, reinforcing the pre-iron-curtain-days mythology. As a champion for the new independent state of Ukraine, Oxana stood for the alien, although not a hostile land, for the non-existing enemy. The nature of the Olympic contest is such that the individual heroic achievements are immediately translated into the symbolic collective achievements of a group, country, or state. Oksana represented a complex semiotic construct — an orphan, she fortunately suited the archetypal heroic model. Her mother's death from cancer provided the required heroic biographical foundation, so much expected from any hero. Her young age and sudden glory made it a heroic occasion miracle (Campbell, 1946; Butler, 1979).

The heroic climax though occurred when, as if by magic, Oxana had the misfortune to endure an injury on the eve of her performance. By ironic twist and the symmetry of the sign positioning vis-à-vis Nancy, Oxana collided on the rink with a German skater, Tanja Shevchenko. Now Oksana was also a martyr. Despite the fact that the circumstances of the collision were different, and officially nobody suspected a deliberate mischief, the attack on a rival was emulated when the memory of the event-matrix was still too fresh. The pre-contest conditions of the two contestants have been evened out by the physical injury. The symmetry of the two traumas, preceding the recognition of a hero, would reinforce the ordinary and extraordinary ratio.

By the miraculous help of the German doctor, the young Ukrainian skater managed to participate in the scheduled performance and even win the gold medal, to the disappointment of the American ice princess. The ugly duckling had turned into a beautiful swan, who symbolically changed the black costume for the archetypal white. "She is a hero", concluded Oxana's coach after the Olympic events. The ordinary victory and the customary choice of an Olympic hero would turn even more extraordinary, the heroic intensity of pain and suffering would elevate the expected extraordinariness. Oxana's gold medal was a reward not only for her performance, grace, youth, but for the extra-martyrdom she had to endure unexpectedly and in the process of the heroic quest. Her gold medal signified not only superiority of the professional training over amateur sport, but the superiority of the government subsidies to sport over the private support. In a sense, it was not a medal to the individual skater, Oxana Baiul, but to the sport organization system in the state-run cultural events.

Gold	Silver
Ukraine	U.S.A
state	private
socialist	capitalist
professional	amateur
non-profit	profit

The persistent desire of the organizers of the Olympic games to ennoble the battle-like essence of the events cannot mask completely the original genesis of the war preparatory exercise. The perfect physical body of the Olympians selected not in the purely aesthetic search — the ultimate purpose of the heroic physique was to use it in military conquest against the future enemies. Several attacks on the Olympic champions during the peaceful games were a mere reminder of the primary essential motives and the subconscious understanding of the ritual. Despite the modern claims, the Olympic games still signify the symbolic state of military readiness, because, as the history of the collective interrelationships has repeatedly shown, the use of force is not yet obsolete.

Sports do rehearse and emulate the military drama. The games have the same meaning as the display of ammunition during the peaceful parades. It is a proud display of physical fitness and potential. The same recklessness and selfless attitude, the same paraphernalia of reward, the same metallic signification of distinction and temporary battle-emulating atmosphere. Even the gross violations of the competition rules, such as deliberate harm caused to the participants, is a practice which is parallel to the military game. Like in a real war, the physical damage to the warring party or destruction of the ammunition is not uncommon. After the incident caused by the attack on the prospective medallist Nancy Kerrigan, the *Times* magazine for February 21, 1994 published a summary of the similar incidents in the history of sport, having had to acknowledge the long record of such regrettable events, repeatedly taking place in the history of the allegedly noble competitions.

The games do arouse the deep-seated primal instincts in the artificially re-created battle-like situation, when the rival actually does not endanger the life of a specie, but merely displays one's extraordinary skills or gifts, what the others might lack. This desire to repossess the property of the Other be it special skills, experience, beauty or endurance, acts as the overpowering drive during the competitive contact of the "I" and the "Other". The modern Olympic and other tournaments encode the essence of the historical and modern social relationships, rooted in the deeply ingrained hierarchy. The high/low ratio functions as the simplest distribution of roles and the display of the heroic mode at its best.

The cycle of selecting the Olympic heroes metaphorizes the existential need in heroes, mimesis and destruction of the old heroes. The hero possesses what the rest of the group wishes to acquire, arousing the desire to imitate the hero. When "the efforts to acquire fail, we are left with a feeling of impotence", or simply envy, as Girard defies this powerful sentiment (Girard, 1965:13). Envy breeds hostility towards the hero and the desire to destroy him/her. The hero may be destroyed indirectly by changing or elevating the standards of the competition when the typology of the heroic selection would eliminate the undesirable Other. New temporal constraints, new speed, size, distance and height standards are being perpetually introduced to destroy the old hero, or to sustain the cycle of the heroic rejuvenation. What is the purpose of it all? To satisfy the growing envy and failure to acknowledge the senselessness of it all? What is the intellectual, spiritual and aesthetic benefit of another extra cm or a split second." Does it improve the quality of life? Does it prolong life? Does it make human life happier? The quick fix, the moment of intoxication only to be followed by another attempt to repossess, destroy, remove the visible hero-sign?

Sports competitions reveal the eternal fascination with the physical harmony of the young trained body, as well as the universal tendency to tie the individual hero to the group, promoting the heroic myth about it. The celebration of the physical extraordinariness is also a manifestation of the death and genetic defect anxieties that invariably haunt the *homo-sapiens*. Each healthy body is the victory over the unknown *biosemiosis*, the successful display of control over the "Other", superior signification.

Steroids used by the athletes, for example, stand for this eternal anxiety of competition with Nature and the *natural signs*. The instant gratification and shortened distance towards the heroic goal are the *false signs*, incapable of control since the Body ultimately exposes this deceptive semiosis. The false signification of health through fitness regains its power over Nature. The damaged body of an athlete responds with vengeance to the disrupted natural semiosis.

5.5. *Beauty Signs and Aesthetic Neurosis*

> *If beauty is considered to be transcendental, it*
> *acquires a metaphysical worth and unchanging*
> *objectivity, and an extension which is universal.*
> The Aesthetics of Thomas Aquinas. U. Eco

> *There once was a tailor who had three daughters,*
> *and they were the most beautiful girls in Greece.*
> *The tailor made the most beautiful suits and*
> *clothes all very beautiful".*
> "The Tailor's Clever Daughter" — a folk tale
> of the Greek Gypsies from Thessaloniki

This short introduction of a Gypsy fairy tale demonstrates the universal beauty motif, which no tale escapes. Beauty is the universal heroic prerequisite and no introduction to the heroic life is spared from this visible heroic decorum. Beauty —the extreme manifestation of the successful physical semiosis— is the required heroic component of any *hero-sign* (Eco, 1986). The physical extraordinariness is not complete and *hero-sign* cannot be fully constructed without the *beauty -sign*. Here the gender parameter plays a differentiating role, since women have always been regarded as signs of beauty, the "beautiful sex" icon encodes another distribution of extraordinariness in nature and culture. If a woman is not described as beautiful, at least her attire is. For instance, Mikevan, the protagonist from the Japanese fairy tale, first sees a beautiful kimono of the "woman who came from heaven", then she is introduced through her clothing, her "second skin" (Seki, 1963:64). Occasionally, the importance of the *beauty-sign* is shown in the semiotic clusters, or colonies of signs such as:

> There was once a widowed king who had twelve daughters one more beautiful than he other *(The Secret Hall,* a Russian fairy tale).

The story introduces the reader into a rich semiotic environment where not a single heroine, but a dozen exhibit beauty. The icon "12" exaggerates the *semiovalence* of the sign, constructing a saturated milieu

(Afanasiev, 1945: 224). Not a single fairy tale hero/ine is introduced without the beauty-sign, a part of the presentment of the Hero-Sign, Beauty along with Force represents the basic structure of the signifier-Hero (Kovach, 1974).

Beauty-sign is not only the permanent prerequisite for the construction of the fantastic reality, but is a vital component of any cultural text. The hero-sign signifies its heroic meaning through the *beauty-sign,* as the superficial manifestation of the semiotic processes during any heroic performance.

Some visual signs and their combinations have been and are preferred over others; the beauty-sign signifies and evokes various feelings. Charles Peirce, who insisted on the mathematical, logical and experiential proof, did not attach much significance to the *beauty-sign.* He basically claimed that such a signification is "without reason" and, therefore, does not deserve any interpretative effort:

> My dear Sir, if you can prove to me that this quality of feeling that you speak of does, as a fact, attach to what you call beautiful, or that which would be admirable without any reason for being so, I am willing enough to believe you; but I cannot without strenuous proof admit that any particular quality of feeling is admirable without a reason (1931: 621-3).

Peirce also suggests that behind any *beauty-sign,* i.e. the "admirable" or beautiful, there is a foundation, a semiotic layer, actually predetermining its expression. The value web arbitrarily designed may affect the presentment of the *beauty-sign.* For instance, the Hegelian notion of what is admirable is deeply rooted into the worshipping of the extraordinariness of the Greek cultural text. To Hegel, not only the cultural signs, the product of the Greek tradition, are admirable, but, as had been mentioned previously, so are their producers —the Greek people. Hegel perceived the physical appearance of the Greeks as the heroic *beauty-sign*, the aesthetic standard for all races. The Greek profiles and hair styles were equally regarded superior to the appearances of other people, along with their philosophical treatises, Homer and Sophocles, Pythagoras and Asclepias, their distinct pottery and monumental superb architecture. Hegel attributed to the Greeks all the features of perfection and forced upon them his ideal of a heroic race, along with the burdensome symmetry between the natural and cultural signification. In a way, as previously mentioned, he echoed Leonardo da Vinci's view that a trace of not so beautiful and admirable might ultimately reveal itself in the *cultural sign,* if its producer happens to have natural flaws. The Hegelian aesthetic credo had reinforced Leonardo's cultural bias, as well as the archetypal universal preoccupation with symmetry and harmony (Leonardo da Vinci, 1802; Hegel, 1975).

Since time immemorial people preferred symmetry between the external and the internal, which would be always transferred onto the acceptable standards of Beauty. The producer of the *beauty-sign* had to be beautiful himself/herself. This ancient universal beauty-anxiety most clearly manifests itself in the modern North-American society where the beauty-sign even regulates the economy and industry. For instance, the performance of an employee is judged less severely, if he/she is beautiful by the common evaluative standard. Any success in the job interview is largely predetermined by the evaluation of the physical beauty of an applicant. A more attractive applicant has more chances then a less attractive one, regardless of the job, be it a clerk, a truck driver, a movie star, or a university professor.

The natural *beauty-sign* may be controversial in a particular semiotic environment. For instance, a black child may wish to become more white looking in the predominantly white neighbourhood. The American popular star Michael Jackson had changed through plastic surgery his African features, in order to fulfil the aesthetic expectations of his predominantly Caucasian audience. He reinvented his *face-sign* to suit the aesthetic expectations, established and valued in the USA. Eventually, even this was not enough, his appearance had undergone further metamorphosis — from a more male to a more female. Jackson's plastic surgeries would signal to the audiences that he had fulfilled the aesthetic expectations of the sign-perceivers (Change, 1976; Seaford, 1978; Gary, 1979; Umiker-Sebeok, 1979). It also communicated the possibility to challenge the natural sign. Since "white" is more desired and valued than "black", Jackson sent the message to the cultural environment that even a *natural sign* could be re-designed to suit the needs and desires of the crowd (Webes, 1984; Ageh, 1992 *The Globe and Mail*). Many Orientals, aspiring to be employed by the Western firms have also duplicated Jackson's efforts. Plastic surgeries in Korea, China and Japan have become increasingly popular. The Caucasian *face-sign* is now used as a heroic matrix, a marker of success so that Orientals could now possess the curently desired beauty.

The cosmetic and apparel industries daily promote the particular beauty-signs as the *desired signs*. Millions of women have been traditionally disturbed by this tyrannical signification, and they still submit themselves to it to fulfil their own heroic impulses and the heroic expectation of the perceivers. False meanings of the *beauty-sign* are unanimously agreed upon. It is temporal, and there is a general acceptance of this fact. The efforts of the sign modifiers are directed at prolonging its heroic stage, it may appear mostly admirable and pleasing. To be eternally young and beautiful is the common, heroic and impossible dream, which we all cherish, possess, ignore, and cannot destroy. The *beauty sign* is another *universal sign* that holds us as hostages to its powerful heroic meaning (Kovach, 1974; Eco, 1986).

5.6. *Healing — Defying the Body*

Beauty, physical strength and endurance —all signify the most preferred heroic stage of one's life— youth. Despite the endless efforts to prolong this heroic phase of the signification of the *natural signs,* we ultimately reconcile with its failure. The mysterious producer of all *natural signs* has staged and pre-determined our limited semiosis in the physical universe. Despite the eternal death anxiety we have accepted the temporal boundaries of our natural signification. However, what we do accept with difficulty, is the disrupted course of the natural semiosis, revealed in illness (Uexkull, 1986; Sontag; Kahn, 1976; Young, 1989).

Since the early stages of culture, even the most primitive humans have always interpreted the *visual natural signs* in order to diagnose, cure and prevent illness. Even modern physicians, equipped with the most sophisticated technology do not shy away from the interpretations of the visual signs which they call *symptoms.* The doctors initially interpret the visual explicit signs of the Body, such as colour, weight, size of the body parts and possible displacements of the regular body tissue. The act of examining the Body in itself is the act of interpreting its signs, either auditory, visual or tactile. The differently sounding healthy and infected lungs are quite familiar to a well-trained physician, as much as the differences between the normal and dysfunctional thyroid (Kahn, 1976; Young, 1989).

Medicine and healing combine two semiotic processes — *recognition* and forced *displacement.* The bulging eyes have frightened our ancient ancestors who have connected them with the outbursts of uncontrollable anger. One may find it in Aristotle' *Physiognomonics* where he argued that " eyes should be neither large nor small and must neither recede, nor protrude" (1984, 1: 1246-7). This Aristotelian statement not only reveals the Greek obsession with harmony and equilibrium, but the global analysis of the *natural signs*, which usually tends to have a certain orderly signification pattern. The motto "nothing in excess", carved on the temple of Apollo, encapsulates the acceptance of the arrangement of the *natural signs*, as well as the general fear of the extra-ordinary in the ancient culture.

To see the bulging eyes, larger than usual, means to notice some unusual quality or extraordinariness in the *face-sign.* To find out that this *displacement* is the result of the thyroid disorder is to connect the internal and external signification and recognize the ailment. The second step is to re-channel this displacement and reverse the process of this disturbing semiosis. It took centuries of erroneous, abortive efforts until the dangerous semiosis could be controlled.

Healing is the most ancient semiotic activity. It is not accidental that healers in all cultures have always been revered and feared. The witch or the witch doctor could occasionally reverse the pattern of the dangerous semiosis and actually cure. The act of cure was the victory of the successful interpreter of signs and fortunate intervener into the shifted, displaced semiotic process. By curing, the healer reinforced his/er interpretative power and ability to recognize the *dangerous signs,* as well as destroy them, bringing back the natural semiotic equilibrium. Healer saw the exterior Body as the mirror of the inner semiotic structures . While healing, the healer adopts the heroic function of the sign-modifier and can actually compete with the primary sign-producer — Nature. The heroic status of physicians in society stems from this awe of their interference into the natural semiosis. Doctors may play God with our Bodies and may frequently be quite successful, but when the recognition and destruction of signs is a failure, the misinterpretation is silenced in shame. Aside from the obvious moral and ethical issues, every failed healer painfully suffers from the failure to interpret the Body. The body overpowers the interpreter when it succeeds in masking and concealing its dangerous and malicious signification. The Body outwits the healer when it closes its secret code container and refuses to offer any transparency to its signs. In this uneven battle of signifiers and interpreters the Body wins, reclaiming its superior heroic status to the original sign-producer. The body and its disease or malicious signification represent a constant challenge to the healer who has to compete with the obviously superior construct. The *natural signs* inspire the producers of *cultural signs,* who create new heroic occasions and compete for new heroic titles — be it discovery of polio-vaccine or cancer cure, insulin or antibiotics, gene or virus, etc..

5.7. *Space Flight or Defying the Earth*

The impulse to perform heroic deeds, the drive for extraordinariness is the inescapable strive for getting beyond the trivial existential opportunities. It is the ongoing creative impulse which constantly shapes and reshapes the real. The rediscription of the real first occurs as fiction, or a dream about the impossible. Many fairy tales have anticipated future scientific discoveries. The future aeroplanes and spaceships first settled as prominent motifs in the fairy tales. A fairy tale is the first testing ground for the impossible. Human imagination first reshapes the boring reality in the fantastic transformations where all the desires are satisfied and where no boundaries could limit human activity (Propp, 1929; Dolezel, 1978, 1984). If the real is structured on the basis of the strict boundaries between the impossible and possible, the unreal could be the actualization of the limitless and boundless, the forbidden and the unknown. The fairy tales carry the images of the broken boundaries and the archetypal account of the extraordinary. Most of such actions, images, thoughts and desires are connected with the life on Earth. However, the utmost extraordinariness has always been connected with its version of extreme Otherness- the life beyond and above the Earth. Thus, the image of the flying objects, imitating the birds, has always been a great challenge.

The Russian fairy tale *Horns,* in the Alexander Afanasiev's collection, has a motif of a flying carpet on which the princess sits and vanishes from the onlookers. The flying carpet captures the desire to fly, to be able to move in the air and leave the tenets of the ground. The impossible mode of movement, which would eventually become a standard mode of transportation, is anticipated by the flying carpet image. The fantastic image signifies the other reality, beyond the ordinary experience, the utter extraordinariness. The Russian fairy-tale is not a unique heroic account of flying. The Greek Daedalus and Ikarus were preceded by the Chinese tale about flying carts, only to be repeated in the Arabian, Buddhist, Icelandic and Scottish stories. The Hindu tale reports about fantastic wings cut off from flying mountains (Hith-Thompson, 1955).

These and numerous other fantastic accounts capture the awe of flying as the utmost extraordinariness, the utopia within the utopian unreality. This worshipping of flying and movement into the upper universe would transcend the world of the fantastic and re-emerge in the real world as worshipping of air industry and space exploration. The Russian "sputnik" had imparted the heroic status to the impoverished third world country, which possessed the secret to the revered and mystified beyondness. The Russian success in space explorations aroused the heroic competitive drive in the two naive superpowers, who would engage in the lengthy and costly training of their space heroes. The conquest of space epitomized the heroic utopia of the fairy tales and realized the dream about the final conquest of nature. All the heroic triumphs on Earth seemed rather ordinary, next to the uniqueness of the movement and presence in space. Man in space, man on the moon-these images and events stood for the utmost human heroism within the present boundaries of the extraordinary and its triumph over the ordinary.

Movement above the earth, in the heavenly skies, has been associated with the extension of the heroic territory and the expansion of the *"utopic space"*, i.e. the location where "the hero accedes to victory" (Greimas,

1979:363). In this sense, all the previous fictional and real heroic performances could be treated as mere *paratopic* spaces, "where competence of the heroic is acquired." Thus, wars, executions, sacrifice, physical agility in sport, physical beauty in beauty contests and mental acuteness in all intellectual pursuits, leading to the heroic recognition, could be seen as mere *paratopic* heroic efforts. They were the necessary heroic prerequisites, the *heterotopic* gaps, preceding the ultimate conquest, the invasion of the utopian, long-desired and imagined upper world (Greimas, 1979: 181).

The vertical movement, in fact, is the most willed manifestation of the *hero-sign*. The hero- sign has the prevalent upper localization in the social space, be it a kingdom, a republic, a party, a group, a committee or a team. The upward mobility in society reveals itself in the perennial verticality of the *hero-sign*. Heroism is associated with verticality, despite the fact that military and geographic exploration involve the non-vertical spread of the heroic universe.

The twentieth-century space explorations have redesigned the canonical *utopic space* and shifted it from the lower to the upper world. The *hero-sign* has expressed its unknown previously heroic meanings which had been vaguely signified in the fictional global narratives. The aeroplane has perfected the dream about the flying cart, bird, mountain and falsely closed the heroic upper space. As it turned out, the embodiment of the archetypal dreams was not sufficient. The *hero-sign* expressed its unknown *semiovalence* in space exploration and revived the seemingly complete semiotic process.

However, despite this new stage of the vertically-oriented heroic activity, the mode of signification of the acting hero-sign had not changed. The hero still had to possess the universal set of the heroic qualities. This is how the Canadian newspaper presented the hero-astronaut Marc Garneau, the "perfect Canadian hero":

> He was born in Quebec city, received a degree in physics from Royal Military College in Kingston in 1970 and went to obtain a Ph.D in electrical engineering from the Imperial College of Science and Technology in London, England, before launching a military career. He also found time to jog, play tennis, squash and scuba dive and he twice —in 1969 and 1970— sailed across the Atlantic in 59-foot yard with 12 other crewmen (*Toronto Star*, March 1/1985).

This astronaut has fulfilled all the archetypal requirements of a hero. He is young, physically fit, intelligent, born, if not into a poor family, but at least into a poorer province. (Quebec is the mythical poor brother among the other Canadian provinces, the unrecognized community of modern martyrs.) Like all the archetypal heroes, Garneau "travels," as far as England to get his Ph.D., and returns back to be recognized among his fellow Canadians. Garneau's set of numerous sport skills and victories is not only a testimony to his extraordinary physical fitness, but the unusual time management, a truly heroic effort in the modern fast-moving industrial world. His scuba diving success repeats the cycle of the archetypal heroic deeds. The hero invades the lower world before he sets for the upper universe, it is his "testing for fitness to be a hero", the eleventh alleged quality of a hero as defined by Bill Butler (1979: 27-30). Butler established the famous set of thirty heroic features, which are presumably the universal heroic requirements, and divided the preparatory stage from the actual quest. The heroic account of the space star fits precisely Butler's heroic model, as much as a fairy tale or legend narrative would. The heroic quest is always a journey to the Other world, full of danger and with the risk of death. In this case, it is a space flight, involving a certain danger and fulfilling all the demands of the archetypal heroic plot.

However, unlike Butler's unlucky hero, Garneau is happily married and is a father of two at the relatively tender parenting age of 36. The post-modern hero defies the post-Freudian anxiety pattern and serves as a model of social stability and adjustment. Contrary to Freud, he is not traumatized by family, nor by society (Freud, 1936). "Only such perfect Canadians could fly into space and become heroes." — this is the leitmotiv of the *Toronto Star* a Canadian newspaper in 1985. The second Canadian cosmonaut, Roberta Bondar, is a slightly different version of a hero. According to Butler, "the divine hero is always a male" (1979:28). She challenges this first precondition, which makes her even more heroic, intensifying the meaning of the new *hero-sign*. This first Canada's woman in space strikes with her single spaced, twenty page curriculum vitae, membership in twelve learned societies, Ph.D in medicine, five honorary doctorates and the fact that

> She flies , rides in hot-air balloons, and participates in canoeing, bicycling, fishing, target shooting, cross-country skiing and squash (*The Toronto Star,* January 21, 1992).

Her conquest of the surface of the Earth had preceded her space conquest where she ultimately fulfilled her existential purpose.

It may be questioned by the future generations of cultural historians why such rigorous standards had been imposed on a female hero. But the fact remains that the 46-year-old female hero had to sacrifice her family life and scholarly career for the sake of a rather questionable role in space. In this sense, she has fulfilled the heroic standard requirements of Butler's divine hero. The little Sault Ste. Marie, the place of Bondar's birth, "gets a boost" as a result of her heroic quest. The *"utopic space"* of the hero involves land, heaven and land again, the heroine completes her heroic cycle in her birthplace and follows the most observable pattern of the territorial expansion (Butler, 1979; Greimas, 1979).

All cosmonauts share all the heroic qualities of extraordinariness with the heroic performers of the past, be it in fiction or in reality, on land or under water. In fact, the latter are regarded as the preparatory testing stages prior to the ultimate quest scene. The future culture critics might probably question even more rigorously the purpose of such heroic undertakings and the disparity between the pragmatic heroic activities on land, their immediate usefulness and the remote results of their presence in space. Nonetheless, we may merely record the contemporary space explorations as a part of the universal heroic semiosis and the expansion of the *"utopic"* heroic space at large.

The lack of contentment partly stimulates the eternal heroic semiosis which results in the new heroic vistas, broken frontiers, redescribed heroic maps. The records of heroism constantly await for the new entries, new actions, new "actants" and new heroic narratives (Bremond, 1970; Greimas, 1971). The surrounding world of difference and "differance" inspires the heroic efforts of surpassing the established perfection, and available extremes, it challenges the perceivers and producers of signs in the ongoing heroic semiosis. Space exploration is just one of the most logical challenges, inspired by the mere natural verticality — space above, the unusual mysterious natural world, and a metaphor for the social pyramid in the cultural universe (Auerbach, 1953; Aristotle, [1985]; Morawski, 1970; Makolkin, 1992, a).

Chapter Six

The Anti-Heroic Semiosis

> *There is something gladiatorial in any competition.*
>
> (A comment by a concert pianist)

> *The people are always in the habit of elevating one man as their champion above all others, and they nurture him and make him great. That is the custom. It is clear that this championship of the people is the one and only root from which dictatorship and the dictator can grow.*
>
> Plato, *Republic*

6.1. *Hero-Demos and Democracy*

The heroic drive, the universal impulse to elevate a particular extra-ordinariness has not always been perceived as a positive necessity in a society. Plato had a rather negative attitude towards the heroes, whom he regarded as the causes of the evil dictatorship. He did not condemn the particular individuals, but blamed the universal human custom of elevating individuals for the undesirable societal order. His ideal republic intended to dispense with heroes and dictators and institute democracy, i.e. the order of the ordinary, equally treated citizens where nobody could be elevated. The act of elevation of a particular individual, the recognition of the extraordinariness was contradictory to the democratic premise of the ideal Platonian state.

The French, American and Russian revolutions, aiming at the destruction of the monarchy and dictatorship, were basically anti-heroic group efforts. The democratic ancient concept dispensed with the heroic when it denounced the principle of elevating a single hero. Thus, the ancient democracy implied the cult of the ordinary demos, depriving the average individual of any opportunity to rise above. To be a hero means to be unequal to the other, better than the majority and anti-democratic in principle.

Centuries after Plato, D.H. Lawrence would attack the anti-heroic essence of any democracy, the cult of the average, the standard, representative of the most common denominator in society. According to D.H. Lawrence, this standard of the ordinary had been invented to keep the talent and heroism in check. It was a pragmatic measure, invented by the pragmatic individuals for purely pragmatic distribution of wealth, equally and conventionally, i.e. the standard boots, standard lamps, standard bread. The standard man appeared as much by the will of the market, due to the archetypal resentment of the extraordinariness. The equal distribution of food, energy, housing, clothing, luxury and wealth, not only meant the realization of the just democratic principle, but the realization of the secret dream — to kill the hero, to destroy the *hero-sign*. The destruction of the hero signified the end to the misery of the average, who are incapable of the extra-ordinary thoughts, actions and events (Haddas, 1965; Frye, 1989). The democratic order of the standard average man satisfied the compelling desire to rest from he eternal competition with the troublesome extraordinary, to be liberated from the eternal fear of the Hero (Girard, 1972: 1978). This anxiety of the exceptional has been associated with our eternal unhappiness, eternal need to respond to the heroic challenge which, after all, is not the need of the multitude.

This anxiety is in all our myths, tales, laws, rituals and daily appraisals of any activity — the crucifixion of the Lord, betrayal of a saint, punishment of the dissident, witch hunt, slander, persecution of the free thinker, envy of the rich and famous, joy at the death of the hero and the hypocritical sadness etc, etc.... Most heroic elevations require the multitude of the average, ordinary worshippers, who are unable to excel, overdo the heroic deeds of the elevated Hero (Adler, 1974; Girard, 1965). Inequality is ingrained not only in the man-made signs, but in the *natural signs* as well. Our language reflects this existential axiom and the producers of signs are not equal either:

> Men are not equal and never were and never will be, save by the arbitrary determination of the some ridiculous human ideal (Lawrence, 19: 701).

Therefore, the democratic ideals which rely on the assumed innate equality of men as producers of *standard signs* tend to suppress the equally innate strive for the extraordinary. Any democratic society rests on the anti-heroic environmental principle which deprives the heroic "I" from expressing itself in the innate remarkable way. "I am myself," — proclaimed D.H. Lawrence, "I do not need anybody to represent me," he stated, rebelling against the hero-killing spirit of the democratic order, which requires uniformity of the signs and sign-producers. Lawrence's sign-producer is always unique in his semiotic power.

> One's — self I sing, a simple separate person.
> Yet utter the word democratic, the word *en-masse.*

This was another evaluation of the conflict between the individual and collective self, between the average and the outstanding, uttered by Walt Whitman. Both statements capture the eternal paradox, the conflict

between the heroic and the anti-heroic, the average and the above average producers and signs. The Platonian, Marxist, Christ's, Rousseau's,
Voltaire's , Lenin's, and numerous other versions of the presumably just
and free societies presuppose death of the hero, the reign of the standard,
average and the comfort of the uniform ordinariness. Democracy is the
tyranny of the average, which finally suppresses excellence and origi-
nality. It is the final solution to the archetypal problem of the Hero, who
is ultimately more feared and hated than loved and worshipped (Frye,
1989).

The heroic energy is the unsettling force which disturbs peace and
tranquillity of the inert group, unwilling or unable to produce signs. The
awe of the hero and the heroic energy evenly balances out with the an-
noyance and hate for the troublesome sign-producer. The democratic
motto is essentially anti-heroic, discouraging any excessive sign-production above the familiar and prescribed level. It is the new sign-producing milieu when the *hero-sign* can no longer be recognized amidst the
standard-conscious, average and content multitude.

6.2   *Freud and Debunking the Hero*

If democracy suppresses the heroic semiosis, shifting the *social signs* in
society and levelling down the extraordinary impulses of the multitude,
the Freudian philosophy and psychology supplied the additional reasoning and justification of such a shift. The Freudian search for the archetypal layers in the human psyche and his architectonics of the human
consciousness was an attempt to find the universal common denominator. The famous Freudian *id-ego-super-ego* triad was his discovered basic
semiotic configuration of the human mind (Freud, 1901; 1905). His *id*, the
primordial force, the dark archaic past of humanity expressed in the ever
powerful libido, was such a common denominator for the entire humanity. The layers of the psyche, responsible for the construction of Culture
and production of the *cultural signs* were treated as the superstructure
above and beyond the prevailing *id*. The superego and ego were the natural sign —suppressants, controlling the universal archaic id and its
trauma— causing effect on the psyche. According to Freud, *homo-sapiens*
applies heroic efforts trying to resist the natural signification and dominance of the *id*. The three main sources of human anxiety are the three
basic systems of signs —family, community and state— which control
human sexuality and re-direct the preeminent sexual desire towards the
"Other". The essence of sublimation is the traumatizing heroism, aiming
at the suppression of the Body (Freud, 1901).

Consequently, the Freudian recipe for the confused and discontent
civilization was the destruction of the civilized hero, battling one's sexu-

ality, one's Body. To listen to the Body and its communicative signs was the Freudian message to the heroic civilized self. Freud mocked the efforts of humanity to depart from one's Body. The Freudian psychology and philosophy filled the vacuum, created by the post-Christian, post-industrial, post-romantic modern semiosis (O'Neill, 1989; O'Neill, 1983). Rooted in the modern anxiety and confusion, his anti-heroic philosophy originates in the Nietzschean heroic delusions and alludes to his *The Birth of Tragedy*. Nietzsche anticipated drastic changes in the system of signs and treated the forthcoming semiosis as a tragedy:

> All that is new called culture education, civilization will one day have to appear before the incorruptible judge, Dionysus (Nietzsche, 1956:120).

Instead of the coming of messiah, or the last judgement of Christ, Nietzsche proposed a new hero-Dionysus. This heroism was perceived as a tragic one, since it would allegedly have marked the end of the cultural signification. The Nietschean heroic anxiety connects the ancient fear of Dionysus as a *dangerous sign*, the initiator of destruction and disorder, with the modern fear of the anti-heroic environment. The post-techno-cratic, post-industrial, post-Victorian demons of modernity have found their solace in the Nietzschean Dionysus, the antidote to Christ, Marx and the embryonic image of Hitler and Stalin. Dionysus signified the utmost submission to the Body and, what Freud would later diagnose as the *id*. However, unlike Nietzsche, Freud did not see it as a tragic mark-er, but rather as a sign of liberation from the purely heroic. The taboos which restricted the Body and required the heroic restraint were sweep-ingly removed by Freud, who demystified the civilized *homo sapiens* and proclaimed that ultimately one is driven by the prevailing *id* (Freud, 1901).

The id-sign was elevated while *homo-sapiens* was levelled to the posi-tion of a slave of one's libido. However, Freud distinguished the heroic possibilities of the two genders. The female part of humanity was reduced to the anti-heroic function of seduction, procreation and oppres-sive sexuality, forcing it upon the males. The entire global community was condemned to the primitive recognition of the *natural signs* while the production of *cultural signs* —sublimation— was after all reserved for the minute group of the exclusive males (Freud, 1977 [1936]).

The Freudian *id* would become the dominant *hero-sign* in the natural and cultural universe, as well as the source for the future debunking of heroes in the years to come. It is the omnipotent "id" which no hero could conquer and which united the average and the extraordinary. The heroes who were as traumatized by the sexual anxieties as the ordinary mortals had lost their heroic aura. The Freudian sexual theories had a revolutionary impact on the depiction of the extraordinary individuals in the traditional genre of the heroic biography. The heroic biography had undergone a drastic transformation, having become a debunking biography of a hero. Heroes, overwhelmed by the pressures of the *id* and the entire dominance of the body, had lost their original semiotic significance (Madelenait, 1984; Makolkin, 1987; Makolkin, 1992a).

Each biography of a well-established hero, a prominent historical individual had undergone a discursive metamorphosis in the post-Freudian period. The possibility to discuss freely and openly the taboo topics have empowered the biographers with the new debunking and anti-heroic modes of depiction. No hero was spared. One's sexual habits, be they real or imaginary, became the object of scrutiny and the sources of the anti-heroic portrayal. The post-Freudian biographers and all writers of heroic lives during anti-heroic stage undermined the basic thesis of heroism as the "brilliant triumph of the soul over the flesh" (Roche, 1987: VII). No extraordinary individual in the post-Freudian accounts could conquer one's flesh. All heroes succumbed to it, trapped in the mire of the powerful *natural signs*.

The Freudian theory of personality levelled all the individuals to a single, basically unheroic level. Incest and sexual inversion, early awakening of the libido and masturbation, desire to break the taboos, imposed by the millennia of the production of cultural signs — all demonstrated the anti-heroic nature of all humans. The Freudian perspective on humanity was rather gloomy. In the Freudian anti-heroic universe, the *homo-sapiens* was doomed to be an ordinary sexual being, totally absorbed by one's own body, having submitted to the ultimate heroic force of libido, the heroic space of the most powerful "id" (Girard, 1972: 182).

Freud perceived the majority of humanity as the passive perceivers of the cultural signs. consumers of "the fantasy pleasures" that are "the agency of the artist opened to those who cannot themselves create" (Freud, 1977: 774). He shared the Victorian worshipping of an artist and his, but not her extraordinariness. Freud, a student of Le Bon, divided the entire humanity into the anti-heroic majority and the heroic minority. The latter, as he suggested in his *Civilization and Its Discontents*, was the manifestation of the so-called "narcissistic personality" who is more self- sufficient [and] will seek his essential satisfaction in the inner workings of his own soul" (Freud, 1977: 775). The pleasure principle allegedly would express itself in the *cultural signs*, produced by the narcissistic heroic types, while the anti-heroic majority would occupy itself with the *natural signs* fixated on their own bodies. In this connection, women, in Freudian view, were automatically dismissed as the inferior "carriers of the id", who "represent the interests of the family and sexual life" (Freud, 1977: 783; Makolkin, 1992: 34-7). The heroic task of producing Culture was reserved for men. Freud was convinced that "the work of civilization has become more and more men's business", that more than half of humanity were incapable of heroic actions, and the production of the cultural signs was the heroic mission of the tiny narcissistic minority.

Freud's concept of the narcissistic personality anticipates the future openness of the 20th century homosexuals and their future competition for the heroic space in society. Freudian elevation of an artist complemented the Romantic hero-worshipping with the philosophical and psychological basis for the new artistic deity. The Freudian narcissist, seeking one's ultimate pleasures in Culture and not in Nature, is the heroic antithesis to the archaic man, who cannot suppress one's libido and cannot disconnect oneself from the woman, the archetypal source of "id" and barbarism. If a narcissist is the producer of civilization the rest of its consumers are nothing more than a mundane primitive crowd of the uncivilized barbarians. However, since the crowd is largely heterosexual, due to its natural ties with the opposite, allegedly unpleasant and inferior sex, only those would be able to create genuine civilization, who are separated from the eternal source of the "id"—the woman. Consequently, the Freudian ideal hero is the narcissistic male artist, secretly seeking the gratification of the sexual pleasure in the Other Self, unnatural space, breaking the taboos of the archaic primitive crowd, doomed to the mundane and "unimaginative" sexual hetero pleasures (Freud, 1977 [1936]; 1983 [1905]; Rice, 1993).

6.3. *The Anti-Heroic Meaning of Some Dominant Signs*

Being *the dominant signs,* all religious systems prescribe a very limited heroic repertoire for the majority of the followers. The ultimate hero is either Christ or Allah, Buddha or the modern cult leader, and no other extraordinary figures are permitted to take their place. Thus, the selection of a single dominant sign precludes the heroic performance of many. The religious icons form the exclusive utterative space that does not allow any further heroic articulation. The monotheistic religions actually limited and narrowed the "utopic space" since they became the reserved heroic universes. for single heroes (Greimas, 1979).

If paganism, animalism, pantheism involved the heroic performances by the various heroic "actants", the monotheistic religions redescribed the localized space and redefined extraordinariness. The extreme extraordinariness was reserved for the singled out dominant signs. The concept of sin actually was a license to act unheroically. The virtuous

God was the only one who would not actually sin, who would be able to withstand the seductive signals of the mundane and worldly. The category of forgiveness was the admission of the eternal anti-heroic behaviour of the sinning believers. Consequently, having stopped asking for the impossible virtues, the religious systems legalized and institutionalized the unheroic act, reserving the heroic deeds for the selected few.

Similarly to the organized systems of spirituality, the authoritarian states designed their social semiotic universes in such a way that the ultimate "utopic space" would be the heroic domain of the principal hero on the top of the social pyramid. Ivan the Terrible or Hitler, Stalin or Pol Pot, Peter the Great or Queen Christina, Ludovic or Louis XV, Bismark or King John of Austria — all craved for their *utopic heroic spaces,* which belonged solely and exclusively to them. The basic claim of all revolutionaries is the desire the express their heroic identities, to compete for the utopic space. However, paradoxically enough, all the utopic spaces are contested on the individual, rather than on a shared group basis. Ultimately, all the rebels against autocracy and tyranny frantically cling to their invaded and captured utopic spaces. The utopic space is the eternal dream of every hero, and it is a selfish desire to reign in it singularly and single-handedly. Every struggle for power is the struggle for the isolated spacial solitude above and amidst the ordinary "heterotopic and paratopic" spaces (Greimas, 1979:1981).

Laws, being *dominant signs* controlling and regulating human behaviour, have initially been designed to reform the primitive man and instill the desired patterns of behaviour. Those desirable customs aimed at the atmosphere of social harmony, prevention of violence and ethical interactions. Even the laws in the most primitive societies embodied the human desire for the ideal heroic specie (O'Neill, 1989). First and foremost, the laws have been invented to protect the biological existence. The incest taboo was, perhaps, the first vital law, dictated by the bio reality to regulate itself properly. It demanded the utmost heroic effort on the part of the community which was not accustomed to observe and practice the new law. To observe any new law means to act heroically until the law becomes a custom, a habit and acquires dominance and is recognized as a *dominant sign.* To observe the law means to overcome the temptation of disobedience and entails a certain degree of heroism.

The family laws were the initial group heroic efforts, aimed at improving the biological specie. Later, the religious taboo would prescribe the societal norms of acceptable behaviour, which involved respect for property, space and rights of the other members of the group. Regardless of the origins, forms and their popularity, all religious beliefs, along with laws, enforced the collective heroism which eventually seized to be treated as such. Laws, practiced, enforced and respected for centuries and millennia, turned the formerly extraordinary ways into the ordinary, respecting sexual taboos, honouring one's family, offering help and obeying the social pyramid pressure have become the societal ordinary ways.

In contrast, the law-breaking incidents have become the new extraordinary acts, which explains the cross-cultural fascination with the detective stories, criminals, vagabonds, murderers and rapists. The forces of semiosis have transformed the *hero-sign* from a carrier of a positive to a negative *semiovalence*. All extraordinary actions involving violations of the law invariably seize the attention of the society members. The social stability, having become a norm, challenges the sign-producers and tempts some individuals to break the law, to defy the *dominant sign* (Kevelson, 1988; Khabarov, 1978; Peirce, 1931-2; Lyotard, 1991).

Democracy may stimulate law-breaking as a natural protest against the common, ordinary and non-heroic behaviour. It way explain the higher crimerate in the Western democracies than in the Eastern autocratic and dictatorial states. The collective conformism otherness in the United States paradoxically may be the cause of the higher law-breaking as a manifestation of the dormant eternal heroic drive, some form of extraordinariness in the impulse to defy a law in the law-obeying society as a a perverse form of heroism. On the other hand, all societies with well-established laws have redefined the meaning of a law as a *dominant sign*. It becomes a deterrent for any extraordinariness, an anti-heroic factor which restricts the self, demands a predictable pattern of self-expression (Adler, 1974; Babad, 1983; Gerzon, 1982; Girguz, 1981; Gergen, 1991; Holland, 1977).

For instance, to be a Protestant, a Jew ,or a Moslem in the predominantly Catholic 16th century Spain would have been not only a law-breaking , but a heroic act. The law-abiding majority would be reading safely the societal prescribed non-heroic code and following the custom. Similarly, to aspire for freedom of information and exchange of ideas in a dictatorial state would be an extraordinary act and defiance of the dominant sign.

It is not only a law, a dominant philosophical belief, or prevalent medical and economic theory, which could be the anti-heroic factors. Fashion or the style of adornment has traditionally exercised similar semiotic effect. To dress in defiance of a style, a prevalent fashion has always been a marker of otherness, strangeness and some madness. Fashion as a *tyrannical sign* insists on and succeeds in the complete mimetic conformity. To dress differently has always meant not to belong to the group. Since dress and adornment are very *potent signs* of visual significance, any group always insists on collective conformity. In the past, no deviation in dress was allowed, all members of a village would select and agree on a particular style and pattern of dressing to the minute details. Each villager would immediately recognize a stranger by a different semiotic arrangement of attire. Dress was a signifier of age, status and locality. The rural dress code excluded any extraordinariness. Eventually, the urban life style permitted some deviations in the dress code. However, even the urban variety still preserved the basic tyrannical and anti-heroic meaning of the attire (Tsselon, 1992; Simpkins, 1992; Rudd, 1992; Mitchell, 1982; Konig, 1973; Kohler, 1928; Heard, 1924). Married women world be recognized by their headwear, wealthy women would be distinguished from their servants and so on. Aside from the sociological typology, clothing has other controlling effects on the group. All military or medics have their own dress code, so do the students. Certain occupations still demand uniform as a trace of the old sign, the desire to suppress the heroic drive. However, the uniform may be explained as a neutralizer, amidst other more semiovalent signs and forms of signification that take place in a hospital, school or police station (Horn, 1968; Bigelow, 1970; Bogatyrev, 1977; Berger, 1984).

Nonetheless, the herd instinct, manifesting itself in the blind following of the particular fashion style offers only a partial explanation to the mass mimesis in dressing. To dress like the other, to follow his/her aesthetic norm is to deny the heroic status to the Other. Consequently, the fashion trend exploiting the variety of collective emotions becomes the *anti-heroic dominant sign*. For centuries, people have been changing the style of dressing, following a certain model, imitating the potential hero-dresser and destroying the mimetic matrix through the precise mimesis. The hero, after all, is the most *despised sign*, despite the common worshipping. If one may not or cannot destroy and eliminate other hero-signs, the fashion hero-model can be destroyed by the precise mimesis. Creating a double means to mirror the heroic self, duplicating him/her *en masse*, achieves the ultimate — robs the hero from the alleged uniqueness and extraordinariness. When the ordinary have such an easy access to the extraordinary, it ceases to exist, intimidate and annoy with its unique meaning. The origin of the metaphor "dressed to kill" may be traced to the deep-seated resentment of the *hero-sign* and the violent emotive functions it arouses in the process of his/her presentment (Danesi, 1993).

Any *hero-sign* provokes intense mimetic energy among the perceivers who desire to re-possess the extraordinary qualities of their mimetic matrix. Girard is convinced that "man is subject to intense desires" and the most intense is the desire to be something he himself lacks and which some other person seems to possess" (Girard, 1972:146). To imitate one's style of dressing is the easiest way of satisfying the intense anti-heroic sentiment. It is much harder to excel in other mimetic attempts.

The idea of military, police, school and medical uniforms as well as other professional attire, has its original intention to suppress the mimetic and anti-heroic sentiments. The uniform is the single external appearance, imposed on all members of the group and excluding any aesthetic variations, any individual creativity and any extraordinariness. Uniform neutralizes and masks the mimetic drive and rivalry, which it invariably involves. Girard maintained that "mimesis generates rivalry, which in turn reinforces mimesis" (Girard, 1982: 53). Jeans and Tshirts have become the American symbol of democracy and equality and a means of neutralizing rivalry.

6.4. *Modernism and Anti-Heroism*

> *The constant in all modernism is defiance of authority.*
> Frederick R. Karl, *Modern and Modernism* (1985:XII)

What Karl labels as authority one may rename as *hero-sign*, the semiotic imperative and the mimetic tyrant. In an attempt to assert itself as a cultural stage, modernism intended to mark the new phase in the production of signs, enriching Culture with new, *unrecognizable signs* that had no connection with their past mimetic models. This protest, dissent, deviation and anti-heroic mode of modern creativity was perceived by some as decadence, degradation and fall of civilization. The rise of fascism in Germany was equally a racist mania and a pathological fear of the modern, anti-heroic aesthetics which rejected the ancient Greek canon, along with the rest of the *familiar signs*, matrices for the ongoing heroic mimesis (Hegel, 1975; Reich, 1970; Karl, 1985; Lyotard, 1984; Kroker, 1986; Hutcheon, 1989).

The roots of modernism and anti-heroism could be traced to Plato, who already in his famous *Republic* cautioned against the society ruled by artists, expressing his dislike of poets. He feared their creativity, which could undermine the authority of the true heroes — "lovers of wisdom", philosophers. What Plato did not articulate was the fear of the lost mimesis. Modern means anti-heroic and anti-mimetic. Any society, pleased with its pyramidal distribution of *social* and *cultural signs*, its stable arrangement and controlled mimesis, fears change and artists, who have always been the initiators of change, producers of new signs and designers of the new order and disorder.

The twentieth -century artists expressed their rebellion, their anti-heroic sentiments through the rejected mimesis. The lost melody in music, disappearing shape and image in painting and narrative in literature — all signified the rebellion against mimesis. Instead of the *recognizable signs*, curbing the organizing principles of the irrational, the unknown forces of the human psyche were allowed to take over the regulated mimesis, with the intense signification of the non-representational art, non-melodic music, uninhibited behaviour and seductive clothing. The modern art intended to be shocking, unfamiliar and irrational. The Russian avant-garde and European modernism inspired the Russian formalists, who would respond to the new trend with their critical diagnosis — "defamiliarization" (Skhlovsky, 1929; Veselovsky, 1940 [1910] Jameson, 1972; Steiner, 1984).

In 1867, the two French engineers, Droux and Rueff, commenting on the essence of the modern creativity, drew a distinction between the "destructive and productive geniuses'" as the producers of signs. In their mind, the future belonged to the new technology, science and engineering and the old heroic canon could no longer be followed (Mousse, 1974:41). Modern art was to be the world of technology, and destruction of the old cultural icons and signs.

In 1909, Tommaso Marinetti would publish his modernist manifesto, which could be described as the most anti-heroic modern message to the Europeans:

> It is from Italy that we broadcast this manifest of ours, to the whole world. Italy has been a junk shop for too long. It is time to burn her libraries, flood her museums, and galleries, tear down her sacred cities. We will sing of great crowds engaged in work, pleasure or revolt (Bradbury and McFarlane, 1974: 243).

Italy is described as a cemetery of heroes which supposedly needs to be first destroyed, prior to building the new modernist universe of pleasure, where heroes would no longer disturb with their extraordinariness. The consciousness of the modernist rebels had been seeking escape from the mimesis, rivalry and the disturbing heroic presence. To find peace it was not enough to retreat into in the irrational, unrecognizable — it was necessary to produce the new non-heroic meaning. Modernism was the escape from the archetypal mimesis and instinctive duplication of the heroic deeds of the Other. It was a negation of heroism, be it morality, ethics, canonical taste aesthetics or sexuality. It was the cultural pause of mocking the hero and the heroic self.

The anti-heroic ethos of modernism went on parallel with the negation of heroism in politics. There was a peculiar symmetry between the protest against the canonical taste and mode in art and the similar shift in the socio-political code as demonstrated by the Russian revolution of the

1917. The most non-representational paintings were produced by the Russian avant-garde artists along with the most incomprehensible poetry and the most violent negation of the hero-tsar, hero-capital. In the Russian case, the modernist spirit and consciousness denounced all the previous forms of signification more energetically and vigorously than in any other European countries.

"To throw away everything from the ship of modernity." — this motto of the Russian producers of the anti-heroic signs was articulated by Vladimir Mayakovsky, the key figure in the Russian avant-garde movement. It echoed Marinetti's manifesto and the similar commitment of the French symbolists. However, its *semiovalue* was much greater. Modernity had an utterly different cultural, political and social meaning for the Russians than for the Western thinkers and artists, for whom it was just another social drama, a mere temporary heroic shift in a limited sphere — namely, in art and fashion. In contrast, the Russian society was faced with the simultaneous transformations in various cultural codes and a complete re-arrangement of signs in various *semiospheres*. It was an intense process, characterized by symmetry in the fashion system, artistic political and economic universes. The change to a uniform dress for all members of society went on parallel with the equalization in property ownership and both signified commitment to equality and suppression of any individuality. The socio-economic revolution tended to reduce each member of society to a sign of a singular semiotic value. Each member of the new proletariat society meant to signify the basic anti-heroic policy, the ordinariness of the Self or the Other.

The inner anti-heroic type of the signification inside the new Soviet proletarian state compensated itself by the collective heroic aspirations beyond the geographical borders. The capitalist West, experimenting with modernism in art, fashion and behaviour, did not venture beyond this anti-heroic territory, the rest of the signs remained in the traditional order pattern. It observed with caution and fear the destruction of the heroic pyramid and the heroic order in Russia. The profound fear to loose the heroic status of the capital, its power and privileges dictated the isolation of the Soviet modernists in politics and economics, having ironically boosted the collective heroic aspirations of the destroyers of the old heroism. The cult of the hero-proletariat became a very successful tool in mass propaganda of the Soviet dictators. The only state in the world, conducting this enormous anti-heroic revolution, debunking and destroying the old forms of signification managed to produce a new hero-sign —the Soviet isolated proletariat, experimenting with new social signs, new arrangement of the social pyramid, and actualizing the myth of the just society of the ordinary. "Land and freedom to all" slogan implied an equal symmetrical order between the people— signs and the pieces of land-signs of equality, excluding any deviation, any expression of otherness any difference. The profoundly rigid order of signs in this first modernist universe was rooted in the anti-heroic semiotic structure. Since heroism implies difference, divergence from the prescribed pattern of signification and carries the danger of conflict and rivalry, the anti-heroic system naively intended to create a rivalry and anxiety-free mythical paradise. This mythical reality might have been more soothing and healing for the psyche of the ordinary majority, but it certainly oppressed the extra-ordinary minority, seeking an outlet for its heroic drive. Eventually, it would express itself in the intense internal dissent.

However, during 1917-1937, the global community of sign-perceivers and producers looked at Russia as the utopic global space, where the community of the ordinary, guided by the anti-heroic prescriptive order, actually had been accomplishing a heroic deed, staging a new heroic social drama. To some, it signalled in certain apocalyptic overtones the fulfilment of the Nietzschean Dionysian prophecy and coming of doom. The transition from the Victorian industrial era to the modern technological universe carried some message of despair, alienation and cultural panic The reversal of the order of signs, accomplished by the 1917 revolution, planted some apocalyptic moods and signified a certain decline of the European civilization. The modernist anti-heroic rebellion and negation went too far in Russia, and, at this point, the collective mythical consciousness set a new heroic task —the task of destroying the new enemy—the Soviet Russia, the icon of evil and global apocalypse. This would preoccupy the signifying universes globally for many decades to come. The task will consist in negating the heroic status of the group, preoccupied with what appeared as a dangerous semiosis, a dangerous anti-heroic policy. This would be another modern paradox, a new heroism, arising from the anti-heroic essence.

David McCullough described the modern century as "extraordinary times", filled with the most paradoxical hideous extremes" (1992: 210-11). On the one hand, the most remarkable achievements in physics, chemistry, biology and astronomy mark this remarkable age, while on the other- there is a profound accelerating ignorance. In the age of television and genetic engineering, space flights and computers, there are numerous global village inhabitants who possess even less information than their predecessors centuries prior. The gap between the *sign-producing minority* and *sign-consuming majority* is getting larger and larger. The sign-consuming majority is the standard, ordinary perceiver of signs who vicariously lives the lives of the "rich and famous", successful achievers and stars. The TV screen has connected the millions of the global village inhabitants, around the same pseudo-heroic plots of Hollywood soap operas and the real horror stories. Modern television reinforces the extra-ordinariness of some individuals and selected events and breeds the overwhelming ordinariness of many. While preaching control over one's life, self-esteem and exploration of one's hidden talent, the modern TV heroes reinforce their own superiority and exploit the basic anti-heroic inclination of the century.

The modern technology resents the original critical thinking more than ever before since its mass-oriented needs could be satisfied only by the uncritical passive consumption of the silent many. The TV and computers have been invented with the massive users in mind and with the standard of below average intellectual potential. Thomas Carlyle, fearful of the day when man would become an addendum to the machine, would have called the modern extraordinary times the anti-heroic delu-sionary stupor.

The negation of the authority could be perceived as the desire to be-come one, a craving for power. The modern sign-producers heavily rely on the mass negation of the *hero-sign* and the mass hero-killing impulse. The debunking mode of the biographical discourse kills the hero-subject and indirectly empowers the perceivers, who look down at the troubled heroic selves. The physiological, psychological and societal conflicts of the modern heroes please the perceivers, who acquire self esteem and anti-heroic superiority while viewing the troubled heroes. Diseases and addictions, bankruptcies and failures of the public figures are the plea-surable material for the ordinary majority. The suspected paedophilia of Michael Jackson, his drug addiction and legal battles, or AIDS-related death of Rudolph Nureev, the sexual escapades and recent Monica Lewinsky affair of Bill Clinton, or the new skinny Ophrah — all fascinate and please the ordinary, who have the options of worshipping, con-demning, mocking and debunking their heroes.

When the well-groomed, attractive and heroically aspiring TV hosts some times cannot determine Kafka's profession. ("a philosopher?!"), or Mayakovsky's popularity ("an orator"?!), the sign-perceivers develop a profound cynicism towards the sign-producers and deny them their desired heroic status. There is comfort in the awareness of the viewing majority that the stars are the Carlylean "fake notes", just mere ordinary individuals who are simply posing as heroes. The lack of the factual knowledge and cultivation of obstacles to knowledge have become the symptoms of our hero-resenting times. The Orwellian dream may be already partly fulfilled in the modern post-sputnik, post-Chernobyl, com-puter-controlled society where the utmost heroism has become the accep-tance of the ordinariness and mediocrity.

The age of the intellectually —"standard"— average is a convenient environment for the emergence of the new tyrants and the new heroic global dramas. Isn't it a modern paradox that a DNA discovery, genocide and flight to the moon have occurred in the same century, only to be complicated by the ethnic cleansing in Yugoslavia and claims of unique genetic endowment of the Orientals, as professed by Rushton, the controversial modern Canadian psychologist?

For centuries, the ratio of one/many and the essential conflict between the heroes and the crowd was being resolved in favour of the individual hero. The cult of a single hero, belief in the superior *semiovalence of the hero-sign* nourished and sustained the traditional global semiosis. The populist movements in France, America and Russia along with the awakening of modernism had shifted the heroic paradigm. The French, American and Russian revolutions have undermined the image of a single Hero-Political leader. The glory of the mass rebellion, mass participation in a societal dissent, mass production and mass rule, rule of *demos* have marked a new heroic or anti-heroic territory of modernity, the new form for expressing the collective anti-heroic self. The modern mass production of the signs of exchange, such as cars, TV sets, houses, computers and other collectively designed and assembled products originated in the Victorian romantic heroism of the industrial era. The romantic semiosis demanded speedy production of identical signs, which required the heroic effort of many individuals and diminished the semiotic value of a single *hero-sign*. The assault on a hero began when the *saturation of the semiotic field* with the identical signs could be achieved only by the heroic efforts of the group. Thus, the modern anti-heroism originated in the forced rejection of a single hero. The new signs required a collective effort of many to actualize the heroic myth of the new industrial paradise.

It is not accidental that the new myth of a nation or a race-hero has been reinforced in this century. All the semiotic acts required group efforts and the myth of the heroic specie went parallel with the Darwinian theory of species, Marxist concept of the hero-proletariat and Rosenberg's superior German nation (Barzun, 1941). The United States of America and American cultural myth have also manifested this profound shift in the modern heroic paradigm. The competition for the heroic title of a nation-hero did not begin in Germany. The American economic success and prosperity, the fortunate combination of the geographical and ethnographical circumstances, helped to create the myth of the heroic America, the modern paradise, the land of plenty and "pursuit of happiness" in this heroic environment (Cantor, 1976; Girgus, 1981; Fishwick, 1979). The new, allegedly heroic country had been founded on mass anti-heroism, the mass rejection of the societal pyramid, elitism and archetypal universal heroism. The American settlers, who had abandoned the traditional icons of the old World, the inherited heroic titles and condemned the worship of ancestry, would also produce the new, exotic, extraordinary American mass culture. Americans cultivated the myth of their own extraordinariness. "America — the land of golden opportunity", "America — the land of democracy and equality", used to and still continues to attract millions of people from other countries and continents. The Statue of Liberty with the inscription "Give me thy tired and thy poor" is the universal symbol, most *semiovalent sign* of the American and modern heroic anxiety.

Through its own economic success, new egalitarianism (albeit excluding women and other inferiors) and exploiting the archetypal heroic drive, America continues to seduce with the myth of its own heroism, the country-heaven, the country-paradise, the collective winner. The popular winner/loser ratio is the essence of the American societal dynamics, follows the heroic prescription of Arnold Toynbee who insisted on the icons — conqueror and saviour. According to him,

> In a growing civilization the creator is called upon to play the part of a conqueror who replies to a challenge with a rigorous response, in a disintegrating civilization he is called upon to play the part of a saviour who comes to the rescue of a society that has failed to respond because the challenge has washed a minority that has ceased to be creative (1961 [1920]: 533, vol I).

The American collective image of nation-conqueror, paradoxically built on the initial denial of heroism, has eventually completed the original anti-heroic route on the new heroic ground. Consequently, the American collective heroic anxiety among the similar states or other groups has manifested the universal pathway of heroism, with the archetypal oscillations between the Hero and Anti-hero, something which Giam-battista Vico perceived as the universal semiotic feature (Vico, 1968 [1801]).

According to Vico, any moments of clarity in the lives of the nations would eventually be followed by the periods of the heroic delusions. He called the heroic age, "the age of the spear", the stage of militant aggressiveness, which, in his view, would invariably prevail over the essentially anti-heroic image of humanity. It has proven to be correct in many respects. "La comune natura delle nazioni", —the common nature of the nations— is the heroic strive to prevail, and until that is somewhat suppressed, or sublimated by the anti-heroic forces, the collective aggressiveness and violence would thrive (Vico, 1968[1864]:949; Makolkin, 1990).

Chapter Seven

Hero-Worshipping Code

7.1. *Sanctuary as a Reward for Heroism*

Places of worship, such as churches, synagogues or temples have been named "institutions", "sacred spaces", "time and history holders", "symbols of cosmic ambiguity", cultural legacy" and so on (Fox, 1988; Kramer, 1988; Burkert, 1988; Knipe, 1988). We would like to view them as signs of heroism in several respects. First of all, they honour and worship particular heroes, immortalize them in the tangible physical structures. Secondly, temples as products of collective hard labour indirectly and subtly honour their builders. To perform the acts of heroism and be recognized as a hero would have been an incomplete *heroic semiosis*. The final stage is the post-recognition phase, the production of signs, immortalizing the hero after his heroic quest. The disclosure of the complete meaning of the *hero-sign* requires the support of the post-heroic semiosis —— some posthumous form of remembrance, and temples built in the honour of heroes fulfil this function.

The sacred edifices embody the archetypal extraordinariness, reminding the ordinary members of the group about their heroic otherness; they also unify the community around the selected, approved heroes, exercising a certain control through the monumental signification. The aesthetic value of temples is fused with their socio-political, psychological, historical and ultimately heroico-semiotic value. The aesthetic aspect of a temple as a structure reinforces the original extraordinariness ,which inspired its construction, in the first place, and masks the relationship between the beauty and hero signs. The *beauty-sign* supplements the hero-sign (Eco, 1986).

Prior to the temples built in the honour of heroes and heroic forces, there were decorated caves even during the early old "stone age" when the primitive people already distinguished between the ordinary and the extraordinary. The food supply, being in the hands of the mysterious heroic forces, was the primary reason for worshipping this kind of the mysterious extraordinariness, exemplified by the Palaeolithic cave sanctuaries in France and Spain (James, 1965, 15-39). The remaining ancient European sanctuaries give an idea about the kind of extra-ordinariness, singled out by the prehistoric inhabitants. One of the frescoes in the rockshelter at Cogul, Spain depicts a fertility ritual by nine women, dancing around one single naked man. This fresco motif on the cave wall may suggest the heroic male family status within this particular community. It may also give an idea about the shorter life span and gender disproportion in favour of females. The maleness is celebrated as an extraordinary physical state. The male hunter was obviously a hero of the Paleolithic era which explains the animal motif of the frescoes and the frequent depiction of a hunting scene. Immortalized in the primitive cave frescoes or drawings, a male is always either in the aggressive hunting position, or in the animal disguise as a clever cunning victor. The pre-historic cave drawings have immortalized the earliest heroic obsessions of the primitive human societies who already knew how to recognize, immortalize and worship their heroes-hunters (Campbell, 1949; James, 1965).

The figurines of the mother-goddess, a fertile female, are also quite frequent artifacts of the ancient worshipping. The Cretan state goddess, or Tripolian fertility figurine, Maltese headless female or a Sardinian witch sculpture — all signify a certain bewilderment over the extraordinary power of a female body, worship of femininity which was apparently perceived as equally heroic (Warner, 1981; Sulliman, 1986; Muller, 1987; Adler, 1993).

The temples were built in their honour in Sumer and India, ancient Greece and Israel, Latin America and Japan. It is a common sign serving the common heroic needs of all humans. S.N. Kramer reports that the ancient Sumerians dedicated their tallest buildings to the heroic war-god, Enki who was simultaneously the god of wisdom and the Inanna, the goddess of love and war (Kramer, 1988: 2). The comfort of human relations and victory of the close tribesman due to the wisdom and power of the gods were those essential needs of the ancient Sumers, fusing the mundane and the heroic. The gods, with their extraordinary powers, guarded the existential universe. Thus, the ancient extraordinariness had a rather profound pragmatic meaning, which eventually would be lost at the more advanced stages of human civilization.

The ancient Israeli House of the Lord exemplified a new temple of simplified worship, instead of the numerous heroes, it worshipped a single hero — the Lord. The Israeli temple building embodied a new system of heroic semiosis , which excluded all the pseudo-heroes, other pagan deities of lesser heroic significance. In contrast with the Greek "temple culture", the Israeli culture distinguished between the places for prayer and the spaces for worshipping the Lord. The temple building as such was not encouraged. The early Houses of God were destroyed and later even the historical periods in Israel were labelled as the First or Second Temple era (Naran, 1988: 25). This signifies the extreme sacredness of the heroic semiosis in the ancient Israel. The temple embodied the Lord, His singularity and single extraordinariness. Consequently, the Israeli Temple was a sign of higher heroism, embodying the monotheistic principles and new semiosis, shaping them.

Unlike the Israeli rare temples, the Greek temples were signs of the pagan heroic semiosis. Their temples were as numerous and abundant as their gods, to whom they delegated numerous heroic responsibilities in the sphere of art and science, politics and trade, morality and piety. The Hellenic man was ordinary and humble, or fearful of his numerous deities (Haddas, 1965). The ancient heroic pantheon of the endless deities reflected the complexity of the ancient societal norms and the nostalgic dream about a simpler life. The Greek temple was the embodiment of their collective anxiety over the burdensome heroism of the ancient Greek society.

The structure and location of the temples have always utilized the canonical notions of centricity, verticality and displacements so that the temples could fully signify the Heroic Otherness. The central positioning of the temples, either on the top of the hill, or in the middle of the square utilized the archetypal centricity of any sign, to which the producers intended to draw their attention. The temple in the honour of a hero required a heroic central location as well as the vertical orientation of the structure to emphasize the utmost significance. The height of the temple embodied the distance, difference and the emotive gulf between the sacred and the profane, the ordinary and the extraordinary, the heroic and the traditionally mundane. The temple intended to differ from the dwellings of the ordinary Greek or other citizens, and this difference was signified by size, height, location vis-à-vis other urban structures, and the degree and sophistication of the aesthetic decorum. Since temples honoured the gods and the important citizens of the ancient world, they could not be separated from wealth and politics" (Burkett, 1988: 44; Turner, 1979).

The hierarchical quality of all deities and heroes is reflected in a variety of temples, signifying the societal imbalance and inequality. The visual ornamentation and location of a temple can mediate the varying status in the social hierarchy. This has been found not only in the Greek, Roman, but in the Mesoamerican and Hindu temples. Due to the central location and distinguished size, temples have been traditionally used as the areas for the exchange of signs — markets and craft-shops. Thus, temples had not only the worshipping function, but they played the role of clusters of signs so that other signs and forms of signification would be organized around them. Being the places of hero-worshipping and rewards for extraordinariness, temples stimulated the *heroic mimesis* and exercised control over other signs, sign-producers and perceivers. They functioned in the same way a *hero-sign* usually does — celebrating the heroic otherness and immortalizing the heroic, through the symbolic representation of the familiar social mythical pattern (Makolkin, 1992a).

7.2 *The Semiovalue of a Monument*

Exegi monumentum
Horacio

The temple of Apollo, Parthenon, Mayan temples, Jerusalem temple, the Cordoba Mosque or Sancta Sofia Basilica — all represent the highest symbolic award given to deities and the highest *semiovalue* of worshipping. In contrast, some monuments stand for lesser heroism and recognize the heroic value of different heroes, who are presumably of lesser heroic significance than the deities. However, temples, portraits, engravings, medals, and monuments share the same basic distinguishing features such, as size, height, aesthetic markers and centricity which are the repeated *semes*, the usual markers of the intended distinctness (Eco, 1979, 89-120). Similarly to all symbols of sacredness and immortalization, all monuments are traditionally erected in the most open, public spaces, exploiting the favourable locations and standing out visually in front of the public eye, i.e. the space reserved for the *permanent sign* (Makolkin, 1992a). All *commemorative signs,* as monuments also are, share their semiotic value while acknowledging the heroic status of particular individuals, but they go beyond the recognition of individual heroes. Monuments are being erected to become symbols of collective particularities, such as the statue of Liberty, a sign of Americanness or an Effel Tower, a sign of Frenchness etc. Michael North (1985) divides monuments into some major types:

anthropomorphic —in the honour of people;
ideographic   —in the honour of ideas,
iconographic   —in the honour of places;
occasional   —in the honour of a heroic event or occasion.

The anthropomorphic monuments, immortalizing and glorifying the chosen national heroes, kings, warriors or priests, are also the cryptic heroic biographies of the real historical figures, whom a tribe, group, or community collectively choses to remember. They tell and retell permanently the life story of a selected hero that had previously passed the collective censorship of the community. In the course of time, the group may decide to dispense with the old monuments and replace them with the new ones. The monuments to Lenin and Marx, for example, had been destroyed all over Eastern Europe after the unification of Germany and the official breakup of the Soviet Union. The first act of *perestroika* was marked by the destruction of the old monuments representing the past, whose condemnation could be truthfully replayed in the drama of beheading the stone figures, the signs of Evil, the emblems of the past. The dominance of the visual perception dictates the physical embodiment of the historical narrative, individual or concept (Jacobson, 1975[1937]).

The monuments to the real individuals represent the Real, selected for iconographic representation while the monuments to the fictional characters, such as Don Juan (the monument erected in Seville, Spain) have a more complex form of signification. They refer to the unreal, the imaginary reality, created by a writer and duplicate the originally intended signification. This duplication intensifies the *semiovalence* of the fictional hero-sign and simultaneously is a monument to the author, Byron, e.g.:

Signifier	Signified
Monument	Byron, English Romantic, a writer
monument	The other
Seville, Spain	England
Man	Don Juan, the archetypal hero or anti-hero
Real	Fictional

The monument to Don Juan mocks the heroism of the Other, the English culture and other real Spanish heroes. Don Juan signifies otherness, the other extraordinariness which is presumably foreign to such hero-appointing institutions as the Spanish Church and State. It is an *ironic sign* which appropriates the ordinary semiotic meaning of a war monument or another expected monument and subverts its intended message. It glorifies the anti-heroic behaviour of the Other, a fictional hero from a fictional universe, constructed by the extraordinary individual, a foreign writer.

7.3. *Medal as a Portable Sign*

Umberto Eco has repeatedly stated that "semiotics is mainly concerned with signs as social forces" (1979: 65). The social impact of medals in contrast with temples, monuments and other permanent signs of heroism displayed in public spaces is less visible. The *semiovalence* of a temple, church, statue, palace, or monument is such that it does not require the extra-familiarity with the internal communal code. The permanent signs of hero-worship are customarily produced to honour a hero, who is known not only to a particular group, but whose heroism had already transcended the boundaries of its community. For instance, the monument to Mozart or palace of Peter the Great does not need any additional information to be perceived as the *recognizable sign*. One need not be a Moslem to acknowledge a mosque.

In contrast, many medals require additional and particular knowledge to be recognized as signs of heroism. One does not have to be a
Christian to understand the meaning of a Christian cross. But one does
need to be familiar with the history of Germany, or Britain to appreciate
the meanings of the German Iron Cross (1865). Medal, limited to a particular significatory universe, carries and endures the drawbacks of its
lesser visibility. Crosses as forms of honouring military conquest actually
duplicate and expand the meanings of the *sign-matrix* — the religious
cross. They monopolize on the metaphoricity of the image, used previously in a greater semiotic context, and emphasize the societal hierarchical system. The crosses, medals for military service, acknowledge the
heroic deeds of a secular nature and refer to the secondariness of the civic
activities, their secondary space occupied after the ecclesiastical symbol-
ism.

Numerous medals of the post-Christian period adopted the familiar
cross-like imagery to denote their mediatory role between the ultimate
hero-Christ, the invisible omnipresent hero of all believers and the particular hero of the Hebrew rebels. The unchanged part of the medals for
valour — the Cross, reflected the endless semiotic possibilities of the
same sign, which could acquire different meanings and be re-used again
and again for various significatory purposes.

The public circulation of a medal is more limited since it could be
exposed only by the hero himself/herself, or a the particular hero-se-
lecting community in an exclusive public space, such as a museum or a
gallery. Those spaces are open to a lesser audience of perceivers than a
street, a square or any other open public space. The medals are intended
to be worn by the hero, who together with his medal, represents a complete semiotic structure. If a person choses not to wear a medal the signification process is then interrupted. Thus, the semiotic boundaries of a
medal are controlled by the sign displayer, who is recognized as a hero
thanks to the medal he/she wears. The exposure of the medal depends
on the will of the hero, who may stop the process of the circulation of the
medal and the signification itself, by refusing to wear it, not displaying
the *recognizable sign* and thus depreciating its semiotic value.

The medals intend to preserve the heroic pantheon in time and space,
either referring to the events, performers or their heroic value. The medal,
commemorating the fortieth year of the Romney, Hythe and Dymchurch
railway, for instance, with the image of the train and the insignia: "The
World's Smallest Pubic Railway", is a tribute to technology and progress.
On the other hand, the gold medallion of Constantinus I Chlorus is an
acknowledgement of the heroic value of a person and a Roman. The train
image in contrast with the human face is a sign of a lesser *heroic value* and

of a indirect signification pattern. The face image simply duplicates the real hero and establishes a direct communication line between the sign and its perceivers (Linegar, 1974; Soboleva, 1986).

All medals have a commemorative and hero-worshipping function. Some record the glorious events, such as battles, construction of the memorable edifices, or immortalize heroes themselves. The latter ones are of greater *semiovalence* since they emphasize the principle of recognition of the most recognizable human sign —the Face-sign, be it the Queen or the Duke, Admiral or a Bible translator— all the representational models possess the highest semiotic appeal. The medal revives the archetypal meaning of a reward, originally obtained in a hunt, battle, or a fishing expedition. Unlike a trophy, its ancient prototype, a medal changes the original internal circulation principle. An ancient hunter could go beyond the boundaries of his tribe and return with a trophy. A medal, awarded to both foreigners and native citizens, widens the circulation of the sign and direction of the signification is changed, i.e. from the outside inside and vice versa.

outside	inside
trophy	medal
inside	outside

Awarding the medal to foreigners, the society chooses to push the sign outside the sphere of the customary signification, borrowing certain qualities from the *portable and exchangeable signs,* such as coin, banknote or cheque. Medals may transmit the heroic commemorative message not only through the direct recording of a face image or an object, but through an elaborate allegorical mode. Linegar, for instance, reports that the British medals recording the reign of George I depicted "the Hanoverian horse, leaping the North Sea from Hanover to Britain" (Linegar, 1974: 117).

7.4. *Coin, Banknote — Sings of Exchange and Heroism*

Scholars report that, prior to the circulation of regular coins in the canonical numismatic sense, there used to exist the peculiar form of knife money cast in bronze (Carson, 1962: 539). This type of money was used between the seventh and fourth centuries B.C. and represents the original tentative moment of the money. Knife as a tool in hunting, killing enemies and performing other necessary tasks was a heroic tool, an instrument of heroic conquest. It is remarkable that the ancient Chinese acknowledged its heroic meaning in the process of exchanging goods and slaves. The saturation of these signs in the hands of a single owner marked one's wealth and heroic status, the resulting extraordinariness was signified by the quantity of knives one used to own. The Chinese tradition also honoured the heroism of the agricultural labour by using spade or pu money, which contained the replicas of the actual spades, earlier used for barter (Carson, 1962).

If one compares the ancient Roman and European coins with the Chinese or Indian coins, there is more representational facial iconology in the European material. The near Eastern or Far Eastern coin samples contain more factual data, such as weight, the years of rulers' reign, or geographical insignia. Carson argues that the initial European coinage was also purely functional with the predominant object representation, the heads of gods and heroes are allegedly later phenomena. The earliest coins from the island of Samos had either lion's mask, or Ox's head and shoulder, such coins were signs of deities, which indirectly referred to them. The lion's skin symbolized Hera in some sources, while others maintained that it signified "the reconciliation between the pre-Dorian hero of Tiryns and the great goddess of the Argolid" (Baron, 1966: 2). Coins and banknotes with the iconic function shorten the perceptive time of the sign. "The topological similarity between a signifier and its denotata is established instantly and so is the heroic meaning of the money-sign" (Sebeok, 1976: 128). The iconic distinctions between various currencies monopolized on the persistent semiotic impulse — to differ and the endless possibility to disseminate a particular iconic image or symbolic message (Sebeok, 1987).

The maple leaf on the Canadian copper pennies signifies Canada, Canadian landscape on one side and the portrait of the Queen on the other, both images reinforce the meaning of Canadianness. The portrait of the Queen on one side of the two-dollar banknotes and the bird-couple on the reverse, serve the same purpose. The obverse and the reverse sides have their inner hierarchy. The front side of the coin or the banknotes, their face, so to speak, is usually reserved for the iconic image that stands higher within the selected pair of signs. The face-sign of the obverse side of the coins or banknotes represents its semiotic puzzle, it is usually the duplicated image of the societal heroic figure. Thus, *money-signs*, in the process of exchange between groups, not only empower the owners with the objects of exchange, which money can buy, but they temporarily exchange the societal heroic pantheon for the material objects. The group heroes, commemorated on money, expand their heroic territory through the currency exchange. The heroic imagery affects the heroic sensibility of the sign-perceivers who are forced to participate in the double layered semiosis, i.e. the exchange of things and ideas. The insecure emperors, tzars and military leaders used to introduce periodically the additional heroic imagery to the new money-signs. This way, *money-signs* performed the semiotic functions of a *laudatio,* statue, monument, temple or medal, unifying economics, politics and art.

Coins and banknotes have a wider semiotic field of signification than medals. They were constantly being circulated and exchanged and had a *perpetuum significatum* function within a particular context, with the possibility of trespassing its geographical and political boundaries. *Money-signs* played a unifying factor within a given group, their socially binding function was reinforced by the image of the most socially significant hero-ruler, king, queen or president. In contrast, medals and medallions included the other, less significant signs of extraordinariness, such as poets, painters, scientists etc. — all could appear as proto-icons (Trapp, 1990; Crawford, 1990).

The archetypal desire to possess more money, the universal avarice could be also explained as a saturation quality of certain signs. Money-symbols of control and power — carry and reinforce their seductive meaning through the saturated fields of heroism, constructed in the presence of the powerful icons. The absent queen, her grandeur and power are imparted to the owner of numerous *money-signs,* along with her iconic image. She is absent, but present through the money-sign. The number of banknotes intensifies her presence. The owner of the banknotes is surrounded by the numerous absent queens and the imaginary belonging to royalty takes over the perceptive powers of the neurotic addressees.

Before the existence of the bank system, individuals kept their money in the special hiding places, either inside the dwelling, or outside. The archetypal motif of the hidden treasures in yards or treasure boxes permeates the heroic folklore of all cultural and linguistic traditions as a testimony to the universal power , heroism, seduction and oppression by the semiotic power of the *money-signs.* Along with the other signs of extraordinariness, money-signs offer the uniformity of measuring the heroic value, referring to the meaning of signs other than themselves, facilitating the particular semiosis — Trade. Aristotle speculated in his *Politics* that the moment of producing the *money-signs* could be concurrent with the general excessive production of other signs in society and the necessity to select and measure the meaning of signs, according to their societal significance (Politics, I, 9). The value of products increased through the money-sign, a facilitator of exchange and a standard of value (Towne, 1900: 80-3). In their turn, *money-signs* communicated another meaning, pointing to the other, the gold standard, or the ultimate measurement of the exchanged objects. Thus, the canonical currencies have served as an intermediaries between the ascribed temporary value and meaning of the sign, embodied in the object that had been purchased with money, and the ideal, absent and invisible object —gold deposit, and the ideal meaning, represented by gold— the *proto-measuring sign*. The money-signs are the true mediators between the two absent or invisible signs — prices of the goods and their gold equivalent assessment.

The choice of gold as an ideal measuring sign was dictated by the innate hierarchical mechanism of human imagination as well as by the variety of different signs in the natural macro-semiosphere. Gold, as opposed to silver, bronze, or copper signified its superiority as a *natural sign*, possessing more seductive visual qualities — permanent shine, beautiful chromatic variation, as well as superior physical feature— capable to withstand oxidation without tarnishing. Having therefore surpassed all other metals in their physical and aesthetic qualities, gold would transform into another *hero-sign*, with the very significant meaning even among the *cultural signs — sign of wealth and social status* and a hero-worshipping device. Gold would start affecting human life in economics, politics, art and daily life, being the most *desired sign* (Barron, 1966).

The search for new gold (e.g. the Alaska gold fever) provoked another new definition of gold- as a marker of honesty. Towne reports the following pronouncement of the American senator Jones:

> Gold is so exact a measure of human effort than when it is exclusively used as money it teaches the very habit of honesty" (1900:35).

This precious metal, assigned a new symbolic social meaning — honesty, the archetypal heroic quality, from then on, would signify the presumably universal standard of the heroic value of sign-producers and signs. It is quite logical to assume the reason why so many of the highest awards for heroism would be later be represented by gold medals, gold figurines, or other symbolic objects of recognition made out of this precious metal, the sign of value and superiority. If the ritualistic objects of heroic recognition were not totally made out of gold, it played at least a partial ritualistic role, e.g. as a frame in a portrait. Its presence , at least in the form of gold glittering, signified opulence, perfection, beauty and general outstanding quality.

7.5. *Portrait as a Semi-portable Sign*

One of the main forms of defining a mature, civilized society is its capacity to remember its heroes. Portrait, along with the other forms of commemoration and immortalization, is a hero-worshipping sign. Lancman, analysing Chinese portraiture, argues that one of the available definitions of a portrait is "a record of certain aspects of a particular human being seen by another" (1966:33). In order to become a hero-worshipping device, a portrait has to emphasize only the heroic qualities of the individual and to exaggerate the positive aesthetic qualities of the *face-sign*, along with their spiritual otherness and social significance. Many ancient painters were respected as the masters of the heroic portraits since they were responsible for the permanent presence of the *herosign* in space and time. Lancman points out that the Chinese portraitmakers were producers of the multivalent semiotic objects that had an aesthetic, historical and socio-political functions. Some Chinese portraits without any landscape background were highly valued since nothing could distract the perceiver from the hero's face and body (1966: 35). It is quite understandable why emperors and members of the court be selected as the most preferable heroic models.

Portraits sustain and further transmit the heroic value of a particular subject, as well as add to its *universal heroic semiosis*. There is a profound symmetry between the innate heroic impulse of human imagination, the actualization of the heroic deeds and their ultimate recording for posterity. A portrait of a hero is an expression of the archetypal heroic and biographical impulse of the discourse at large. The ancient Chinese portraitmakers were the writers of specific heroic biographies, who were required to have a psychological insight into the inner self of the herosubject. The biographical narrative power of a portrait was noticed very early on. The portrait of the deceased encapsulated what had been traditionally recreated verbally in the funeral orations and mourning songs (Makolkin, 1987: 225). The parallel between the verbal and visual portrait had been observed by various scholars (Friedländer, 1955: 231; Lancman, 1966: 30-5).

The Egyptian mummies were the variations of the special portraiture, the most faithful representational display of the utmost fidelity to the *proto-sign* — the deceased. The profiles of the inhabitants of the palace of Knossos, along with the early cave drawings in Dordogne, France and in Spain, also provide examples of the earliest "fragmentary statements", i.e. the profile portraits carrying only a half image. The universal appeal of the portraits lies in the portability of the intended heroic meaning, be it beauty, inner spirituality or intellect, and the universal fascination with the human face (Panofsky, 1982; Panofsky, 1967). Since antiquity, many rulers recognized the semiotic power of portraits and kept the portraitmaking as a part of their court rituals(Foucault, 1970). The galleries of the royal family portraits were kept at any royal palace. Portraits, exchanged between countries as a part of the diplomatic ritual, acquire new sociopolitical, historico-cultural meanings, beyond the primary representation of the Hero-sign, Face-sign or Beauty-sign. They immortalize cultural conquest, influence, economic bond, occasionally tied to sexuality via royal marriages, some arranged and some as authentic attraction. The portraits were frequently presented as a royal gift, from one royal palace to the other, with the specific heroic message, e.g. the portrait of the Russian tzar Peter the Great in the national Historical Museum in Amsterdam reinforces the superior cultural role of the Western country upon the Eastern one, another trace of cultural conquest.

Unlike money, coins or medals, portraits are less portable and function differently in the preservation of the scattered global heroic pantheon. Portraits are kept in particular spaces and are more private. Galleries, museums, walls of public buildings, palaces are their public designated spaces. Special public events, such as demonstrations, funerals, carnivals or celebrations invite the display of the pertinent portraits publicly and openly. Heroic occasions are tied to heroic portraits and vice versa.

Leonardo da Vinci's theory of portraiture emphasized upward position of the figure portrayed, the high aesthetic quality of the image and the power of the various face features-*sememes*. Leonardo, the originator of the Renaissance portraiture, revived its heroic mode in his famous rules of painting. Among others, as mentioned earlier, those rules maintained that only a beautiful artist was capable of mediating the beauty of his subject. He insisted on the symmetry between the heroic qualities of the sign-producer and the sign-itself (Leonardo, 1802: 131). This fear of the non-heroic signification in portraiture reveals the universal heroic obsession of the sign-producers, who were particularly interested in the superior heroic individual and were anxious to tell a heroic biography of the renaissance *homo*, the particular hero of the time.

The shift in the genre of the portraiture from the iconic to the impressionistic and expressionistic portraiture would undermine the hero-worshipping value of the portrait and the ritual itself. Both impression and expression style concentrated on the particular vision of the portrait maker, who was no longer concerned with the heroic image of the individual. The heroic value of the portrait was diminished with the ironic mode of the expressionist portraits and the light/darkness ratio of the impressionist portrait. The trend towards distortion of the *proto-sign-Face*, playing with the proportions of the face and the mirror reflections within the portrait boundaries, would transform the original commemorative and hero-worshipping function of the portrait. For instance, Armand Guillaumin's portrait of Camille Pisarro (1868) is hardly a "portrait in a conventional sense" (Mcquillan, 1986: 58). The subject is depicted, facing the portrait, the viewers are able to see the back of the painter who is painting a blind man. The mini-portrait within a portrait signifies the mirror image, and the blind man may symbolize the lack of vision in the modern world and lack of need to see. The central and focal point of any portrait — a *face-sign* had lost its significatory power. With the disappearance of face image per se, the portrait has also disappeared and what has remained was a trace, a memory of the past signs.

Many impressionistic portraits by Degas and Manet, Monet and Renoir are akin to caricatures. For instance, *Study for Singer with a Glove* by Degas(1878) is an ironic statement, an image, mocking a female singer and her artistic efforts. It debunks the female singer, her raised hand, clad in a black glove, is depicted parallel to the singer's face and mouth, clearly overemphasizing the significatory value of a hand. The singer's hand, clad in a black glove, is actually akin to a foot and could be viewed as a metaphoric pair and allusion to the idiom — "to put a foot in one's mouth." Degas' design is purely anti-heroic and debunking, if not misogynistic.

The expressionist mode of portraiture would complete the anti-heroic initiatives of the impressionists. The irony, sarcasm and play with the visual parameters, exercised by the impressionists, meant the absolute reversal of the *proto-sign*-Face, its distortion in order to mediate the expression of anger, protest and disdain for the natural heroic matrix. The Nietzschean apocalyptic predictions would be partly fulfilled in the sinister images of Emil Nol de, Alexei Jawlensky, Richard Guster, Ernst Kirchner and Oskar Kokochka. The expressionistic world of portraiture frightened many perceivers and revived their nostalgia for the ancient pagan and Christian heroism. The National-Socialist and Communist aesthetics of the social realism were basically the hysterical responses to the anti-heroic modern experimentations with the anti-mimetic imagery. The anxiety of death of the hero stimulated the counter-current of modernity. The cult of the ugly and distorted needed to be counter-balanced by the new myth of the strong beauty and force, new hero-race or proletariat (Whitford, 1987).

The myth of the *hero-race* and *hero-nation* in Europe was being created symmetrically against the myth in aesthetics. The aesthetic credo of the modernists could not offer any support to the mythopoesis in politics, so the cult of the hero was revived and imposed from above. The national-socialists banned the modern anti-heroic experimentations as the symptoms of the cultural degeneracy, while the Soviet leaders conducted a vehement battle against the Russian modernism and formalism. Both trends were exemplary expressions of the collective fear of losing the *hero-sign,* even in the seemingly insignificant portraiture (Cantor, 1968; Karl, 1988).

Hitler and Stalin, for example, were very fond of the heroic mode. The display of their own heroic portraits reinforced their status within the respective societies. In contrast, the condemnation of those heroes was marked by the disappearance of their portraits from circulation. The absence of a portrait is a customary indication of the doubtful position of the hero. The *hero-sign* loses his/her heroic meaning with the diminishing presence of one's portrait. A heroic portrait, as much as the heroic biography, is a hero-supporting structure and a *permanent social sign*, signifying one's visibility and status.

The early portraits of a hero in one's life time could be interpreted as symptoms of the heroic instability and the collective desire of the crowd to preempt his death and destroy the *hero-sign*. After all, the hero is equally despised as worshipped, and the *post mortem* worshipping is more welcome. The heroic pantheon of the global village seeks constant renewal and new portraits on display. The overly energetic display of a particular hero, the saturation of the heroic meaning in a particular space is usually indicative of the heroic tension, and the potential need for a renewal of the *semiofield* in the anticipation of the coming heroic displacement.

Chapter Eight

Heroines and Extraordinariness

Mother and maiden was never none but she;
Well may such a lady Goddess mother be.
From a 15th -century carol

8.1. *The Universal Mother — The Universal Sign*

The global heroic pantheon is full of special heroic icons whose *semio-valence* varies in time. Female heroes or heroines have a separate history of semiosis, with uneven shifts in the heroic meaning — from adoration, glorification and worshipping to invisibility and oblivion. The abundance of female hero-worshipping artifacts, dating to the Neanderthal, Cromagnon, Copper and Iron ages, lead to a conclusion that worshipping of women and their primary extraordinariness — fecundity is a *universal cultural sign*. The universal mother, female deity could be found in Africa and Asia, Europe and the New World. Cave paintings, pottery decoration designs, stone paintings and primitive sculptures —all largely immortalize the universal mother and express the human fascination with one of the most extraordinary human rituals— the ritual of birth. The exaggerated buttocks and breasts on the numerous stone engravings and cave paintings focus on the anatomical and biological otherness of the female body, intended for procreation, the act of natural heroism (Panofsky, 1967; 1982[1939]; Stephenson, 1988; Sulliman, 1986; Muller, 1987). The duty, responsibility and ability to give birth have placed the female specie in the natural heroic position. This remarkable ability was not always positively described, but even the prehistoric stone caricatures of female bodies mediate the universal bewilderment, the awe in front of the mysterious, heroic female body —be it the Ice Age deity, or the Upper Paleolithic buttock amulet, Mother Goddess or Bird Goddess, the key elements of the Neolithic architecture, the squatting deity from Malta, 25 century B.C., or the 17-14th century B.C. headless female figures from Dordogne, France, — all exhibit the archetypal fascination with the female body (Johnson, 1988: 1-75; Sonesson, 1988; Warner, 1976; Sulliman, 1986).

The prehistoric and ancient monuments glorify, depict, mock and debunk the heroic otherness of the female body, its natural ability to outperform the male. They also point out to one of the first and earliest admissions of the human heroism. It was understood and accepted very early on that motherhood outweighs fatherhood in its existential complexity. Prior to becoming an *aesthetic sign*, a cult of the external beauty, physical woman, was universally acknowledged for her ability to conceive, give birth and nurture another being. Motherhood, rather than physical appearance, was one of the basic heroic preconditions for the *universal sign* — woman. The *semiovalence* of this sign taken in diachrony was not always even-handed. The ancient Venus, found in France and belonging to the late Magdalenian period (10,000 BC), is a figure with the head of a bird, exaggerated buttocks and enlarged belly, which could be hardly defined as a *sacred sign*. In contrast, Madonnas of the Byzantine and Renaissance period worship motherhood and could be defined as *sacred signs*. The female biological function was elevated to the level of sainthood, utmost heroism and exemplary femininity. The body part responsible for giving birth —the womb— is absent from these new hero-worshipping and motherhood worshipping icons (Uspensky, 1971; Panofsky, 1982). The icons depict only the angelic faces of young beautiful mothers, with children at their breasts. Breast, the later Freudian fetish-sign signifies glorious motherhood on the Byzantine and Renaissance icons. The belly and buttocks, so much idolized by the prehistoric and ancient masters, would disappear from the later *cultural signs,* which would focus on the body parts, embellishing and glorifying motherhood. The ancient *women-signs* in sculpture, painting and architecture were simultaneously the seductive, Eros and motherhood-denoting-signs. The post-pagan *cultural signs* would attempt to purify and elevate the *woman-sign* through the primary heroic feature-childbirth. The presence of a child next to a mother is a visual displacement and shift in the heroization of femininity. Rather than fantasizing about the female biological possibilities, the later sign-producers would stop displaying the erotogenic zones of the female body —belly and buttocks— and would instead bring in the child. The sex-object, the concubine, Hetaera or mistress would be replaced by a Madonna, giving the aesthetic pleasure, re-inventing motherhood and marginalising the erotic pleasure. The child at Madonna's breast pointed to the ideal singular feminine function, her utmost existential heroism. The child image had also created the illusionary redescribed universe where women do not engage in such mundane, vulgar or primitive activities as intercourse. The predominant half-cut female bodies on the post-pagan portraits, sculptures and murals referred to the shifted representation of women and their changed social signification. The post-pagan societies, which attempted to establish some new order and reorganize sexuality, needed new sacred signs, and women-mothers would became such signs, revealed by the rich artistic tradition of the early Christianity, Byzantine, Renaissance and even in the new national-socialist and Marxist aesthetics (Panofsky, 1982; Uspensky, 1971; Muller, 1987).

Umberto Eco also defines women in terms of child birth, as soon as the woman becomes a 'mother', she is no longer a physical body, but a sign which indeed "connotes a system of social obligations" (Eco, 1979: 26; Lévi-Strauss, 1947). The Madonna images of the post-pagan period re-described the role of females in setting the new boundaries of human behaviour, expressing the new societal approach towards the female body. The single biological function was granted a supreme heroic sta-tus as a primary signification of the body and the sacred role in society.

The cult of Madonna and worshipping of motherhood through cen-turies exposed the canonical conflict between the two semiotic universes —the Body and Mind, as well as two symmetrical semiospheres— Na-ture and Culture. Despite the obvious parallel between the animal and human procreation, it is not enough in a human society to follow the nat-ural signification. Humans reflect and analyse the given patterns of semi-osis in order to control the Body and form new semiotic relationships. In this process, the sign-producers may wish to ignore the real for the sake of the imaginary, the possible for the impossible.

The religious rituals have all established an additional, secondary system of signs, which could control and manipulate the Body. The celibacy ritual of the monks and priests as well as the sacred sign of vir-gin Mary — all refer to the impossible dream of purifying the Body from the ties of sex and male/female contact, desire either to expel sex, or puri-fy sexuality from the archetypal animalistic features. The religious semi-otic structures strictly divide the human and animal biosignification. Animals are associated with the ordinary biological forms and primitive signification. All taboo concepts of the religious prescriptions are dictat-ed by the ultimate goal of elevating the *homo-sapiens* and one's *sapienza* and creating the hierarchical system that follows the high/low ratio, by which humans are placed higher than animals. It is the order in the realm of the sexual relations that is largely responsible for the higher status of humans (Makolkin, 2000).

Suppression of one's sexuality could be sustained only partially by the Church and State, so the religious fathers had to invent a new *woman-sign*, which would point out to the imaginary sexless image of a mother, gives birth miraculously and mysteriously, in an unknown, way and place. The Church, was uncomfortable with sex-connected birth, has pro-duced the myth of immaculate conception, which emphasized the extra-ordinariness of motherhood and, exploiting the birth anxiety, offered a new mythical version of birth (Warner, 1976).

The anxiety of the coitus-connected birth would resurface in the con-temporary artificial insemination attempts. Aside from the medical rea-sons, there are similar naive semiotic strategies which had been invented by the Church centuries prior. The lesbian worship of motherhood in a sanitized, male-free environment is strikingly similar to the archetypal religious structural impositions. The selected stages of the organic semi-osis,i.e. the miraculously conceived new life, are still perceived as the extraordinary ones. Even the females, who are sexually inward-looking and prone to what Freud characterized as the "sexual inversion" cannot overcome the archetypal attraction to the *mother-sign*. Their seduction by the Madonna image is akin to the experience of the Church fathers, the producers of the Madonna myth (Freud, 1977 [1905]: 50-51).

Some parts of the Freudian psychoanalytic semiotic universe had been constructed around the a-sexual anxieties and Madonna-related complexes of the post-pagan sign-perceivers and producers. It is enough to allude to   the archetypal Freudian statement about the ultimate desire of a mother's breast, the famous breast syndrome (Freud, 1977: 98, 100-2, 144). Freud maintained that "the man is afraid of being weakened by the woman, infected with her femininity ˙(Fred, 1977, 271). The elevated mother-Madonna is the embodiment of this universal sexual fear and the a-sexual fantasy. The universal mother-goddess is the segregated sexual territory, limited to procreation alone. By depriving a woman of her innate sexual power, the sign-producers had neutralized the complex semiotic universe of femininity. The *semiovalence* of a *woman-sign* was reduced to a single heroic function — production of children, still suffi-cient for the heroic semiosis.

Mothers were selected as the *perfect signs,* the guardians of the high-er authority "and moral watchdogs" (Mullins, 1985: 20). They rep-resented the standard of moral and ethical behaviour to which men al-legedly could not rise due to their limited biological role. Motherhood gave women automatically a double societal signification function — to produce offspring and legislate morality. The post-pagan societal semi-otic division made sure that sexual restraint and femininity were placed near by. The most ideal heroine of course was Mary, the most perfect among the perfect, the mastermind of the immaculate conception. However, next to her, there was the chaste, woman, whose primary goal is "to produce sons" (Eco, 1979: 26).

8.2. *Virgins Temporary and Permanent Heroines*

> *Thou youngest virgin — daughter of the skies,*
> *Made in the last promotion of the blest;*
> *Whose palms, new plucked from paradise.*
> *In spreading branches more sublimely rise.*
> John Dryden, *Ode* (1631-1700)

Before and after the exceptional impossible heroism of the Saint Mary, virginity as a phase in a woman's life was universally venerated.

Virginity stood for the stage of innocence and goodness, as well as sexual weakness. The woman, who possessed the knowledge of sex and manifested her biological superiority towards men, was more ordinary in the real social system. The wide-spread law of premarital virginity introduced a certain temporary heroic phase into the life of women, elevating their societal value as signs of exchange. A woman as a sign was marked by the *universal seme* of virginity, whose loss might devalue her as a *social sign* in marriage and could even lead to ostracism. Virginity would become a universal heroic passage prior to marriage. The Old Testament has many evidences of the strict punishment of the deflowered virgins. Originally imposed as a natural birth and population control, virginity contributed to the construction of an additional mythological layer, standing for control over the Body in the realm which was most difficult to control. The female virginity, guarded and imposed by the male elders, whom a tribe entrusted with control and experiment with the human sexuality, demonstrated the possibilities of human mind to control the body. That which men did not wish, or could not restrain in themselves, they could impose on women. It also signified "the excessive possession of a woman, which forms the essence of monogamy." as Freud claimed (Freud, 1983: 205). It was a prescribed heroic passage from virginity to monogamy, a form of "sexual bondage" (Krafft Eging, 1892). Freud went much farther, labelling virginity and woman in general as *taboo-signs:*

> It is not only the first coitus with a woman which is a taboo but sexual intercourse in general, one might almost say that women are altogether taboo (1983:270).

He provided some insights into the other possible reasons of the elevation of virginity that could have been motivated by the general fear of women and of "being weakened by women". Granting a heroic status to virginity and chastity, men have removed themselves from the object of anxiety, from the possibility of being overpowered by women during the sexual intercourse. The archetypal *id* and *libido* signs, women-virgins have neutralised their archaic natural signification and have become a part of what is known as "civilized society" based on heroes and hero-worshipping.

The virgin did not pose any danger to men, since she was incapable of castrating the male. Ultimately, it is the fear of castration that is among the causes for worshipping the virgin, the comfortable and valuable sign of exchange. The primitive *homo* who naively perceived woman as the culprit of all misfortunes, including their own sexual drive and inconveniences of the heroic asexual semiotic universe, where libido had to be suppressed. The attractiveness of virginity needed to be advertised to increase the special marketable value of the *woman-sign,* adding a new heroic meaning to it. The coitus was temporarily sacrificed for the eliminated castration danger and promise of the permanent sexual pleasures in the future ideal marriage.

The steps toward monogamy and preservation of pre-marital virginity were conscious extraordinary efforts which demanded some sacrifices in the conflict between Body and Mind. The innate semiotic energy was behind the new *hero-signs.* The primitive *homo,* who had invented the concept of virginity, was definitely and clearly in search for the *dominant signs,* which could overpower the *natural signs,* such as libido and coitus. The separation from the female/male ties, the disrupted sexual bond could partially explain the sexual inversion and attraction to the same male sex, as a safe way of by-passing the prescribed route of the Body towards the Other. At least, this is the way Freud used to fantasize about the human sexuality.

Virginity, as a marker of extraordinariness, perhaps preceded the chastity of monks since the insistence upon virginity dates far back in history and precedes the introduction of a religious code. Virgins had to guard their virginity and frequently committed suicide if subject to rape, all this intensified their heroic value. In turn, the defence of virgins could involve the heroic actions of the male members of the family or community so it was significant as a heroic occasion as well (Warner, 1981; 1976). Virgins were *temporary hero-signs,* who would lose their heroic meaning in marriage. The woman, who would chose a religious life, would signify the ideal heroism, associated with virginity, purity, chastity and sexual otherness. The first venerated virgin saints who had successfully competed for her heroic status was the well-known Virgin Mary. The virgin saints extended the stage of virginity for the rest of their lives. Muller reports about some-fourteen auxiliary saints were among the earliest venerated virgins (Muller, 1987: 92). Their images were immortalized by the anonymous artists across Europe, the most famous of them were the virgins Catherine and Barbara, the earliest recorded examples of feminine sublimation, going back to the 9th and 10th centuries, now preserved in the museums of Germany, Netherlands and Belgium. The pipe clay statutes of Barbara and Catherine dd 15-16th century (Netherlands) depict two women holding books. Virginity was associated with education, another form of female heroism after the devotion to Christianity. In contrast to Madonna-like saints with children, Barbara and Catherine are always depicted with books. Their lives were recorded in numerous written legends as well. A virgin, educated and religious, dedicating her life to Christ, would become a new sign of increased *semiovalence.* According to Mueller, "The *Speculum Historiale* by Vincentius van Beavais and the *Legenda Aurea* by Jacobus de Varagine are the most commonly used sources" (Muller, 1987: 93). Eventually, the two women would become the patronesses of philosophy and knighthood. The saints, their legends and visual images circulated the new *hero-sign* — a permanent virgin, who dedicated her life to learning and loving Christ. Their education and intellectual pursuits illustrated in a primitive way what Freud would later classify as "narcissistic personality" type (Freud, [1905] 1983, 33-170). They refer to the incredulous possibility of living in the asexual world and reveal the eternal drama of the sexual being, who cannot reconcile with the tyranny of the libido and fancies the asexual world. The virgin saints, who had escaped the trappings of their sexuality, had been granted the utmost heroic titles after the supreme heroine — Virgin Mary ,and refer to the ideal asexual universe of truly civilized humans, the impossible dream of the non-heroic multitude.

8.3   Women — the Archetypal Beauty Signs

> *The virtue of her lively looks*
> *Excels the precious stone*
> *I wish to have none other books*
> *To read or look upon.*
> *A Praise of His Lady.*
> Toffel's "Miscellany," (1557)

Seeing and admiring a physically attractive person has always been a very highly pleasant emotional and aesthetic experience and a part of the heroic paradigm. The choice of heroes and heroines in any cultural tradition, as we know, had been usually tied to the assessment of one's physical appearance. This natural signification of the body, resulting in the well-proportioned facial and body parts, contributed to the societal approval of physical the extraordinariness. Being beautiful and more beautiful than the rest of the group is one of such heroic prerequisites. In this sense, the male/female beauty contest has been canonically won by women, who were and are customarily described as the "beautiful half" of humanity. Partly, this division along the aesthetic lines is due to the fact that, unlike the animal kingdom, the human cohabitation pool is characterized by a more profound gender differences. Male and female human bodies are more visibly different than their animal counterparts. This difference in appearance has been defined and described as the heroic advantage of the females, who appear more beautiful. Is this a real or an imaginary signification of the female body? Beauty has been traditionally associated with magic and mysterious power. The world folklore recorded the universal associations of beauty with power, happiness and prosperity. Be it a Russian princess. Vasilisa the beautiful, a Chinese beautiful maiden, who is not even named other than the "beautiful", the Greek Helen, or Aphrodite, the Etruscan Artemis, or the Assyrian Ishtar, the Phoenician goddess Tanit, or the Persian Anahita, the Sumerian Inanna, or Hebrew Ester, the Hindu Durga, or the Egyptian Selket — all are the migrating and universally present *women-signs* whose major semiotic value is their beauty, magically empowering them for the heroic deeds for the benefit of their respective groups.

Carl Jung maintained that the ancient people used to regard animals more beautiful and powerful than themselves (Jung, 1938: 114). Beauty was equated with strength and survival. The biological otherness of females as life-givers imparted them with the obvious superiority and strength, which was allegedly originating in their beauty. Buffie Johnson's *Lady of the Beasts* based her main arguments about the universal fascination with the feminine beauty as power, parallel with the attitude towards the *zoosigns*. Avoiding the contemporary prevalent paradigm, organized by the patriarchal attitudes, the scholar emphasizes the centricity of Beauty to the man/animal and man/woman relationships. The archetypal heroine is the lady of the beasts who conquers them with her eternal beauty. Johnson's "Lady of the Beasts" is the universal *beauty sign*, which manifests its semiovalence in the world of art, sculpture, architecture, folklore, mythology and pottery. The pervasiveness of the woman as a *beauty-sign* eventually contributed to the extreme position in aesthetics, operating with one single principle of beauty, namely feminine beauty, and, what Kovach labels as "gyneism" (Kovach, 1974: 159). The female form, colour, proportion and the impressions it arouses, constitute the essence of "gynesim", the cult of a female appearance, apparently shared by the generations of artists, poets, musicians, sculptors, choreographers and costume designers as well as some ancient philosophers. Hippias was quite convinced that a "beautiful maiden was beauty" and that was his response to Socrates (Plato, 1968: 160). The saturation of *beauty-signs*, embodied in the various images of women, has not surprisingly interested majority of the philosophers, who wrestled with the concepts of Beauty and the beautiful. Parallel with the proliferation of *women-signs* in art, sculpture, and painting, there is a striking absence of the *analogous signs* in the philosophical discourse. Women as aesthetic objects were only partly rediscovered by the feminists as sex-objects. For example, Umberto Eco makes no references to women as aesthetic objects in his famous *Art and Beauty in the Middle Ages* (Eco, 1986 [1959]). Despite the fact, that he recalls the related question by Thomas Aquinas "What is beauty of the body?", his response is : "A harmony of its parts with certain pleasing colour" (1986: 28).

Eco would continue to rely on the views of Cicero and Galen, Poly-clitus and the Stoics, totally void of references to the female body. Eco's approach is a summary of the general trend in the Western and Eastern philosophy and aesthetics, arising from the archetypal misogyny. The female body as an art object and archetypal *aesthetic sign* would be a taboo topic even before the post-modern openly misogynist images. The subversion of the *beauty-sign* standing for a female body, or face has been completed in this century when the distorted *proto-sign* —the real woman— would stop dominating the artistic imagination of the artists and being the most desirable and preferable image of the artists. Since Degas and Picasso, the expressionists and the surrealists, the images of women in art have progressively deteriorated in their respect to aes-thetics. The span of semiosis from Venus, with its innumerable copies, to the *Blue Woman* by Picasso, or *Rape* by René Magritte, captures the trends towards the obvious destruction of the Beauty-sign, embodied in a rep-resentational image or a *recognizable analogous sign.* André Breton would choose Magritte's pseudo-portrait as a suitable cover illustration for his manifesto, entitled "What is Surrealism?" The critics tried to justify the disturbing and obviously aesthetically unappealing pseudo-face of Marie-Terese as a reaction to the Franco's Spain. The "Blue woman" is a distorted proto-sign image, which breathes post-modern misogyny and neuroticism. It is a horror picture in a nightmarish dream. The double-headed creature, with strange huge paws, the archetypal feared female, who threatens with her intense sexuality. Magritte's image is a face, con-structed "from the salient features of the female anatomy." The eyes are displaced breasts, mouth is the pubic triangle. The outcome is the extreme caricature, with a very anti-aesthetic impact on the viewers. Leaving aside the surrealistic code, and simply following Venus — the perfect beauty-sign up to Magritte's displaced beauty signification, one may conclude that the "aesthetic function of sign" has been abandoned in favour of the "erotic one" (Mukařovsky, 1950: 350-70). The abstract and concrete beauty was deliberately rejected to suit the erotic fantasies of the sign-producer, fearful of the natural distribution of signs and meanings and the heterosexual order.

8.4. *Presentment of a Woman Sign: Peirce versus Plotinus*

One does not find women-signs among the *degenerative signs* in the clas-sification by Charles Peirce, despite the fact that they could have been included into "any object of direct experience" or *decent sinsign* as much as his favoured weathercock (1932: 2, 255). Peirce also acknowledges feel-ings evoked by various signs and labels them "as presentments" and sep-arate signs (Peirce, 1932: 1. 313). Thus, for Peirce, object and attitude towards it are separate signs, so women and feelings, aroused towards them, would be separate semiotic structures. The idea of black or white, male and female, hard or soft is a *monad* in Peircian terms. Accordingly, a person, thinking of a woman or beauty, redness or softness, would be in a *monadic state of feeling*. He insisted that :

> We must think of a metaphysical monad as a pure nature or quality, in itself without parts or features, and without embodiment. Such is pure monad (Peirce, 7932: 1,303).

To reach a *pure monad*, one has to overcome the feelings towards the object, or quality — to step over the Firstness of the Sign, initiating the analysis of qualities, or *qualisigns* and ultimately, upon comparison, recognizing similarities and reaching the monadic state. Another option, suggested by Peirce, is the apriori emersion into a monadic state, bypassing all the transitory stages of battle and feeling, and simple belief in the abstract pure monads. A Platonist and a Christian are united in one Peircean theory of the monadic state.

The Peircean, nearly chemical, approach to the classification of signs originates in the Platonean ideas as the primary foundation signs. It is the Platonian worldview that Peirce embodies in his *pure* monads, which appear more as doubles of the Platonian ideas. Consequently, a woman and a beautiful woman, beauty and gender would be his separate signs. Equally, the idea of sex and sexuality, beauty and beautiful sex would all be separate *monads*. Charles Peirce had to accommodate the changing societal attitudes towards women in the 19th century and separate various signs, according to his own semiotic classification.

Plotinus (215-270AD) perceived Beauty and Being as one. He claimed that "Beauty is loved because it is being" (1962: 430). Thus, to him, *women-signs*, especially those loved for their beauty, meant something different — they were beautiful because they were, existed. Neither did they have monopoly on physical perfection. To Plotinus, any being, thing, event, or feeling was beautiful as a manifestation of Being, Presence, and Existence. However, the beauty of "the battle-sought Helen", or lovely Aphrodite had nothing to do with their femaleness. To stress this idea, Plotinus argued that:

> It has nothing to do with the blood or the menstrual process; either there is also a colour and form apart from all this or there is nothing unless sheer ugliness or (at least) a bare recipient, as it were the mere Matter of beauty (1962: 423).

His Aphrodite is not a goddess of desire as the canonical Greek myth maintains, but she is a sign of several meanings. "To us Aphrodite is twofold," — says Plotinus. First of all, she is "the heavenly Goddess who

presides over the sexual unions." Secondly, she is the Intellectual principle, the "Soul at its divinest" (1962: 193). Plotinus maintained that "Eros
was not the child of Aphrodite, but was simply born on her birthday. He
was allegedly the child of Poverty and Possession. Consequently, the
canonical sign of lust, beauty and seduction had been transformed into a
sign of intellect, divinity and spirituality. People love Aphrodite, the sign
of female extraordinariness, for her intellect, generosity as much as for
her beauty. Plotinus purified the *perfect sign*, Aphrodite, having imparted
her with even more heroic qualities, such as her relationship to Eros. His
pure Eros is the child of a poor soul and possessive male, but Plotinus
does not agree with that :

> Love is represented as homeless, bedless, and bare-footed; would not
> that be a shabby description of the Cosmos and quite out of the Truth?
> (1962: 196)

He refused to believe that love was totally void of goodness, reason, and
introduced another sign — Kind Reason, as a characteristic and integral
part of loving:

> All the natural Loves, all that serve the ends of nature, are good"
> (1962:198).

They are good because they are, and therefore are beautiful. To love is as
beautiful as to be, and to be is also beautiful. Thus, women, who love and
are loved, are already beautiful because they live. It is not the beauty-
monad, which would be simply a *dominant sign* in Peirce's classification,
but Being, the *existential comprehensive sign*. Thus, Plotinus widens the
canonical meaning of a *woman-sign*, which would reign in the universe
of art and *cultural signs* for centuries to come. Plotinus unified the erotic
and aesthetic functions of the sign in the single Being, as if anticipating
the future split and misogynist sign-production of modernity.

8.5. *Women as Sign-Begetting Signs*

Omne symbolum de symbolo
Peirce (1935-66:2,302)

Signs beget signs.
Thomas Sebeok,
"Messages in the market place" (1987:25)

Thomas Sebeok reminds the semioticians and consumers of signs about
the special semiotic universe — "the market place, the arena of a society,
in which signs are bought and sold", incidentally elaborated earlier by
Frances Bacon (1987: 22). While Sebeok only disclosed the false meanings

of the modern consumers' universe, cautioning not to trust the "idols of the market place", he did not dwell on the underlying semiosis which takes place during buying and selling, nor did he explain the role of the *women-signs* in bartering. The American market place had been designed and is being perfected daily ,with the help of numerous signs and semiotic structures. Women, their bodies, faces, bodily parts, attire and items of personal hygiene had been turned into the sign-producing machines, responsible for the ongoing perpetuum engine of the capitalist market place. They simultaneously assist in stimulating the consumers' desire and signify the ultimate existential goals — to be possessed by men. Neither car, nor a new driver, neither a detergent, nor a house are sold without the active, conscious and visible manipulation of a *woman-sign*. Usually, an attractive young white female is used as an exciting, seductive promise in exchange for the product bought. A *woman-sign* begets various other signs in the process of advertising buying and selling. A *woman-sign* transmits the present, past and future mythical allusions connected with herself as a female specie. She points out to the unfulfilled desires, aspirations and memories. A woman, sitting in, or standing in front of a car for sale, is also sold on a symbolico-mythical level. She triggers the forces of the semiosis in a direction that activates the imagination of the intended consumers in the most acceptable, profitable and market — desired fashion. The consumer's forum is not the place for the consumers-produced signs, but rather for their submission to the tyranny of the *dominant signs*. This submission is analogous to the fulfilment of the natural bodily functions.

The *woman-sign*, the archetypal symbol of the erotic to the unassuming perceivers, is also a facilitator of another semiotic process- buying and enriching certain owners of the signs. Her erotic function, the in/visible libido, and her aesthetic presentment, refer to the mythical universe of signs, to the paradisiacal world, where all the wishes of the consumers are fulfilled. The consumer is assumed to possess a zero-interpretative level and needs to be reminded of the otherness and extraordinariness of the promised ideal world, created with the help of the purchased products(Sebeok, 1987).

First and foremost, the *woman sign* revives the store of the semiotic memories in the memory-bank of the consumer. She is the sign of kinship — a mother, sister, daughter, or of sexual pleasure— wife, mistress and concubine, but she also stands for the childhood, adulthood and pleasurable maleness. A *woman-sign* is instrumental in bringing in together various signs —*recognizable, pleasurable, natural* and *cultural*. She is entrusted with the mission of arousing the "energetic interpretant" (Peirce, 1931: 53: 5.475). The desired consumer is the energetic interpreter of the *woman-*

sign, who would automatically obey her communicative messages, enticing consumers to buy another item —— a car, a house, a swimming pool, a beer, a wine, ... etc. In advertising, a *woman-sign,* using the erotico-aesthetic functioning, imitates the sexual foreplay, producing a *false sign* — the parody of the sex act, turning the familiar *pleasurable sign* into the unfamiliar— pleasurable buying of an object. Her own body is just a pass into the market place, and into the bedroom. The *woman-sign* offers space, the intermediacy between herself and the product to be bought, becoming a new semiotic system where the *natural signs* are being transformed into *cultural, social, desirable, pleasurable,* etc.

The ordinariness of the new *recognizable signs* is just a transitional point between the Body and the pleasures of owning the consumer goods , towards the ultimate paradise, the extraordinary dream world for the hero-consumer. The ultimate victory is the possession of the products, advertised with the help of the women-signs. Women, the *begetting signs,* lead the gullible interpreter from the *thymic space,* limited to the perception of the body to the *utopic,* where the allegedly heroic status could be achieved (Greimas, 1979: 346, 362).

Possessing the *woman-sign* alone has also been a marker of male heroism in many popular cultural traditions. The archetypal Don Juan, the conqueror of the female imagination and her body, has been the popular male hero in many societies. The sexual conquest and its repeated pattern has passed the collective censorship of many groups and has been approved as a version of a peculiar societal heroism or extra-ordinariness. In contrast with the monogamial demands of the state and church, some groups have legitimized the subversive alleged herism of adultery. Its illegitimate heroic glamour reinforced the role of a *woman-sign* as a *glory-begetting sign.* The macho-man could not gain his victorious space within the subversive mythical collective universe without the ownership of a *woman-beauty-sign.*

Despite the fact, that the natural signification of the female body has been traditionally used to assert the male heroism and to promote the exchange of the other signs in society, the appeal of the woman-sign has sometimes been of a different nature. For instance, a woman-sign plays a significant role in the Dostoevsky's messianic delusions. Dostoevsky advocated the exclusive heroic nature of the Slavs and particularly Russians, who were allegedly destined to play the extraordinary historico-cultural role in the twentieth century. The Russian woman was presumably destined to play a major role in this heroic ascendance of the Russians. Dostoevsky claimed that

> The essential and the most redeeming rejuvenation of the Russian society would inevitably befall upon the Russian woman. One cannot doubt

the high calling awaiting the Russian woman, particularly after the current war, where she had revealed her high, pure and sacred essence (Dostoevsky, *Writer's Diary*, 1877; 236).

He insisted that the Russian woman would help her barbaric state to conquer, overcome the ages-old prejudices, and eventually stand heroically above other European nations. By educating the woman, allowing her to be equal to men in all respects, Russia would elevate her position as a European country: "We burden her with all our hopes for future elevation of our society." — Dostoevsky wrote shortly after the Crimean War and the Balkan crisis of the past century. Being aware of the general subservient and unequal position of women, Dostoevsky perceived a woman as a *potent sign* in the general cultural mythology. The educated and emancipated female participant of the future Russian society could contribute to the general elevation of the Russian cultural text among other European nations. The messianic role of Russia could be performed with the strong helper to the hero. The Proppian fairy tale categories are perfectly in place within Dostoevsky's mythological universe. The Russian *woman-sign* is the glory-begetting sign of the Russian hero-nation. Prior to conquering Constantinople, the new modern heroic task facing Russia after Rome and Jerusalem, was allegedly in attempting to conquer the European public imagination. The Russian woman, the future physician and educator, engineer and philosopher, painter and lawyer was destined to outperform the archetypal mother, nurse and spouse. Extending the domain of her extraordinary deeds, beyond the private territory, and being aware of the general reluctance to grant visibility to women, Dostoevsky maps the road of women as *sign-begetting signs.*

He claimed that only women possessed this "newly revived energy the noble desire to act, to sacrifice and commit heroic deeds" (1877, October, 325). The Russian women would allegedly be the societal fermentation force, the engine of the extraordinary messianic behaviour of the Russians as a heroico-mythical entity. The heroism of the Russian women would recharge, reactivate the heroic activity of the group, historically passive, and having an enormous creative potential. They would serve as a mimetic model to be emulated by the entire Russian nation:

hero-nation

Russian
nation-sign

Russian
woman-sign

Heroic matrix

Dostoevsky anticipated the drastic changes in the universal woman-sign. Not knowing precisely what these new meanings might be, he could foresee the shift beyond the traditional private sphere and the intensity of the future societal semiosis, which would eventually manifest itself in the various feminist significations of the future. The twentieth century super woman image was still very distanced from Dostoevsky's time, but the romantic code had already invented an extra-heroic locus for the *woman-sign*.

Unlike Nietzsche and Freud, Dostoevsky associated femininity with neither   inferiority, nor weakness. His myth of the collective Russian grandeur in the near future was chiefly constructed on the basis of high semiovalence of the woman-sign. In Dostoevsky's exaggerated vision, the future of the superior Russian civilization was to be constructed by a Russian woman, contrary to the Freudian theory of civilization. If, according to Freud, woman stood for the archetypal primitive human state, the pre-civilized phase of humanity vis-à-vis the male, the mythical superior specie, who would be capable of being engaged in the activities, requiring total sublimation. The Freudian woman signified only the intense libido, the forces of the "id", while Dostoevsky's woman-sign was a *potent sign*, combining a variety of culture-related meanings and was an active producer of *cultural signs* herself.

Paradoxically, Dostoevsky's perception of the woman-sign was much closer to the contemporary social semiosis and the current battle for the signifying power and role of women, as new sign-producers. In contrast, the Freudian interpretation of the women-signs would be less acceptable to the feminists and progressive intellectuals in the 20th century. His obsession with the female nature-oriented and libido-fixated mode of signification reaffirms the archaic division between the male and female sign-producing capacity. Freud could not accept the Peircean "*Conjointed Sign*", or "something [that] can be selected as to be an once a Chinese and a woman, a mother and a physician, a wife and a concert pianist' (Peirce, 1932: 2.441). To master the conjointed signification meant to embrace the polyvalence of existence and harmony between the two main semiospheres, embodied in Nature and Culture. Freud and his post-modern followers, producers of signs, rejected the *conjointed sign* and contributed to further alienation, having widened the gulf between the signs, sign-producers and perceivers. The organic empire of *conjointed signs* began to disintegrate into *semes* and *sememes*, according to the singular functions and presentment. This *qualisign*, one of the multiple meanings of the *woman-sign* — the most obvious gender difference, would be the new classificatory principle, by which "women" be separated from blacks., Jews, homosexuals etc. The begetting power of any sign-producer was being energetically denied proportionately with the rising significatory power of *women-signs*. During this process, the desire to uphold the conjointed mode of signification or *polyvalence* would be another heroic or extraordinary challenge.

Conclusions

In the spirit of defiance, the contemporary producers of signs in the era of skepticism have embarked on a journey of debunking the *hero-sign* and undermining the heroic foundation of the "Empire of signs". Paradoxically, during the process of displacing the old heroes, the sign-producers have reaffirmed the recurrent acts of reversal, repetition and return, after all, "as soon as the new sign emerges, it begins by repeating itself", as Derrida summarized in his *Writing and Difference*. (1978: 269). Even the cynical post post-modernists could not do without heroes. The birth of the anti-hero is merely another prelude to the birth of the new hero and a testimony of the eternal conjecture of the ordinary and extraordinary.

The multitude of the contemporary *hero-signs* reflects the post- modern freedom to select and reward any extraordinariness in its unrestricted presentment, be it a celebrity, a hockey, or a film star, a cancer, or AIDS victim, a criminal, or a spaghetti-eating contest winner. The boundaries of the heroic universe have been stretched in the unprecedented manner, the notions of the extraordinariness have been pushed to the limit, but they all shockingly repeat the universal eternal search for the *recognizable* and *familiar sign* — Hero, whose universal seductive qualities did not fail even in the cynical, worship-denying times.

Hero is the point of the eternal repetition and return. It is the *eternal sign*, whose immortality is sustained by the transtemporal, trans-linguistic and transcodal reproduction of the same, of the analogous ideal structure. Hero is the *dominant sign*, that which is universally desired and universally despised. We are simultaneously slaves and masters of the heroic universe. We willingly participate in the heroic contest, being seduced by the familiar *perfect sign* and unable to challenge its eternal tyranny. This universal seduction is rooted not only in the expected pleasure of the unconditional love, adoration and acceptance, but in the joy of overcoming the obstacles, crossing the boundaries of the unknown and the impossible.

Hero is the preferred locus in the cultural space, since it is there where victory occurs and conquest takes place, regardless of what we collectively and individually designate the sign to represent. The individual display of heroism, a transcultural invariant along with the collective extraordinariness, is much more acceptable as a *semiotic phenomenon*. In contrast, the heroic clusters or groups claiming a heroic title are perceived negatively. The cultural space does not tolerate colonies of *hero-signs* while the distance between them in the semiosphere guarantees the expected conditions of semiosis and secures calm reversal, displacement and renewal.

The heroic acceptable semiosis is characterized by verticality, by striving upward and above. However, the semiosphere does not tolerate the simultaneous horizontal spread through the heroic clusters, competing for "utopic space." The heroic clusters or collective heroism disturb the natural balance between the ordinary and the extraordinary. The saturation of the *hero-signs* in a single locus turns into a violent display of force. Any military conflict in the past and present is not merely a battle for the physical geographical boundaries, but for the sphere of the heroic manifestation, which is simultaneously desired and rejected. The universal impulse for equality invariably denies extraordinariness and submits to its occasional displays while the appearance of the heroic clusters provokes the innate rejection of the extraordinary. The other is tolerated as an *exotic* and *entertaining sign* in its occasional presentment, but the field, saturated with otherness becomes a threat and is perceived as an invasion into one's existential space.

The heroic paradigm , viewed from the semiotic perspective, with the *hero-sign* as the key cognitive device, offers some methodological advantages in processing the *natural* and *cultural signs,* as well in the analysis of the confusing *social signs* — revolutions, elections, protest movements, liberation independence movements, strikes, tournaments etc.

Certain forms of extraordinariness may have become obsolete, after numerous cycles of return and repetition, e.g. one may, perhaps, question the need to jeopardize one's life for the sake of another inch above the mountain slope. Perhaps, it is time to reconsider certain heroic rituals, which endanger life , involve unnecessary cost, sacrifice, or meaningless physical effort. To redescribe the image of the hero does not imply to exclude the sign, or make it invisible. It could merely signify the change in its outward presentment ,since to expel the hero would imply to destroy *homo-sapiens*. After all, living is a heroic act and a heroic occasion to be celebrated, the conjecture of Nature and Culture, the given and the attained, a gift and a conquest, with and without return.

Bibliography

Aarne, Anitti and Thompson, Stith, *The Types of the Folktale; A Classification and Bibliography.* Helsinki: Suomalainen Tiedeakademia 1961.

Aaron, R.I., *The Theory of Universals.* London: Oxford University Press, 1952.

Adler, Alfred, *Superiority and Social Interest.* New York: Norton & Co., 1974.

Adler, Kathleen, ed., *The Body Imaged.* Cambridge: Cambridge University Press, 1993.

Aeschylus, *Agamemnon.* Trans., Walter Headlam, Cambridge, Mass.: Cambridge University Press, 1925.

Afanasiev, Alexander, *Russian Fairy Tales.* New York: Pantheon, 1945.

Alekseev, M.P., ed., *Epoha Romantisma.* (The Romantic Epoch), Leningrad: Nauka, 1975.

Aquinas, Thomas., *Commentary on the Sentences.* Pocket Aquinas, ed., V. Bourke, New York: Washington Square Press, 1960.

Aristotle, *Categories* in *The Complete Works of Aristotle.* Princeton, N.J.: Princeton University Press, 1985,vol. 1., 1985 edition, pp. 3-25.

——, *Metaphysics* in *The Complete Works of Aristotle.* Princeton, N.J.: Princeton University Press, 1985, vol, 2., pp. 1552-1729.

——, *Physiognomonics* in *The Complete Works of Aristotle.* Princeton, N.J.: Princeton University Press, 1985, vol. 1., pp. 1237-1250.

——, *Politics* in *The Complete Works of Aristotle.* The revised Oxford trans. ed., by Jonathan Barnes, Princeton, J.J.: Princeton University Press, 1985, vol. 1., pp. 1986-2130.

——, *Rhetoric to Alexander* in *The Complete Works of Aristotle.* Princeton, N.J.: Princeton University Press, 1985, vol. 2., pp. 2270-2316.

Armstrong, Arthur Hilary, *Hellenic and Christian Studies.* Alder, Hampshire: Variorum, 1990.

Armstrong, David Malet, *Universals.* Boulder: Westview Press, 1989.

Auerbach, Erich, *Mimesis.* New York: Doubleday Anchor Books, 1953.

Babad, Elisha, *The Social Self.* Beverly Hills, Cal.: Sage Publications, 1983.

Babbitt, Irwing, *Rousseau and Romanticism.* New York: Meridian Books, 1966.

Bald, Marjory A. *Women-Writers of the Nineteenth Century.* Cambridge, Mass.: Cambridge University Press, 1923.

Barthes, Roland, *Empire of Signs.* Trans. Richard Howard, New York: Hill & Wang, 1982.

——, *The Fashion System.* Trans. M. Ward and R. Howard, New York: Hill & Wang, 1967.

——, *Mythologies.* Trans, Annette Lavers, New York: Hill & Wang, 1972.

Barron, John Penrose, *The Silver Coins of Janos*. London: The Athlone Press, 1966.

Barzun, Jacques, *Darwin, Marx, Wagner*. Boston: Little Brown & Co., 1941.

Bentley, Eric Russelll, *A Century of Hero Worship* Philadelphia: J.B. Lippincott, 1963.

Berger, Aza, *Signs in Contemporary Culture*. New York: Longman, 1984.

Berkeley, E. *History of Rome*. Edinburgh: n.p. 1900.

Berlin, Isaiah, *Vico and Herder,* London: The Hogarth Press, 1976.

Bettelheim, Bruno, *The Uses of Enchantment*. New York: Knopf, Random House, 1976.

Blonsky, Marshall, ed., *On Signs*. Baltimore: The Johns Hopkins University Press, 1991.

Bogatysev, Peter, "Costume as a Sign" in L. Matejka & Titunik, eds., *Semiotics of Art*. Cambridge, Mass.: The MIT Press, 1977, pp. 13-20.

Boulding, Elize. *The Underside of History*. Boulder, Col.: Westview Press, 1976.

Bradbury, Malcolm and James McFarlane, *Modernism: 1890-1930*. Harmonds Worth: Penguin, 1976.

Bremond, Claude, "The Morphology of the French Folktale" in *Semiotica*. N2, 1970., pp. 247-77.

Bremond, Claude, "The Logic of Narrative Possibilities" in *New Literary History*. vol, XI. Spring, 1980, 1980, N3. pp. 387-413.

Brombert, Victor, ed., *The Hero in Literature*. Greenwich, Conn: Fawatt Publications, 1967.

Burkett, Walter, "The Temple in Classical Greece" in *M. Fox, ed., Temple in Society*. Winona Lake: Eisenbrauns, 1988, pp. 27-48.

Butler, Bill, *The Myth of the Hero*. London: Rider & Co., 1979.

Campbell, Joseph, *The Hero with a Thousand Faces*. Princeton, N. J.: Princeton University Press, 1949.

———, "Transformations of The Hero" in Richard M. Ohmann; ed., *The Making of Myth*. New York: G.P. Putnam's Sons, 1962, pp. 99 - 135.

Calvino, Italo, ed. *Italian Folktales*. Trans. by George Martin, New York: Pantheon Books, 1980.

Cantor, Norman, *Twentieth Century Culture: From Modernism to Deconstruction*. New York: Peter Lang, 1968.

Carlyle, Thomas, *On Heroes, Hero-Worhip and the Heroic in History*. ed. by Carl Niemeyer. Lincoln, Nebraska: Univeristy of Nebraska Press, 1966 [1841].

Carson, R.A.G. *Coins of the World*. New York: Harper & Brothers, 1962

Champigny, Robert, *The Ontology of Narrative*. The Hague: Mouton, 1972.
Change, Michael, "About Face" in *Semiotica*. vol. 18:3, 1976; pp. 289 - 297.

Chomsky, Noam, *Language and Mind.* New York: Harcourt Brace Jovanovich Inc., 1972.

Christiansen, Reidar Thorwald; ed. *Folktales of Norway.* Trans. Pat Shaw Iversen. Chicago: Univeristy of Chicago Press, 1964.

Clark, W.J., *International Language Past, Present and Future.* London: n. p. 1907.

Confucius, *The Analects.* Trans. Arthur Walley. London: George Allen & Unwin Ltd., 1956.

Crawford, M.H., C.R. Ligota and J.B. Trapp, ed. *Medals and Coins from Budé to Mommsen.* London: The Warburg Institute, 1990.

Czarnowski, s. *Le culte des héros et ses conditions sociales.* Paris: n.p. 1914.

Dakin, Douglass, "The Historical Background" in P .G. Trueblood, ed., *Byron's Political and Cultural Influence in 19th Century Europe.* Atlantic Highlands: Humanities Press, 1981, pp.1 - 18.

Danesi, Marcel; ed. *Metaphor, Communication and Cognition.* Toronto: Toronto Semiotic Circle Publication Series, 1987-88.

Danesi, Marcel, *Vico, Metaphor and Origin of Language.* Bloomington, Ind; Indiana University Press, 1993.

Danilevsky, Nikolai, *Rossiia i Evropa* (Russia and Europe). Moscow: Kniga, 1991.

Derrida, Jacques, *Margins of Philosophy.* Trans, Allan Bass, Chicago: Chicago University Press, 1972.

Derrida, Jacques, *Writing and Difference.* Chicago: The Univeristy of Chicago, Press, 1978.

Dissanayake, Ellen. *Homo Aetheticus.* New York: The Free Press, 1992.

Dostoevsky, Feodor, *Dnevnik pisatelia* 3 vols. (Writer's Diary). St. Petersburg: Tipografiia Putsykovicha, 1878.

Dunlop, J. *The Faces of Contemporary Russian Nationalism.* Laurenceville, N.J.: Princeton University Press, 1986.

Eberhard, Wolfram, ed., *Folktales of China.* Chicago: The University of Chicago Press, 1985.

Eco, Umberto, *Art and Beauty in the Middle Ages.* Trans., by Hugh Bredin, New Haven: Yale University Press, 1986.

Eco, Umberto, "How Culture Conditions the Colors We See" in Marshall Blonsky, ed., *On Signs.* Baltimore, M.D.: John Hopkins University Press, 1991, pp.137-175.

Eco, Umberto, *A Theory of Semiotics.* Bloomington : Indiana University Press, 1979.

Eliade, Mircea, *Myth and Reality.* Trans. R. Williand, New York: Harper and Row Publishers, 1963.

Eliade Mircea *Patterns in Comparative Religion.* London: Sheed & Ward, 1958.

Farnell, Lewis Richard, *Greek Hero Cults and Ideas of Immortality.* Oxford: Clavendon Press, 1970.

Fishwick, Marshall, W. "The Hero in the Context of Social Change" in John Hague, ed., *American Character and Culture in a Changing World*. Westport, Conn.: Greenwood Press, 1979.

Fishwich, Marshall, *American Hero, Myth and Reality*. Westport, Conn: Greenwood Press, 1975.

Fox Michel, ed., *Temple in Society*. (Winona Lake: Eisenbrauns, 1988).

Freud, Sigmund, *Group Psychology and the Analysis of the Ego*. Trans. James Strachey, New York: Hogarth Press, 1959.

   On Sexuality. London: Penguin Books, 1983 [1905].

   , *Civilization and Its Discontents*. Chicago: University of Chicago Press, 1977 [1936].

Friedlander, Max J. *Landscape, Portrait, Still-life*. Oxford: Bruno Cassirer, 1955.

Frye, Northrop, "Myth, Function and Displacement" in *Fables of Identity*. New York: Harcourt Brace Jovanovich, 1963, pp. 21-39.

   , *Study of English Romanticism*, New York: Random House, 1968.

Gary, Mark "Gaze and Facial Display in Pedestrian Passing", in *Semiotica*. V. 28, 1979 pp. 323-327.

Gergen, J. Kenneth, *The Saturated Self*. New York: The Basic Books, 1991.

Gerzon, Mark, *A Choice of Heroes*. Boston: Houghton Mifflin Co., 1982.

Girard, René, *Deceit, Desire and the Novel*. Trans, Ivonne Freccero, Baltimore. M.D.: Johns Hopkins University Press, 1965.

Girard, René, *La Violence et le Sacré*. Paris: B. Grasset, 1972.

Girgus, B. Samuel, ed., *The American Self*. Albuquerque: University of New Mexico Press, 1981.

Gobineau, de, Arthur, *The Inequality of Human Race*. New York: H. Fertig, 1967.

Gobineau de, Arthur, *Selected Political Writings*. London: Jonathan Care Ltd., 1970.

Godwin, William, *The Pantheon*. London: Garland Publishing Co., 1984.

Gordon, Sarah, *Hitler, Germans and the "Jewish Question*. Princeton, N.J.: Princeton University Press, 1984.

Grand *Dictionnaire Universel du XIX Siè*. Paris: n.p. 1865-90.

Graves, Robert, *The Greek Myths*. 2 vols. New York: Penguin Books, 1977.

Greimas Algirdas J. *Sémiotique: un dictionnaire raisonné de la theorie du language*, Pairs: Hachette, 1979.

Greimas, Algirdas, *Semiotics and Language, An Analytical Dictionary*. Bloomington, Ind.: Indiana University Press, 1982.

———, *Of Gods & Men*. Trans. Milda Newman. Bloomington, Ind: Indiana University Press, 1992.

———, & Fontanille, J. *Semiotics of Passions*. Paul Perron & F. Collins, Minneapolis: University of Minnesota Press, 1993.

_____ , *Semiotics and Cognitive Discourses*. London: Pinter, 1990.

Groom, Frances, *Gypsy Folktales*. ed., Diane Tong. New York: Harcourt Brace Jovanovich, 1989.

Haddas, Moses, *Heroes and Gods*. London: Morton Smith Co., 1965.

Hallett, Judith, *Fathers and Daughters in Roman Society: Women and the Elite Family*. Princeton, N.J.: Princeton University Press, 1984.

Haydon, A. Eustace, *Biography of the Gods*. New York: The Macmillan Co., 1941.

Hegel, *Aesthetics: Lectures on Fine Art*. Trans. by T.M. Knox, Oxford: Oxford University Press, 1975. 2 vols.

Herder, Johann Y. *Reflections on the Philosophy of the History of Mankind*. Chicago: University of Chicago Press, 1968.

Hitler, Adolf, *Mein Kampf*. Trans. James Murphy. London: Hurst & L. Blackett [1939] 1981.

Hobbes, Thomas, *Leviathan*. New York: Collier Books, 1962.

Hobsbawn, E.I., *Nations and Nationalism Since 1780*. Cambridge: Cambridge University Press, 1990.

Hodge, Robert & Gunther Kress, *Social Semiotics*. Ithaca, N.Y. Cornell University Press, 1988.

Hogain, Daithio, *The Hero in Irish Folk History*. Dublin: Gill and Macmillan, 1985.

Hogg, James, ed. *Romantic Reassessment*. Salzburg: Institut für Anglistik und Amerikanistik, 1985.

Holland, Ray, *Self and Social Context*. London: The MacMillan Press Ltd., 1977.

Horn, Marilyn, *The Second Skin*. Boston: Houghton Mifflin Co., 1968.

Hook, Sidney, *The Hero in History*. Boston: Beacon Press, 1967.

Humboldt, Wilhelm, *On Language*. Cambridge: Cambridge University Press, 1988.

Hume, David, *A Treatise of Human Nature*. 2 vols, London: J.M. Dent & Sons Ltd., 1974.

Hutcheon, Linda, *The Politics of Postmodernism*. London: Routledge Co., [1989] 1991.

Irwin, James, *An Introduction to Maori Religion*. Bedford Park: Australian Association for the Study of Religion, 1984.

Ivanov, VV. *Ocheski po istorii semiotiki v SSSR*. (Essays on the History of Soviet Semiotics), Moscow: Nauka, 1976.

Ivanov. V.V. "The Role of Semiotics in the Cybernetic Study of Man and Collective" in Daniel Lucid, ed. *Soviet Semiotics*. Baltimore: The Johns Hopkins University Press, 1977.

James, E.O., *From Cave to Cathedral*. New York: Frederick A. Pralger, 1965.

Jakobson, Roman, *Main Trends in the Science of Language*. London: George Allen & Unwin Ltd., 1973.

_____," On Russian Fairytales" in *Russian Fairytales*. NewYork: Pantheor, 1945, pp. 629-656.

_____ , *Raboty po poetike*. (Works in Poetics). Moscow: Progress, 1982.

Johansen, Jorgen D. "Sign Concepts/ Semiosis/ Meaning", *Danish Semiotics*. ed., J. Johansen and Morten Noigaard. Copenhagen: Munkgaard, 1978; pp. 173-177.

Jung, Carl, *Collected Works*. Trans. R.R.C. Hull, "The Origin of the Hero." New York: Pantheon Books, 1956, vol. 5. pp. 171-206.

_____ , "The Phenomenology of the Spirit in Fairytales" in Jung. C, *Collected Works*. vol. 5. Tran. R.F.C. Hull, New York: Pantheon Books, 1959; pp.207-55.

Kahn, John "A Diagnostic Semiotic" in *Semiotica*. 1976, p. 75-107, v.22.

Kamenetsky, Christa, *The Brothers Grimm*. Athens: Ohio University Press, 1992.

Kant, Immanuel, *Observations on the Feeling of the Beautiful and the Sublime*. Trans., John T. Goldthwait, Berkeley, Cal.: University of California Press, 1960.

Karl, Frederick R., *Modern and Modernism*. New York: Atheneum, 1988.

Kerenyi, C., *The Heroes of the Greeks*. London: Thames & Hudson, 1959.

Kevelson, Roberta, *The Law as a System of Signs*. New York: Plenum Press, 1988.

Khabarov, Ivan, *Philosofskie problemy semiotiki*. (Philosophical Problems in Semiotics) Moscow: Vysshaiia Shkola, 1978, .

Kohn, Hans, *Nationalism in the Soviet Union*. New York: Columbia, University Press, 1933.

Kohn, Hans, *Pan-Slavism*. New York: Vintage Books, 1960.

Konig, René, *The Restless Image: A Sociology of Fashion*. London: George Allen & Unwin, 1973.

Kotler, Philip, " Semiotics of Person and Nation Marketing" PP. 3-13 in Jean Umiker-Sebeok, ed., *Masketing and Semiotics: Definingg the Scope of Their Partnership*. Berlin: Mouton de Gruyter, 1992.

Kovach, Francis J., *Philosophy and Beauty*. Norman, Oklahoma: University of Oklahoma Press, 1974.

Kramer Samuel Nia, "The Temple in Sumerian Literature" in M. Fox, ed. *Temple in Society*. Winona Lake: Eisenbrauns, 1988.

Kroker, Arthur & David Cook, *The Post-modern Scene: Excremental Culture and Hyper-Aesthetics*. Montreal: New World Perspectives, 1986.

Lancman, Eli, *Chinese Portraiture*. Ruthland, Vermont: Charles &. Tuttler & Co, 1966.

Lavater, Johann C. *Essays on Physiognomy*. Trans. Thomas Holcroft, New York: Worthington, 1891 [1775].

Lawrence, D.H. "Democracy" in D.H. Lawrence, *Reflections on the Death of a Porcupine*. Cambridge: Cambridge University Press: 1988[1918] pp. 61-85.

Lawrence, D.H. *Movements in European History*. London: Oxford University, 1971.

Le Bon, Gustave, *The Crowd*. London: Unwin, 1910.

____ , *The Psychology of Revolution*. London: Fisher Unwin, 1913.

____ , *The World Unbalanced*. New York: Longmans, Green & Co., 1924.

Lehman, B.H. *Carlyle's Theory of the Hero: Its Sources and Influence on Carlyle's Work*. New York: Ams Press Inc., 1966.

Linecar, Howard W.A. *The Commemorative Medal*. Detroit: Yale Research Co., 1974.

Leibnitz Y. Wilhelm, *Works* (in Russian). Moscow: Mysl', 1982, 4 vol. ed., of the Academy of Sciences.

Leonardo da Vinci, *Treatise on Painting*. Trans. John Francis Rigaud, (London: 1802).

Lévy-Strauss, Claude, *Antropologie Structurale*. Paris: Gallimard, 1958.

Liszka, James Jacob, *The Semiotics of Myth*. Bloomington, Ind.: Indiana University Press, 1989.

Living Webster Encyclopedic Dictionary. ed. by Prof. Mario Pei, Chicago: The English Language Institute of America, 1977.

Lock, John. *Conduct of the Understanding*. ed. Thomas Fowler. New York: Burt Franklin, 1971.

Lotman, Juri. "*Semantika chisla i tip kul'tury*. (Numerological Semantics and Cultural Types) in *Soviet Semiotics* ed. Daniel Lucid, Baltimore: The Johns Hopkins University Press, 1977, pp. 227- 233.

____ , *The Structure of the Artistic Text*. Ann Arbor, Mich: University of Michigan, 1977.

____ , *Universe of the Mind*. Bloomington, Ind: Indiana University Press, 1990.

Luria, A.R., *Language and Cognition*. Washington, D.C.: V.H. Winston & Sons, 1981.

Lyons, John, *The Invention of the Self*. Carbondale: Southern Illinois University Press, 1978.

MacCannell Dean & Juliet Flower MacCannell, *The Time of the Sign: a Semiotic Interpretation of Modern Culture*. Bloominton, Ind.: Indiana University Press, 1982.

MacCormac, Earl. R. *Metaphor and Myth in Science and Religion*. Durham. N.C.: Duke University Press, 1976.

Makolkin (a), Anna "On the Poetics of Biography: Transformations in Some Biographies of Byron and Pushkin", doctoral dissertation, Universisty of Toronto, 1987, 370 pp. (unpublished).

Makolkin(a), Anna "Resurrection of the Old Saints in Biographical Discourse in *Biography*. vol.11, number 3, Summer 1988, pp.223-235.

Makolkin Anna, "Temporality as a Fictional Device in Biography" in *Comparative Literature East and West*. ed., by Cornelia N, Moore and Raymond A. Moody, Honolulu: University of Hawaii Press, 1989, pp.11-24.

——, "The Absent-Present Biographer in V.V. Veresaev's *Pushkin v Zhizni* in *Canadian Slavonic Papers*. Winter, 1989, pp.44-57.

——, "The Dance of Dionysos in H. Khodkevych and D.H. Lawrence" in *Journal of Ukrainian Studies*, Summer, N. 27, 1990, pp 31-39.

——, *Name, Hero, Icon: Semiotics of Nationalism through Heroic Biography*. Berlin: Mouton de Gruyter, 1992 a.,263pp.

——, *Semiotics of Misogyny through the Humor of Chekhov and Maugham*. Lewiston, N.Y.: The Edwin Mellen Press, 1992 b,239pp..

——, "Galt versus Byron: "I" and the "Other" in Biography" in *Boswells Children*. ed, by Ray Fleming, Toronto/Oxford: Dundurn Press, 1992 c.,57-67pp.

——, "Displacemnt of Signs in Biography: Semiosis of a Popular Genre" in *Signs of Humanity*. ed. by Michel Balat and Janice Deledalle-Rhodes, 5 vols, Berlin: Mouton de Gruyter, 1992 d. pp. 547-553.

——, "Probing into the Origins of Literary Biography"' in *Biography*. 1996, vol. 19. N.1, pp. 87-105.

——, "Vico's Firstness, Secondness, and Thirdness" the Common Essence of Nations as Signs" in Danesi, Marcel, ed., *Vico and Anglo-American Science*. Berlin: Mouton de Gruyter, 1994, pp. 121-126.

——, "Victorian Precursors of Freud: Deromanticizing a Romantic Poet", in *The 20th Century Prose Journal*. 1995, pp. 63-73.

——, *The Genealogy of Our Present Moral Disarray*. Lewinston, NY: The Edwin Mellen Press, 2000, 220 pp.

Maliuta, Alexander, *Gip[erkomplexnye Dinamicheskie Sistemy*. (Hyper Complex Dynamic Systems) Lvov: Izdatel'stvo pri Lvovskom gosudarstvennom universitete, 1989, (in Russian).

McCullough, David, *Brave Companions: Portraits in History*. New York: Prentice Hall Press, 1992.

McLuhan, Marshall, *The Mechanical Bride: Folklore of Industiral Man*. New York: Vanguard Press, 1951.

McQuillan, Melissa, *Impressionistic Portraits* London: Thames Hudson, 1986.

Mead, George H. *Mind, Self and Society*. Chicago, Ill: The University of Chicago Press, 1949.

Mitchell,-Williams, Christobel, *Dressed for the Job*. Pool, Vorsett, England: Blanford Press, 1982.

Mitchison, Roselind, ed. *The Roots of Nationalism*. Edinburgh: Edinburgh University Press, 1980.

Momigliano, Arnaldo, *The Conflict Between Paganism and Christianity*. London: Oxford University Press, 1963.

Mořawski, Stepan, "Mimesis" in *Semiotica.* 1970, N2, pp.35-59.

Mosse, George L. *Germans and Jews.* New York: Howard Fertig, 1970.

Mukařovsky, Jan. "Art as Semiotic Fact" in L. Matejka and I.R. Titunik, ed. *Semiotics of Art.* Cambridge, Mass: The MIT Press, 1977, pp. 3-11.

———, *Structure, Sign and Function.* ed and trans. G. Burbank and P. Steiner. New Haven: Yale University Press; 1978 [1966]

Muller, Ellen. "Saintly Virgins" in Lene Drosen-Coenders, ed. *Saints and She-Devils.* London: The Rubicon Press, 1987.

Murray, Henry, "Definition of Myth" in R. Ohmann, ed., *The Making of Myth.* New York: Putnam's Sons, 1962, pp. 7-38.

Naran, Menahen. "Temple and Community in Ancient Israel" in M. Fox, ed. *Temple in Society.* Winona Lake: Eisenbrauns, 1988.

Nietzsche, Friedrich, *The Birth of Tragedy and the Genealogy of Morals.* Trans. Francis Golfind. New York: Doubleday, 1956.

North, Michael, *The Final Sculpture.* Cornell: Cornell University Press, 1985.

Nuessel, Frank, "Metaphor and Cognition" in M. Danesi, ed, *Metaphor, Communications and Cognition.* Toronto: Monograph Series of the Toronto Semiotic Circle, 1987-88, pp.9-23.

Ohmann, Richard, *The Making of Myth.* New York: Y.P. Putnam's Sons, 1962.

Olney, James. *Metaphors of the Self.* Princeton, N.J. Princeton Unviersity Press, 1972,

O'Neill, John, *The Communicative Body.* Evanston: Northwestern University Press, 1989.

Otto, Walter, F. *Dionysus.* Bloomington, Ind.: Indiana Univeristy Press, 1965.

Parmegiani, Mariavittoria, "A Critical Review of Traditonal Theories of Metaphor and Related Linguistic Issues" in M. Danesi, ed., *Metaphor, Communication & Cognition.* Toronto: Toronto Semiotic Circle, 1987-88, pp.1-9.

Pavlov, Ivan, *Experimental Psychology and Other Essays.* New York: Philosophical Library, 1957 [1923].

Pecham, Morse, *The Triumph of Romanticism.* Columbia, S.C.: University of South Carolina Press, 1971.

Peirce Charles, *Collected Papers.* Cambridge. Mass: Harvard University Press, 1931-32.

Plato, "Hippias" in Plato, *Sochineniia* (Works) 3 vols. Moscow: Mysl', 1968; vol.1. pp. 149-187.

Plato, *Republic.* Trans. Grube. Indianapolis; Hachett Publishing Co., 1974.

Plotinus, *The Enneads.* Trans, Stephen Mackenna. London: Faber & Faber Ltd., 1962.

Ponzio, Augusto, *Man as a Sign.* Berlin: Mouton de Gruytuer, 1990.

Propp, Vladimir, *Russkii geroicheskii epos* (Russian Heroic Epic) Leningrad: Iz-datel'stro Leningradskogo Universiteta, 1955.

___, *Istoricheskie korni volshebnoi skazki* (Historical Roots of the Magic Fairytale). Leningrad: Izdatel'stvo Leningradskogo Universiteta, 1946.

___, *Morphology of the Folktale.* Bloomington, Ind.: Indiana University Press, 1958. Trans. Lawrence Scott.

Raju, P.T. and Alburey Castell, ed., *The Problem of the Self.* The Hague: Martinus Nijhoff, 1968.

Raglan, Lord, *The Hero.* London: Watts & Co., 1949.

Reed, John R. *Victoian Will.* Athens, Ohio: Ohio University Press, 1989.

Reich, Wilhelm, *The Mass Psychology of Fascism.* New York: Pocket Books, 1970.

Rice, James, *Freud's Russia.* New Brunswick Transaction Publishers, 1993.

Rocker, Rudolf, *Nationalism and Culture.* New York: Covici Friede Publishers, 1937.

Rose, Herbert, *Gods and Heroes of the Greeks.* London: Methuen & Co., 1957.

___, *A Handbook of Greek Mythology.* London: Methuen & Co., 1953.

Rose, Holland J. *Nationality in Modern History.* New York: MacMillan Co., 1916.

Rosenberg, Alfred, *Race and Race History.* New York: Harper & Row Publishers, 1970.

Schenk, Y., *The Mind of European Romantics.* Oxford: Oxford University Press, 1979.

Seaford, W. Henry, "Maximizing Replicability in Describing Facial Behavior in *Semiotica,* v.24, 1978, pp.1-33.

Sebeok, Thomas, "Culture and Semiotics: The Doctrine of Signs" in Walter Koch, ed., *Culture and Semiotics.* Bochum: Brockmeyer, 1989; pp.86-96.

___, "Messages in the Market Place" in J. Umiker-Sebeok, ed. *Marketing and Semiotics.* Berlin: Mouton de Gruyter, 1987.

___, *Contributions to the Doctrine of Signs.* Bloomington, Ind.: Indiana University Press, 1976.

Seltman, Charles, *The Twelve Olympians.* New York: Thomas Y. Crowell Co., 1960.

Simpkins, Scott, "The Fabrication of the Sign" in *Semiotica,* vol. 91., 1992, pp.15-27.

Smith, Antony D.S. *Nationalism in the 20th Century.* London: Martin Robinson, 1979.

Snyder, Lousi, *German Nationalism: The Tragedy of a People.* Harrisburg: The Stackpole Co., 1952.

Soboleva T. A. Superanskaya. *Tovarnye Znaki* (The Consumer Signs). Moscow: Nauka, 1986.

Solomon, Michael, ed. *The Psychology of Fashion*. Lexington MA: Lexington Books, 1985.

Steadman, John M, *Milton and the Paradoxes of Renaissance*. Baton Rouge: Lousiana State University, 1987.

Stephenson, June, *Women's Roots*. Napa, Ca: Diemer Smith Publishing Co., 1988.

Suleiman, Susan Rubin, ed., *The Female Body in Western Culture*. Cambridge, Mass: Harvard University Press, 1986.

Tokarew, Sergei, *Religiia v istorii narodov mira* (Religion in the World Cultural History). Moscow: Izdatel'stvo Politicheskoi literatury, 1965.

Tokarew, Sergei, *History of Religion*. Moscow: Progress, 1989.

Tolstoy, Leo. *War, Patriotism - Peace*. London: Garland Publishing Inc., 1973.

Tong, Q.S. "Myths about the Chinese Language" in *Comparative Review of Comparative Literature*. March June, 1993, pp.29-47.

Towne, Edward C., *The Story of Money: Gold Bimetallism*. New York: G.W. Dillingham Co., Publishers, 1900.

Toynbee, Arnold J. *A Study of History*. 6 vols., New York: Oxford University Press, 1947.

Turner, Harold, *From Temple to Meeting House*. The Hague: Mouton, 1979.

Uexkull von Thure, "Medicine and Semiotics" in *Semiotica,* vol. 61, 1986. pp. 201-219.

Van Dijk, Teun A., *Communicating Racism*. London: Sage Publications, 1987.

Veselovsky, A.I. *Istoricheskaiia poetika* (Historical Poetics), Leningrad: Khudozhestvennaiia literatura, 1940.

Vico, Giambattista. *The New Science of G.Vico*.Trans. By T.Bergin and Max H.Fish. Ithaca,N.Y.: Cornell University Press, 1968.

Vinci, da Leonardo. Treatise on Painting. Trans. John Francis Rigaud, (London: 1802).

Von Franz, Marie Louise, *Interpretation of Fairytales*. Dallas, Texas: Spring Publications, Inc., 1970.

Vygotsky, Lev, *Sobranie Sochinenii* (Works) 6 vols. Moscow: Pedagogika, 1982-4.

——, *Razvitie vysshikh psikhicheskikh funktsii* (The Development of the Higher Functions of the Psyche). Moscow: Izdatel'stvo Akademii Pedagogichoskikh nauk, 1960.

——, *Psikhologiia iskusstva* (Psychology of Art). Moscow: Iskusstvo, 1986.

——, *Thought and Language*, Cambridge, Mass.: MIT Press, 1962.

Waith, Eugene, *The Herculean Hero*. London: Chatto & Windus, 1962.

Warner, Marina, *Joan of Arc: The Image of Female Heroism*. London: Weiderfeld & Nicholson, 1981.

——, *Alone of Her Sex: The Myth and The Cult of the Virgin Mary.* London: Weiderfeld & Nicolson, 1976.

Watson, Hugh Seton, *Nationalism, Old and New.* Sydney: Sydney University Press, 1965.

Webster's New World Thesaurus. ed. Charleton Laird. New York: Simon & Schuster, 1985.

Wilson, James D, *The Romantic Heroic Ideal.* Baton Rouge: Louisiana State University Press, 1982.

Wistrich, Robert, *Hitler's Apocalypse.* London: Weidenfeld & Nicolson, 1985.

Whitford, Frank, *Expressionist Portraits.* New York: Abberville Press, 1987.

Wolf, S.J. ed. *European Fascism.* London: Lowe & Brydone, Ltd., 1970.

Yeardsley, Macleod, *The Folklore of Fairytale.* [1924] Detroit, Mich: Singing Trees Press, 1968.

Yoshimiko, Ikegami, ed. *The Empire of Signs.* Amsterdam: John Benjamin, 1990.

Young, Katharine, "Disembodiment: The Phenomenology of the Body in Medical Examinations" in *Semiotica,* 1989, v.73, pp. 213-67.